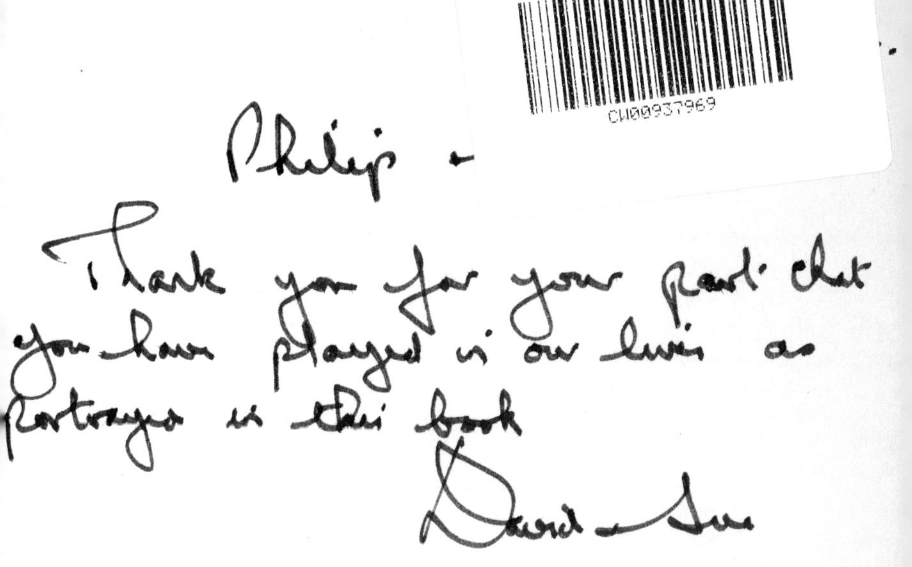

The Luck You Have is the Luck You Make – The Story of David Pickering

Stephen Wundke

The Luck You Have is the Luck You Make — The Story of David Pickering

Olympia Publishers
London

www.olympiapublishers.com
OLYMPIA PAPERBACK EDITION

A CIP catalogue record for this title is
available from the British Library.

ISBN: 978-1-80074-308-3

This is a work of non-fiction.

First Published in 2022

Olympia Publishers
Tallis House
2 Tallis Street
London
EC4Y 0AB

Printed in Great Britain

Acknowledgements

Pulling together the history of a life as varied and interwoven as David Pickering's involves an awful lot of people, without whom the details would have been unverified and sketchy, at best. My sincere thanks go to Holly Royle, who, whilst starting her PHD, at the University of Chester, has found time to research and compile so much of the background and present it in a professional and timely manner. It was a superb job. I am certain she will succeed in whatever chosen field she determines is right for her. The work ethic she displays is exceptional.

My thanks to David's friends who penned their own thoughts; Peter Overmeer, who, after reading his account, may have been a better choice to write this book than me. Neil Large MBE, Noel Barraclough, Tage Weiss, Andrew Chadwick, Trevor Trigg, Bob Clough-Parker, Jo Sykes, Bill Tye, Richard Francis, Barry Smith and Peter Ladd, all added confirmation of timing and facts as well as colour. It was extremely helpful, and I will be interested to hear if they agree that this is a fair representation of their friend and colleague, as well as an acceptable conclusion.

Special mention as well for Mike Huntriss, who now looks after Pickering Enterprises (PE). Whenever I called, nothing was too much trouble and he presented the information in a manner even I could digest. Much appreciated.

Sue Pickering is under written in this book; of that I am certain. Her enthusiasm and feedback during the months of writing gave me all the encouragement necessary when I sometimes wondered, how on earth, I would pull this together. For me, this was just a small inkling of her immense value to her husband.

Finally, COVID-19 gets a mention. Perhaps the only complimentary one for all of 2020, and that is only because, had it not been for lockdown, I would not have been able to write this story. I am sure someone else would have written it if I hadn't because it is a story that should be told but I have genuinely enjoyed doing it.

Prologue

It is my honest belief that for a twenty-year period, it was impossible for any person living in or around Chester not to have some aspect of their life touched by a business, association, or school, where David Pickering was not, somehow, involved.

I have known David since I started business in Chester, back in 1994, and I worked closely with him for the years 2007–2014. If you were in the hospitality or the food and drink sector, you knew of the Pickering family and their business Bodfari and if, like me, you were involved in horse racing, you knew all about Bodfari Stud. From the mid-1990s until we eventually worked together on Chester Festivals and Chester City Management, everywhere you went, everything that was the very core of Chester and Cheshire, had in some way been affected by David Pickering.

He was either on the board of the company you wanted to do business with, or his company supplied the company you wanted to do business with. Besides his involvement with his own businesses, Bodfari and Meadow Foods, there was The City Club of Chester, The Chester Business Club, Chester Race Company, DEFRA, The North West Development Agency, The Skills Partnership, The University of Chester, North West Accountants, Queens Park High School, The Chester Conservative Party, Chester FC, Dee Radio, Chester Zoo, The University of Chester, North West Farmers, they all had David at their heart or head in some way. I guess you get the picture, he was omnipresent in

Chester.

When David asked me to write this book it was because he had an idea about cataloguing the many things he had done, so that in years to come his family might be able to read a little about where they came from and what he and others had done in the Pickering name. At seventy-eight years of age David thought the time was right to make sure that he at least had a record of the varied life he had been living. To that end he asked various people to write about their involvement with him over the years. As someone who had worked with him for seven years, he initially asked me if I would cover that period of work. I agreed. The Coronavirus Lockdown had just started, and I enjoyed the challenge. I presented it to him post lockdown and, after he and Sue had read my account of our time together, he asked if I would write his book.

Before I agreed, I needed to know the ground rules. The first and most important was, is this a catalogue of your life to which only the family will refer, or would you like this book to be published so that the public can read it? Each is a different book and I needed to know which one I was writing. He said that we should write it to be published and if we believe it does not merit that at the end of the process then so be it. My second rule was that if we were to write a book to be published then a story about 'rich kid does well' would turn out to be a somewhat boring tale. This had to be 'warts and all' or there was no point. This he agreed. So, that is the context of this book. An honest account of an extraordinary life to date.

My time working with David covered several projects and, in this book, where I was directly involved, I talk in the first person and cover those stories from my perspective. In all the other matters relating to David and his family life I have relied on his extraordinary diary notes, the recollections of his many friends and of course his amazing wife Sue, without whom I genuinely believe there would not be a book that covers such an astounding story.

I do not profess to know more about David, how he thinks and what he feels, than anyone else and I am certain many of his close friends would say, in their case, that is not very much either but I am confident this is an accurate and truthful portrayal of an extremely interesting life. A life that very few will have ever experienced.

I soon realised that despite having worked with David for seven years and having known him for twenty years that I really knew extraordinarily little about what makes him who he is. I had rarely seen any emotional response in our dealings together. I could not remember ever seeing him drunk or out of control, I could not honestly remember ever seeing him laugh, beyond a smile. It was like there was a cloak, behind which stood David Pickering and, apart from his wife Sue, no one saw beyond the cloak. That was my challenge — find and explain what was behind the cloak. What I have uncovered is what appears to be an ordinary man, who has lived an extraordinary life. There is no story about someone' else's life that is even vaguely like this one. Yes, we are all unique human beings, but this is a story that goes way beyond unique.

There is a widely held belief that, "when we die, we will only ever have achieved 10% of what we were truly capable". That is not true in the case of David Pickering. From twenty years of age until seventy-five David found a way to cram something into every corner and crevice of his life. His microscopic handwriting filled his tiny diaries with dates and times of meetings and commitments, enough to fill ten normal lifetimes. If you contributed details about David's life and they are not included, then my apologies. I simply edited to ensure this story moved along at a reasonable and believable pace.

Here is what you are about to read. A family that rose from peasant farm labourers to landowners and of one individual who simply refused to accept that you couldn't do more.

This is my first and possibly last book and for my shortcomings as a writer, I apologise but those shortcomings will not stop it from being a truly incredible story of one man's life. I will wait until the epilogue to tell you who I think David Pickering is — let us see if you come to the same conclusion. I hope you enjoy reading David's story as much as I enjoyed bringing it to print.

Chapter 1
The Peasant Pickerings of Cheshire

The first question a reader may have, is why anyone would be interested in the story of David Pickering? That is a fair starting place as you contemplate investing good time and money in a book. The answer must be, that in the reading of what appears to be 'ordinary' people's lives, we see that it is not just the celebrities that live extraordinary ones; this we hope you agree, is one such story.

We are all the sum of our experiences, that much is true, but there is so much more to our make-up. How we react to our experiences is also very much shaped by the circumstances into which we are born. Not dictated to by them but they are certainly a significant factor in our reactions and development as a person. This is certainly true of David Pickering.

David's family have farmed the land at Rough Hill, Marlston Cum Lache, some three miles from the centre of Chester, for over three hundred years. David's story is one of generations who passed, from peasant farm hands to farmers, to landowners and latterly business operators. Bettering themselves through hard work and innovation. It is a compelling story of success, failure, and perseverance. Of determination, sacrifice and giving. A human tale of real people doing amazing things and it all starts on Cheshire land some three hundred years ago at a time when the country was undergoing significant changes.

George II was on the throne in the early 18th century but he took little interest in the day-to-day affairs of the country, leaving Pitt the Elder as Prime Minister to get things moving. In a country that had been at war for so long it barely knew any other life. It is not the only time in this story that the ending of wars brings about a time of revolution in agriculture but this was one such time. England wanted to feed herself and Pitt the Elder convinced many of the wealthy landowners to invest in farming. One such farm was the Eaton Estate, just outside Chester, owned by the Duke of Westminster. The landowners and the Duke, more importantly, accepted the challenge and set about growing crops and grass for animals.

Whilst the predominance of salty soil with its clay base across most of Cheshire was not ideal for all crops, there was no doubt Cheshire farmers could grow grass. Up to four crops of grass in a season have been taken off fields at times in Cheshire and with grazing pasture like that, it is little wonder that Cheshire quickly developed a reputation as a county of dairy. The cows not only had wonderful grazing in the summer but a bountiful supply of feed throughout the winter to keep them healthy. But there was more to the Cheshire cow than just milk. It was the taste that people loved. In fact, there is reference to Cheshire Cheese, the first cheese mentioned, in the Domesday Book and a review of the wonderful salty taste this cheese provided.

The French use a word called "*terroir* "and it refers to the natural environment making things taste the way they do. A sense of identity for a product that cannot be replicated anywhere else, simply because no other location has the unique set of circumstances that create that flavour. The French wines are, of course, the classic example. Soil that is stony and flinty in certain areas producing some of the great wines and sandy soil in other areas, a different type of wine. So too, their Camembert and Brie

Cheeses. Well, the same was true of Cheshire milk. The salty soil produced grass, eaten by the cows, who in turn delivered the milk that had a flavour people loved. This was most evident when farmers used the excess milk to make cheese which became the crumbly, salty, Cheshire Cheese. Cheese was made from the excess milk as a way of preserving the produce and of course to get through winter when milk was in short supply. Cheshire farmers were jolly good at making it. The milk was ideal to produce the unique taste and texture of what we now know and love as "Cheshire Cheese".

In fact, during a period in the 18th century the UK simply could not get enough of this unique cheese. Almost six thousand tons, annually, of Cheshire cheese was finding its way to the markets in London and beyond. It was the number one cheese in the United Kingdom up until the mass produced, and thereby cheaper, Cheddar Cheese from Somerset took over much later. Not that the competition did much to dampen the Cheese market, it simply meant the UK was eating even more cheese and so the demand for the produce of Cheshire remained extraordinarily strong.

During the 18th century, the Duke of Westminster created his ten-thousand-acre estate on the edge of Chester, and it was not long afterwards that David's ancestors were farming the land for the duke. Regular work was in short supply and the Duke, treated his workers well. It was a prized position of employment to be working on the duke's estate and the first time we are aware of the Pickering family and their day-to-day life.

Chapter 2
A Farmer's Life

The first recorded Pickering to work the land was David's Great, Great Grandfather, Thomas Pickering. According to a valuation of the farm, done in 1832 by William Jelico of Shifnal in Shropshire, the farm was described as "in a very fair state of cultivation and that the tenant appeared to be an industrious man". High Praise indeed. Thomas was succeeded by John Foster Pickering — more commonly known as Fred. Fred was born in 1848. Records suggest that he had followed in the footsteps of four generations before him. It was the type of employment that was passed from generation to generation and still does today.

For us, our story really begins in the late 19th century with Fred farming the land alongside his brother Robert and so to the first of the extraordinary tales of an ordinary man. Robert marries a lady called Eliza Drew. Eliza is the Granddaughter of Samuel Drew (1765–1833), who is famed as an outspoken and Bible-thumping Methodist Theologian, colloquially known as "The Cornish Metaphysicist" for his written work on the human soul. Drew himself was an incredible man. He was from a poor family, he taught himself to read and write and despite living in Cornwall managed to get a degree from Aberdeen University. In doing so he effectively did what so few could achieve. He crossed the class barriers and went from the bottom of society to the top, but I digress.

Eliza marries Robert. There is no mention in the records of

how a girl, whose relatives all live in Cornwall, meets a Cheshire farm hand but meet they did and shortly after, without the marriage bearing children, Robert dies. John, Robert's brother, and Eliza become "an item"." It was not uncommon at the time for a family to look after a widow. Eliza is living in the working accommodation provided by the estate for her and Robert and under normal circumstances it will not be long after his death before she will be asked to leave by the Estate. They will have to replace Robert in the workforce and that accommodation will be needed. Sadly, this was also quite common at the time as both widows and single mums found their way into a wretched life of despair, cast aside by society. For Eliza these must have been extremely worrying times.

Either for practical reasons or for matters of the heart, John (aka Fred) and Eliza's relationship blossoms, but the law (it was not changed in the UK until 1921) forbids a man to marry his brother's wife. The facts tell us that in 1881, John, now aged thirty-three, and Eliza get on a boat and go to Switzerland and they get married there. As so often happens the facts do not always reveal the true story and often leave many unanswered questions.

The first question is about Fred's circumstances. Fred is a farmhand; farmhands were not known to appoint solicitors. The average farmhand's wage would have precluded him from having the budget to appoint a lawyer to take advice but surely one would have been needed and consulted to confirm that by marrying in Switzerland it would be a legal marriage recognised by the UK courts. Who knew it was legal to marry in these circumstances in Switzerland? How did they raise the money to simply get a boat over to Europe, find a church and a compliant vicar who would marry them and for it all to be conducted in

English so they could understand what was being said? Maybe, there was a roaring trade in Swiss marriages in the 1880s? What we are certain of is that neither spoke Swiss or French. However, this gives rise to the theory that Fred might have been a bit more than just your average farmhand on the estate and that the duke's office were happy in lending a helping hand to the plight of a key worker.

The duke and his advisors would definitely have been aware of which countries were "friendly", where marriage and divorce were concerned, as we know that the aristocracy used whatever laws suited them most for affairs of the heart! Marriage at the lower levels of society had always been used as a controller of men and it was in the estate's interest to look after good workers. Far better to have a key worker, happily married, than one who might be a little footloose and fancy-free. It is reasonable to surmise that Fred and Eliza had some help in getting married and generations to come were glad they did.

Regardless of speculation, the records show they were married in Switzerland in 1881 and from that union arrived a son, born in 1882, his name, John Foster Pickering (Jack), David's grandfather.

Chapter 3
The Farm that Jack Built

As has been to this time, the Pickering family tradition, Jack works on the farm, learning the trade from his father and clearly becoming a leader amongst the farmhands. His father, Fred, is farming Decoy Farm and Rough Hill. The two farms adjoin each other and remain very evident to this day. The work was hard and, whilst machinery was getting better, it was still very physical and the unpredictability of the UK weather was always a challenge.

In 1909, young Jack marries Helen Wade at Backford Church and life continues to get better for them. In November 1911, they have a son and name him John Denis Pickering (Den), David's father. The need for the country to feed itself through the First World War precludes both Fred and Jack from serving in the war and in 1919, as the Duke of Westminster tries to raise money to cover huge losses from the war, Jack is offered the opportunity to buy the two hundred acres that is Rough Hill Farm. He raises the money and becomes the proud owner of two hundred acres of prime Cheshire grazing land, populated with cattle, pigs and sheep. It must have felt incredibly special to both Jack and Fred, knowing your family had worked this land as employees for over two hundred years to finally be the ones who now owned the land and to at last be masters of your own destiny. This did not happen to many families and again, like his mother's grandfather, Samuel Drew, Jack was starting to cross the class divide, from labourer to landowner and in doing so setting the path for Pickerings to come. Life is good on the farm, the animals are healthy, the yield is satisfactory, and the family are doing well.

The joy is short-lived. In 1921, as young Den is attending the Kings School, situated at the time in the grounds of Chester Cathedral, his father dies. Jack has acute tonsillitis for three days and then eight agonising days of Lobar Pneumonia before his heart gives out and he passes. It must have been an incredibly sad and very worrying time at Rough Hill. Whilst it cannot be proven, these symptoms are like those of Spanish Flu, which had killed so many, just two years earlier, a coronavirus that killed over fifty million people worldwide and was highly contagious. For this to come so soon after the purchase of the farm seems incredibly cruel. Helen and her ten-year-old son, Den, now have the daunting prospect of running a two-hundred-acre farm and the responsibility of paying off a significant mortgage. Helen's advisors tell her she needs to sell the farm, repay the loan, and move on and so, despite the fact that the decision to sell up is breaking her heart and that she fears for the future of her son and herself without income, she places the farm up for auction. What would become of them after the sale?

If the farm fetches a big price that leaves a profit, they will be fine, but they have not owned it for long and there surely cannot be much equity in the farm. Money is scarce after the war and those who could buy know the value of their cash. They will most definitely want a deal. What will happen if the sale simply clears the debt and they are forced to leave their family home with no profit and no money to live? Maybe Fred will take them in on Decoy Farm but then what?

In one of those rare twists of fate, without which, life could be so different, the farm fails to attract the price necessary to clear the debt. Cleverly, they sell off just thirty-five acres, which presumably creates some cash and allows a couple of years of payments to the bank, which buys time for them to build up the farm again. Surely a great sense of relief for Helen, but now the job of running the farm. A woman in a man's world. She must make the farm work without Jack.

Step in — Thomas Fox, the kindly bailiff working for the duke's estate. Thomas goes out of his way to aid Helen and, before some of you race off with ideas of any impropriety, there is no sense of anything happening here. This was no more to the relationship than caring for other human beings and acts of kindness from someone who knows the family well and what they are up against. That help is sorely needed because apart from running the farm, dealing with the workers, and bringing up a teenager, Helen is sorely tested again in 1924 just three years after Jack's death. Foot-and-mouth strikes the herd, and all the animals are removed from the farm. Another devastating blow, this time the farm is without animals for at least three months while it is completely cleared of the disease. The job now comes to restock and start again. The watchful eye of Mr Fox would have been even more important. Together they restocked, with a selection of cross-bred shorthorns and a British Friesian bull and they made it work.

Chapter 4
Taking the Reins

In 1927, aged 16 and somehow without major interruptions to his schooling, Den leaves the Kings School with a decent education, to go home and run the family farm. He and Mr Fox, by now Den's mentor, become good friends and Den shows a real aptitude for farming. He is keen to learn and keen to challenge the norms and see how they can do things better. It is only a matter of three years later, in 1930, that Den and Helen have put the farm on such good footing that they can raise the capital to repurchase the thirty-five acres lost when Helen was forced to sell, back in 1921, to furnish the debt. Jack would have been enormously proud. Sadly, Fred, who was still farming Decoy, died in 1930, from what was described on his death certificate as a Cerebral Apoplexy, with a Cardiac Dilatation. Fred had what we now know as a massive stroke. He was eighty-two years of age, an exceptionally good age in 1930 — he might disagree! He had seen his hard work and his family go from labourers to landowners. His grandson was doing well on Rough Hill Farm. The Pickerings of the 1930s had a lot to thank him for.

During the 1930s Den built up the dairy herd. He worked to develop the breading ewes and increase the fat lamb production. He also ventured into pig farming. This became his greatest challenge. The insulation where the pigs are housed throughout the winter was inadequate, so they got cold and for that reason they struggled to keep weight on. Den designed double-skinned roofs with asbestos and hardboard filled with wood shavings to raise the temperature. Asbestos was seen to be a marvellous innovation in 1930s England; clearly we now know of its dangers, but they didn't then, and this was a ground-breaking investment. The new housing did the trick of keeping the pigs warmer and they flourished. A healthy pig is a fat pig and a fat pig makes good money at the market.

Den was every inquisitive and always wanted to know more about farming. He even made a trip to Denmark to learn just how they were producing even better results with their pigs than anything that had been achieved in the UK. It was from one of these trips that he decided that all his three-day-old piglets would be injected with an iron supplement called Imposil Intramuscular Iron. He hoped that by doing this he could overcome the iron deficiency prevalent in so many young pigs across the UK. It was an instant success. The previous oral iron tablets were relatively ineffective, as well as being expensive. The new, injected dispensing system was getting right to the problem and creating stronger, healthier pigs. He also increased the profitability by switching the sale of the pigs from traditional markets like Mold, Tarporley, Chester and Ludlow to an assured price of sale through the Fatstock Marketing Board. Den was an early adopter and as such got the best prices for his livestock. Another canny piece of business from the Rough Hill Farm.

The 1930s weren't without their challenges though. The records show that 1933 was the worst drought the country had seen for fifty years with milk output down by 50%. Den was the Treasurer from 1933 to 1935 of the Cheshire Young Farmers and was elected their chairman in 1936. He gave various talks to the Cheshire Young Farmers of his trips abroad and his new techniques, as farmers struggled to contend with increases in basic wage, changing weather patterns and in 1935 the demand that anyone wanting to drive on the road must be tested for a licence. The implications for farming of this latest government imposition were far reaching as most farmhands had learnt to drive on farms from the age of ten to twelve and had never been tested before. Worse was to follow in 1936 when Cheshire was heavily affected again by Foot-and-Mouth disease. As 1939 approached with its rumblings from across the channel, the decade would not end much better either!

Chapter 5
An Extended Marriage

It was during this turbulent period that Den met young Margaret Owen, David's mother. During their courtship, Margaret's brother, George Owen, was making a good living as a professional jockey and, in 1935, George rode 'Lazy Boots' to a credible fourth in the Grand National. Den was hooked, not just on horseracing but on the jockey's sister, Margaret, as well. This proved to be a match made in heaven and in 1939 at Eccleston Church, Den married Margaret Owen and so began not just a good marriage but also a long association with jockey turned racehorse trainer, George Owen, his brother in-law. It was a stellar year as not only did George Owen get a brother-in-law, but he also rode the winner of the Cheltenham Gold Cup, 'Brendan's Cottage'. For those not familiar with horse racing, the Grand National, held at Aintree, is probably the most famous horse race in the world. The second biggest race to be staged in the UK, by betting turnover and reputation, is the Cheltenham Gold Cup. George was making quite a name for himself. Den was enjoying a successful bet on the horses from time to time and despite the news emanating from Ruhr, Hungary, Poland and beyond, things at Rough Hill were going simply fine.

Chapter 6
War on every front

We are now at the point in the television soap opera where the chief protagonists tell each other how happy they are and ask what could possibly go wrong. Which, as we all know, is the signal for almost everything to come crashing down around their ears. Well, in this case it was of course the Second World War and life would never be the same again. Den was in a reserved occupation, as his father had been in the First World War, and would not be able to enlist. This time, however, there was a very real chance of invasion and the subject of much satire, The Home Guard, is where Den volunteers, something he takes very seriously.

Life on the farm is tough now and fear from the nightly bombings of Liverpool and the nearby proximity of the family house to Hawarden Airport, should that be targeted, all play on the minds of those at Rough Hill. One bright spot is the birth of David's elder brother in 1941, John Michael Pickering. This is quickly followed by David, who is born in 1942. War time babies and two new mouths to feed at Rough Hill Farm, which is really starting to come under pressure, a pressure that just gets greater as the war rumbles on.

There is less feed available for the animals as the country tries to feed itself and its troops. Out of necessity Den was forced to reduce the pig numbers substantially, just as he was making it pay but he will do nothing to jeopardise the dairy herd. Worse was to come. In 1942 the herd was put through a compulsory Tuberculin test and all but one of Den's milking cows test positive and must be destroyed. The average "milker" was producing 900–1000 gallons of milk a year and this return on seventy cows was the bread and butter of the Pickering income. It was a devastating blow at a time when every day brings a new disaster from the continent, more loss of life and fear of a German invasion. There was one small glimmer of light. By an extraordinary piece of luck, brought about by the separation of the younger stock from the "milkers", only one of his ninety heifers tests positive. Den has a plan; but he needs his bank to help and more than just a little luck. He has tried cleaning and moving stock as they calf, but it is just too tough to stop reinfection by moving the animals around Rough Hill and trying to disinfect as they vacate an area. There is only one way to make it work. He needs to close everything down and completely disinfect Rough Hill and that's when fate plays yet another hand.

Gorstella Farm, which, to this day, sits just down the road from Rough Hill, was then owned by the extravagantly named Baron Wolf Erhadt Anton George "Wolo" Von Trutzschler. The name may suggest to you, that "The Baron" is not from these shores; indeed, he is a German by birth, although he is commuting between America and the UK on a regular basis. Another extraordinary man. He was one of the first people to go from the UK to Canada and buy cattle for his farm and, more importantly for Den, his farm had recently been attested, with twenty-five animals, as clean. Rumour has it, the somewhat eccentric Baron would entertain business clients and conduct negotiations completely naked. No explanation exists as to why. He was a larger-than-life character, but he was of course German, at a time when being German in the UK was not a good thing.

The Baron decided coming to the UK was too dangerous. For fear of being imprisoned, he decides to sell his farm and we never hear of him again in Cheshire. He did live to a decent age of eighty-seven, spending his later years living in America.

Opportunity knocks for Den. Gorstella Farm is placed on the market in the spring of 1943, some twelve months after the first problems arose at Rough Hill and with the backing of his bank Den can buy Gorstella farm, with the twenty-five attested clean animals. Now his plan can work. He shifts all his clean stock to Gorstella to join the other twenty-five animals and he deep cleans every inch of Rough Hill. Once Rough Hill is attested clean, he can move the stock back. He now has no need for Gorstella and places it back on the market selling it to Bill Chadwick.

When you write it like that it all seems so simple, but the legal work involved between banker and client, between vendor and purchaser, the time delays as handwritten and typed letters and contracts went back and forth in the post must have been excruciating. All the time not knowing if you will be successful in getting Gorstella, so vital to your plans; as German bombers fly overhead and you wait for the air raid sirens to sound, with a young family to feed and protect. It must have been an incredibly tense period.

Somehow though the people of that time just "got on with it" and even managed a laugh or two amongst all the carnage that surrounded them as our next story shows.

Den took his Home Guard duty seriously and was rewarded with a rank, which allowed him and his commander certain privileges. It seems part of those privileges involved the procurement of some petrol, something in short supply. The two of them decided to take a motorboat up the River Dee to fish for salmon. A nice escape from the rigours and pressures of day-today life. Some normality in a sea of stress and worry. Den, however, lost interest in the fishing, as was his wont to do, and the commander dropped him off on the side of the river near a small pool. The commander headed further upstream in search of the big fish. Whilst lying down next to the pool and watching the clouds go by, Den noticed a full-grown salmon basking in the pool almost asleep, he moved in on the salmon and literally "tickled" it out of the water. When the commander returned having drawn a blank with his fishing, Den is sitting there with a large salmon by his side much to the commander's dismay. Den just seemed to have that sort of luck. The luck of a gambler in almost everything he did. The end of the war, saw Den, awarded the honorary rank of Lieutenant, of which he was rightly proud. That was of course for services to the Home Guard and not for catching salmon!

Chapter 7
Feeding the Nation

Despite the war, back at Rough Hill, the two brothers John and David were getting on well. They both had a nanny who doted on them. May Guest looked after David and Kathleen Davis was charged with caring for John. David recalls that they were both close to their respective nannies and childhood was enjoyable. David and Mae would stay in touch for years and she would always find time to write and enjoy his many successes. Farmers during war time were able to grow many of their own vegetables and of course meat and dairy was in plentiful supply on the farm, so they did not experience the food shortages that many had to endure during these lean years.

There were always cows, pigs, sheep, horses, chickens and dogs around the farm and life seemed to be one big adventure for the two youngest Pickerings. There was a stream that flowed through the farm and any number of fields for the young boys to explore and they did. The two brothers got on well but what childhood would be complete without the odd coming together. If you look closely on the bridge of David's nose, should you get that close, you will see a significant scare. It reminds him always of the time the two set about each other with shovels and the blade end of John's caught David between the eyes. Much blood flowed but, other than a telling off, there was no significant damage. It could have been so much worse.

It was during the '30s and '40s as Den replaced stock lost to the cull, that he started to introduce Canadian Holstein cattle to his British Frisian stock. The Baron, then of Gorstella Farm, had shown Den the qualities of these animals and together they purchased large numbers from Canada and brought them into the UK. The Canadian Holstein was a bigger animal and produced more milk; it was yet another piece of adventurous innovation. Den was at the forefront of the development of the British Canadian Holstein Frisian Association formed in 1946, later changed to the British Holstein Society. Given the success of the herds and some good pre-marketing, the first crops of heifers and bulls were put up at a market that Den helped to organise and the take up of stock was significant. The cattle averaged a price of £235 with over two hundred people at the sale. By way of comparison in today's money that would be well over £2800 and good "milkers" today fetch in the region of £1500 so you can see these animals achieved a tidy premium. People were paying good money for this new breed and business was brisk. It is probable that the Pickerings have the Baron to thank for this as well. He was farming in America and Canada and had connections to make the importation of quality animals from Canada possible. Given that he had farmed just down the road it would be naive to think Den was not influenced by his herd and their distinctive make up and of course the Baron's connections in Canada made the purchases that much safer and easier. In a rare speech that Den gave back in 1960 he explained to Cheshire Young Farmers how he believed that he learnt more from the Baron than anyone bar Mr Fox.

With the war over, in 1947 both boys were now under the care of Miss Giles, at Abbey Gate Nursery in Abbey Square, Chester, for their primary schooling and there was a sense of calm and purpose around the farm. Den, who had worked hard to make his farm that much more successful, came to the attention of the North of England Home Radio programme, "It's Farming Time", where he was interviewed about his farming successes and asked how he saw the future of farming. He replied.

"I think that the future prosperity of British Dairy Farming depends on combining the best of the old traditions, like those embodied in hundreds of farms such as my own, with the best of what's new — wherever in the world that may come from."

It was not just a sound bite, he lived by that mantra every day. Den's statement is set against the backdrop of an economy that was on its knees. We may have won the war, but we really lost the peace. The Americans called in their debts and all but bankrupted the country. Had it not been for the six months of pleading in 1946 by John Maynard Keynes, securing further loans from the Americans and Canadians; an effort that would eventually lead to his early death, things might have been oh so different? But succeed he did. Another £3.75 billion loan from America and a further £1.1 billion loan from Canada gave the UK the opportunity to rebuild herself.

In 1947 we could only supply 10% of the food we needed to feed ourselves and we had no money for imported foods. Things were dire. Rationing would carry on until 1954 such was the shortage of goods on the High Street. The politicians realised that a hungry electorate is an angry electorate and that people had now endured enough of the shortages; enough of going without. They wanted some rewards for their wartime sacrifices. The Government, led by Clement Atlee, recognised that again it was the time for them to invest and to mobilise the Agricultural land of the UK and begin project "Feed Britain".

In a significant move for farmers the UK passed The

Agriculture Act of 1947 — the Act gave farmers an assured market and guaranteed prices for their produce as well as a good climate to borrow for investment to modernise the industry. The objective of this being, according to the Minister of Agriculture, Tom Williams was "to promote a healthy and efficient agriculture capable of producing that part of the nation's food which is required from home sources at the lowest price consistent with the provision of adequate remuneration and decent living conditions for farmers and workers, with a reasonable return on capital invested."

The Act was a success: from 1938 to 1939 the output of agricultural machinery in Britain was valued at £2,500,000 (£1,400,000 of this was exports); in 1951 output was over £100,000,000, Den and his fellow farmers had got the country fed and they were making a good living along the way.

Chapter 8
Gambling on the Future

It was clear that Den and Margaret Pickering wanted the best for their boys, and they were united in their schooling choices, but the war years were harsh. And what of the young David Pickering, during this time of uncertainty, as he embarked on the start of his schooling life? How did he manage? Early end of school reports in 1947 show that,

"David has begun well and has settled down very happily at School. He shows keen interest in all of his lessons and enters in to all the activities. Conduct — excellent."

G Parry/Hilda M Giles

John enjoyed similar reports a year earlier, so both boys seemed none the worse for the effects of the war and the huge upheavals at home. As they started the summer term at Abbey Gate, the cost for the two boys in 1948 set the Pickering's back the princely sum of £12, 12s but given they had cattle fetching them £235 and an ever-expanding milk round it seemed this was well within the family budget.

Meanwhile, Den's brother-in-law, David's Uncle, George Owen, retired as one of the country's top jumps jockeys and set up a Racehorse training establishment. Initially on Decoy Farm, Fred's old farm, he started with some point-to-point horses and then in 1948 took out his full trainer's licence. Such was his fame in the jumps racing world as a jockey, that Lord Phillip

Leverhulme, the family after whom one of the main stands at Chester is named, the same family that created Port Sunlight and current owners of the wonderful Thornton Manor Estate, decided he would have a horse with George and so too, of course, does brother-in-law Den. Den's first horse was called Grand Truce and is the first of many he would have with George. George was enticed, after a sending out a few winners, to set up his training base on Lord Leverhulme's property at Cholmondley, very near the current stables of Ginger and Donald McCain. It proved to be a good omen for all the trainers, as over the coming years they recorded some fabulous victories on the biggest stage the sport can offer.

Putting horses with George Owen proved to be quite a canny move by all involved in 1949. Fernie Williamson, a keen horse breeder from another of Cheshire's distinguished farming families, had, some years previously, sent a home bred horse called Russian Hero to work under Owen's guidance. The horse was making giant strides as a significant chaser. The nine-year-old was responding well to his lower-class assignments and even though Mr Williamson had never imagined having a runner in the Grand National, George and he decided to enter this one. Fancied by not one person in the trade press, he was almost friendless in the betting markets, except for the stable lads, one or two shrewd stable followers and family members, as he drifted in the betting on race day.

Russian Hero went on to win the world's most famous race by eight widening lengths, at the price of 66/1. It was a great day for the bookies as there was big money on those at the head of the market who were all well beaten and very few backed Russian Hero; very few except those "in the know" who had kept the faith.

Russian Hero's jockey Leo McMorrow was staying with Den and Margaret Pickering at Rough Hill over the weekend of the Grand National at Aintree and Den decided to have £16 e/w on Russian Hero with the Tote. With his typical gamblers luck, the Tote paid an amazing 150/1 return and Den is sent a cheque for £3066, 1s,6d. To give some context to the size of this win, the average house price in the UK in 1949 was £2,500. It was a significant result by any standards.

As a postscript to the race Den agreed to drive winning jockey Leo McMorrow back to his home in Doncaster on the Monday, it seemed the least he could do after winning so much. It was a trip which almost came to a nasty end as they t-boned a rather large truck just outside Sutton Coldfield. Fortunately, neither was hurt and in the true tradition of the time, it was reported in the local papers, that "after a cup of tea at the offices of Messrs Bennet, the truck owners, they were transported to Birmingham station to continue their journey". It topped off an exceptional weekend of drama.

Cholmondley would prove to be an amazing place to train horses for the biggest race in the world, as George Owen's 1949 Grand National success with Russian Hero would be followed later by Ginger McCain with the incomparable Red Rum in 1973 and 1974 and again in 1977 and his son Donald, who would send out Amberleigh House to win the 2004 renewal of the race from the same establishment.

As an owner Den would go on to have more than sixty winners with George, not a bad return. Some of his better-known horses were, Linkslade. The champion jump jockey and trainer Stan Mellor, who rode Linksdale, named his training stables in Lambourne after him. Resurgent, Odd Man Out, Candid Friend and Tea Fiend were all winners in Den's racing colours. As good as these were, their exploits would be eclipsed by another in years to come.

Den had his own horses run in the Grand National as well, the first being Grand Truce, a horse he bought from David Miln, owner of the Mollington Banastre, Chester — Telephone number, Mollington 112, according to the family letterhead — that is before it became an hotel! In his letter to Den, attempting to sell the horse, he writes.

Grand Truce, who is by Flag of Truce out of Grandma, we gave two races as a two-year-old and he has grown to a terrific size. My own opinion is that he is pretty well 17 hands and rather fat at the moment... and has the makings of a grand chaser.... Would you or any of your friends be interested in him.

I hope your good lady, your family and yourself are keeping well and with kind regards, believe me,

Yours sincerely
David L Miln

He was indeed a chasing type as Mr Miln had spotted. The horse ran in the 1953 Grand National. The entry created quite a bit of excitement in the local press, as he was yet another live Cheshire chance of success being sent out from the all-conquering Owen stable.

He had won many of his races both as a novice and a handicapper easily and his future looked bright. He was well touted in the local press and was not the huge price of Russian Hero when the tapes were raised. Life does not always go to plan and even though the horse had fallen just once in his previous twenty-six appearances he did not make it past the first of the unique, large, Aintree obstacles. A faller at the first is not how you want your national horse to be described but that did not detract from what was an exceptional career for Grand Truce and Den took it as part and parcel of the game. His untimely death from Colic was yet another reminder of the fragile existence of animals.

Things in the Grand National got significantly better in 1960 when George Owen filled second place with Lord Leverhulme's horse, Badenloch, at 14/1 and fourth place with Den's horse Tea Fiend at 33/1. It was a remarkable performance by the Northern based trainer. As David recalls, the families of all concerned filled the private dining room at the Grosvenor Hotel in Chester to celebrate with an amazing meal. This was a wonderful achievement and, whilst winning would have been good, place money and each way bets stacked up tidy profits for team Owen and his owners. George really did know what a Grand National horse looked like and how to get one ready for a big race.

Chapter 9
Education and Learning at Rough Hill

Over at Abbey Gate School, David's brother John had a severely interrupted 1948 schooling year as illness kept him at home. A burst appendix required urgent surgery and he missed a substantial amount of term time in recovery. He went back to school a little early and suffered complications that also hindered his next term's attendance as well. These days keyhole surgery makes life and recovery times that much faster but the invasive procedure back in the 1940s made for a complicated recovery time.

No such problems for young David; he received a strong second year report. His English was described as Excellent, so too was his Arithmetic — although there was a comment about careless mistakes and lack of concentration that dampened an otherwise glowing report that revealed he was very accomplished with his figures and was rarely tested. This was a comment that would re-appear throughout his schooling life. It was the last such report from Abbey Gate as he advanced to Hampton House School for boys in 1950.

For those unfamiliar with Hampton House, it was a preparatory school based on the site where the Deeside Ramblers Hockey Club now stands, at Tilston, near Tarporley. Both David and John were enrolled, and they were week-long boarders, meaning they stayed on site Monday to Friday and returned home at weekends. It was the perfect preparatory conditions, before boys of secondary school age were sent away to board, as was the norm back in the '50s and '60s, for those who could afford it. A private education was quite a status at the time and did not come cheaply.

Back at home, things on the farm were "buzzing". Den had expanded the Milk business and was now delivering right across Chester and beyond. His clients included Chester Zoo, The Blossoms Hotel, The Nags Head, Chester College and the Grosvenor Hotel. All over Chester families were waking up to a bottle of "Picks Pinta" on their doorstep. The product range was expanded with eggs and yoghurt on the daily menu as well. The Holsteins were producing quality yields, the pigs were working well and paying their way but Den was convinced they could be better.

Den's investigations and thirst for farming knowledge revealed that the Swedish Landrace pig, a derivation of the Danish Landrace, was sturdier, a better breeder and was able to put on weight at a very good rate. In raising animals for meat, the faster they can put on weight the less feed they require in the long run and with less feed costs in the life of the pig, the profit per pound increases. The Swedish Landrace was more known on the continent as a pork meat pig rather than just bacon. At this stage of the British farming recovery and with rationing still in place, pork was a favoured roast and a pork chop was just as popular as bacon for the morning feed so the Landrace had a lot going for it. He imported the breed and set about upgrading his stock. In 1953 when he bought three of the Swedish Landrace pigs, the cost averaged £1000 an animal. This was no small gamble or investment, but they were amongst the finest of their type and Den was happy to purchase quality to improve the herd. He wanted the best on his farm and was prepared to pay for it.

One cannot help feeling that the success of George Owen's horses also helped with some of the costs as well. It was during the 1953–4 jumps season that George's stable jockey, a young Dick Francis, who would later become a leading crime fiction writer, became champion jockey. To win the jockeys title you have to ride more winners than anyone else in the season, so it's not hard to imagine that the family would have enjoyed a few good touches at the bookies with that amount of success and Den's bank balance must have looked quite healthy on the back of his racecourse successes.

George was not only a fine trainer of horses but three of his stable jockeys went on to be Champions. Some five years after Dick Francis was Champion, Tim Brookshaw achieved the feat and then the following year Stan Mellor was also successful. Mellor would win the Championship for the next two years to make it three out of three For three Northern based jockeys to become champion jockeys all within six years, was testimony to the level of success being enjoyed over timber by the many trainers across the Midlands and North and of course to George's immense skill as a mentor. In the history of jumps racing this fact seems to have been forgotten and it is hard to think of any trainer who has sent out three champion jockeys attached to their stable in modern day racing. Martin Pipe had Peter Scudamore, Richard Dunwoody and Sir Tony McCoy and the latter definitely dominated jumps racing for a very long period. The fact that the only other name to be in the same company as George Owen is Martin Pipe, who is revered as a legend of the sport, speaks volumes for George and his ability.

Such was the success on the farm and Den's love of horse racing that Den took out his own racehorse training licence. He started using the gallop on Decoy Farm that had been left when

George Owen moved from Rough Hill to Cholmondley. Working on the farm at the time was Don Cowley and his daughter Muriel. Don had a jockey's licence and he and his daughter rode out daily for Den. There was a real sense of horseracing everywhere you turned at Rough Hill and Den now, with his cows and pigs working well, fancied a new challenge. The two boys, John and David, loved riding on the farm. They also enjoyed the odd race day out to Haydock Park, Manchester Racecourse or Bangor on Dee, to see the famous family colours of light blue with a dark blue diamond on the body and cap, colours that survive to this day.

David's term report from Hampton House at the end of 1950 was the kind many parents have seen over the years. It showed he had a real aptitude for learning, but they too had noticed some carelessness and in some cases a lack of motivation, particularly for Geography where in contrast to most other comments it said— "rather poor but he tries hard". Given the other subject comments, it was possible the teacher was not sure which child he was! It was all satisfactory but far from glowing. However, it was Year 1 and he was getting used to living away from home and the strange habits and expectations of boarding school. He soon adapted to Hampton House and the strong reports started to appear as a matter of course, with the only negative comments being the continued "careless errors" through lack of concentration. He just found the maths subjects extremely easy and for that reason rushed through things, according to his teacher. Meanwhile his business acumen started to rear its head as David decided to set up a shoe cleaning business. This went down very well at Hampton House, his personal bank balance started to grow, and he liked having money in the bank.

There was a hiccup in November 1951, the date is the 5th,

and the boys are playing with fireworks at the farm. An explosion of fireworks saw David running from the scene into the dairy with parts of him on fire. He reached for water to extinguish the blaze but only succeeded in taking hold of the boiling water used to treat the milk and his legs were covered in scalding water. He had extensive burns to his legs and, whilst bandaged up, was kept from school for quite some time, as the wounds healed. A setback but not a disaster and lessons learnt by all involved. Never one to waste time he taught himself to knit and crochet whilst recovering, another string to his bow!

It is interesting to note that the price of school and a week's boarding for a term at Hampton House for the Pickering brothers in 1952 was £104, 10s. Ironically the ten shillings was for extra milk for David. That must have irked Den to pay for milk for his son, given he had an entire dairy full of it back at Rough Hill!

David described school life at Hampton House as enjoyable rather than eventful. He loved the sport and was in all the teams, playing Football, Cricket and Hockey and while he was not one of the stars, he was always in the team and played key roles in each. One of his proudest moments was on 4th July 1953, in the Hampton House Sports Day where he won the Junior Cricket ball throw and broke the previous school record, the trophy has survived for sixty-seven years. History does not reveal if his record survived the school, which was knocked down to make way for houses in 1985. David returned many years later to play hockey for Deeside ramblers on the very same site. His interest in hockey was sparked at Hampton House by the Master of Sport and Welsh International Hockey player, John Saunders Griffiths.

In September 1955 David enjoyed a great summer holiday and had now finished his schooling at Hampton House. He was set to join brother John at Rossall School, where both boys would board. For those who do not know Rossall School, it sits on the beachfront half-way between Cleveleys and Fleetwood, on the rugged Fylde coast. The Irish Sea winds regularly pound the coastline there and in 1955 it must have seemed as remote a place as you could imagine. Of course, joining your brother at a school always makes life a little easier but terms are now a long time away from home and schools of the '50s are not without their discipline. Student number 770 — D O Pickering — is charged £114 for a term and, with John there as well, private education was not a cheap option. In 1955 the average wage was just 217 shillings a week, or just under £11 a week before tax, with a take home of about £9.50. That is less than £600 a year. The Pickering boys' schooling cost was just short of £700 a year. It was quite an investment in the boy's future by Den and an indication of how the farm was really paying its way and of his determination to provide his children with the best available schooling.

Chapter 10
Challenging the Norms

In his never-ending quest to improve the efficiency of his farm, in 1956 Den embarked on a radical piece of thinking; between training racehorses and going to the races! Up until now farming convention dictated that cows come in during the worst of winter and sleep on concrete floors padded out with straw to protect them from the hard surface. To keep the cows healthy there is a huge amount of labour required to remove both the cow manure and the old straw on a regular basis and then to replace the straw. It was also expensive to keep buying fresh straw. Den was convinced there must be a better way. Going against convention is always risky, particularly in farming. It has been done like this for a long time, for a good reason, the old farmers will tell you. But Den knew both the labour and straw were expensive and his thinking was that if you didn't have to do this as often it would save money. However, the cow's health will suffer if you make their living conditions worse and that is of course counterproductive. Den decided, over the summer, whilst the cows were in the fields, to dig out the floor of his barn to a depth of almost two feet. He then got railway sleepers and built a false floor with a two-inch gap between each sleeper and added sawdust to the surface. The principal of his plan was that the cow manure would be pushed through the gaps in the sleepers and would act as further insulation over the winter and far enough away from the cows as to not affect their feet. The floor could then be washed easily with scrapers that then loaded what remained into a hopper for distribution on the fields. The wooden floor would then be far more comfortable and warmer for the cows than sleeping on concrete. It is fair to say Den was excited about the winter of 56–7, as he further invested in blocking out draughts in his barn and made it a much more comfortable environment for his herd, but would it work?

When it came to Spring and the cows were let out, he was elated. Firstly, the Cows seemed in great health and had wintered well, secondly there was a significant cost saving over winter, at a time when the farm produced less money. Almost as important was that the mucking out job, so hated by the workers, had been reduced substantially and made that much easier. The additional bonus was that the previous cost of bedding with straw was £3 a day; by moving to slats and using sawdust he had reduced the cost to just one shilling a day and that was before the reduction in labour. It was a significant saving. He declared it a great success and there are many articles in farming magazines and local papers heralding the new slatted floors. 'The innovator 'came up trumps again and farming moved on with slatted floors right across the UK. In time Den would change the wooden sleepers to concrete ones and deepen the hole underneath so that the task of clearing happened less often, this too would become the standard for Dairy farming.

Chapter 11
The Fighting Rossall Bookie

On the windswept Fylde Coast, the young Pickerings were progressing well. David was loving his sport, they even got to play Hockey on the beach when the tide was out, which made for a wonderful smooth, fast surface on which to pass the ball. He was also making a great fist of Rugby as an open side wing forward and occasional outside wing and he had restarted the shoe cleaning business. His life was a happy one.

A fagging assignment tasked for both he and John proved somewhat problematic as David was given the responsibility of waking John so that the two of them could commence their duties at seven a.m. Sadly for John, who liked his sleep, David confused the time and he had John ready by six a.m. It took a long time for John to forgive him and it was something he never failed to remind David of later in life. David would always retort, better to be ready and waiting for the day, a motto he would carry forward for most of his life.

This time, whilst in school, as well as the shoe cleaning, David added bookmaking to his businesses and he ran the book for all the big horse races for his classmates, no doubt helped by the knowledge from Uncle George and his father. David was always happier holding the book than being the punter and this must have been quite a coup, having all the kids who fancied a bet coming to you to place their wager. Knowledge being power, I am sure the prices for fancied Owen horses in any race were significantly worse than those available with other bookies. One could also imagine the second and fourth of Uncle George's Horses in the 1960 Grand National was a triumph for the Rossall book.

In 1957 Rossall school took David's year group to Spain. It was a cultural exchange to a Pension Hostal to experience the life of school children in and around Barcelona. One of their cultural day trips out included a classic Bullfight. Whilst some were appalled, David was enthralled by the spectacle. He saw the event and the occasion as something that was important to the people, something that brought about a real passion as they cheered every move of the matador. He left excited and impressed. On the journey back to the railway station a call of nature struck. He made his way into the huge public toilets at the railway station, which had four entrances and exits. On finishing his comfort break he came out of a different exit from the one he had entered and became separated from his group in what was a very crowded station. Perhaps his master at Hampton House who had suggested he was poor at Geography was not quite so wide of the mark after all!

In what, by today's standards would be described as a "disaster", the group simply moved on, either oblivious to being a student short or confident he would return. They made their way back to the Pension without him. David had the sense to enlist the help of a local policeman, who put him on the right train and within hours he was reunited with his group, disaster averted. One could only imagine the investigation into that event should it happen on any of today's school outings. The risk assessed world of today has most definitely changed from the one that existed in 1957.

David's brother John left Rossall in 1958, having achieved his GCSE equivalents and he headed for his intended vocation, taking over the running of the farm from father, Den. John missed the main event of 1958 at Rossall, when the school was the subject of a massive blaze. David and his classmates, many wearing cricket flannels and sweaters, some operating hand-held extinguishers and others dispatched to remove as many books as they could from rooms, before the Fire brigade arrived, fought bravely to save the school. Again, in today's world, it's doubtful, that a school and its teachers would send many children in to burning buildings to save text and library books, but these were different times and in the press cuttings from the day the headmaster praised the attitude and resolve of his students, saying that "they behaved wonderfully". The fire brigade saved most of the buildings and schooling continued, much to the disappointment of the students!

David stayed on at Rossall beyond his GCSEs to do his A Levels. The first Pickering to do so. The farm did not need another wage and so he was encouraged to pursue his academic qualifications. He took English, Maths and Physics at A level, all subjects he enjoyed and found relatively easy. He was also now one of the leading Cadets at Rossall and in June 1960 he and a few of his specially chosen colleagues were presented to Field Marshall Sir Claude Auchinleck. It was a celebration of one hundred years of Cadets at Rossall. Back in 1860, the Rossall cadets were amongst the first to take the oath of allegiance and this centenary day was commemorated with a special visit. The chosen cadets wore the original scarlet uniforms of the 65th Rifle Volunteers, specially hired in for the day. It was a grand occasion as the cadets took the salute from the Field Marshall and the Pickering family were rightly proud of their son's achievement.

David's time at Rossall came to a close and his summer term report for 1960 showed he was in the top half of the class for every subject and doing exceptionally well in both Maths and Physics; now, just the exam results to come. His aptitude for figures was evident for all to see and shone through his reports, from infant school all the way to A Levels. Confidence in his results was rightly high. He proclaimed to his mother that he really does not have to work hard at these subjects, he can just see the figures really well. It was the sort of conversation he felt more comfortable having with his mother having felt closer to her than his father.

John was, by now, the spitting image of Den and whilst David never felt jealous of his brother's relationship it was obvious John, with his bigger build and rugged looks, was always being groomed to be the natural successor on the farm. Den and John were at ease together in a way that David could never achieve. David always felt slightly intimidated by his father. Of course, whilst David did not resent the relationship it did mean his career path was less than certain, as he would have to do something no Pickering boy had done for three hundred years — making a living outside farming.

Margaret presumably felt that difficulty and uncertainty for David and, as most parents do, she compensated to ensure the youngest son felt the same importance in the family pecking order. The mother-son relationship between these two would remain a strong one. She would encourage, mentor and support and try to explain the vast opportunities that David would have in the rapidly evolving world of Britain in the 1960s.

When the time came to leave Rossall, the end of school report was very complimentary, with his Headmaster commenting,

"David has developed sound qualities and made a distinct contribution to the general well-being. I hope he too has the success, (in his exams) he deserves it, and I have no doubt he will go from strength to strength".

Chapter 12
Givuss' a Job?

David passed his A Levels but now he had a dilemma. He had not given a moment's thought as to what he could do after Rossall. Life had always been decided for him. Which Nursery, which school, what time to eat and drink and sleep and what to do every day of his life. If it was not rostered as a lesson, it was probably sport and if you were at home there were always chores to be done, helping with the cows, making deliveries, or supporting the horses — what do you do now?

Despite the encouragement of his tutors at Rossall, David had no idea what he wanted to do and in the absence of a university vocation that he genuinely wanted, the ever pragmatic Den again took a leading hand. David was taken on as an intern to be an articled clerk at leading Chester Accountants, Walmsley Henshall, under the watchful eye of Senior Partner, Norman Johnson. The office address was 29 Eastgate Row, Chester and it was a significant address. They had the Boot Inn Pub on one side and Pat O'Hearns Bookmakers on the other. One of these, the pub, still trades from the same building and the other on racecourses across the UK.

David described his early working life as easy. There was little supervision and if they completed the task set for them in the allotted time, the articled clerks were left alone. They were having the time of their lives, betting, drinking, playing snooker and socialising, not all of it out of hours either! It was not long before David became aware that he could have a bet in the bookies, then go to the upstairs filing room in his office, on the pretence of sorting a client's accounts and sit directly above the bookies where you could hear the race commentary. With the quality of racing information coming from home, life was again sweet. The wages were not huge, at £2.50 a week, but David had always found ways to supplement his income and here was no different.

During his time at Walmsley Henshall, David was exposed to both Chester Racecourse and Oulton Park Motorsport Race Circuit, as his company did the accounts for these two thriving businesses. Walmsley Henshall were also responsible for the ticketing operation at both venues.

In 1961 the May Festival at Chester Racecourse was as popular as ever, but the three days in May were the only time they raced on 'The Roodee'. It was not until much later, after the fire of 1985 that burnt down the mains stand, that the programme was expanded to run from May until September.

For the articled clerks, the ticketing operation at both the Racecourse and Oulton Park, was a welcome distraction from the drudgery of preparing mundane accounts for clients. During the May festival, the Clerks would arrange for the distribution or collection of tickets, they would then go to the racecourse and put the names of people on to the seats in the stands and they would assist with marshalling and stewarding. It was a great time. With each day a sell out, you can well imagine there was a thriving business in touting tickets, and these were smart lads! In years when rain fell, David would take the family Land Rover down to the centre of the course and pull people out of the Mud. His weekly wage was just £2.50 as an articled clerk but he was regularly getting £5 per car for freeing them from the earth.

Twenty to thirty cars a day for three days brought in well over three years' wages. This was rich pickings indeed and yet another example of him being prepared to do that bit more than the rest to make a living.

Getting his head down and beavering away in the Henshall office was never David's chief priority, far from it, but it was hard to imagine another job where you could work the system so effectively. He did what was needed and stayed employed and this suited him fine. It was worth persevering with, as he was enjoying a great standard of living. He had his daily routine, which was: arrive at a leisurely nine to nine thirty a.m., at eleven a.m. he would disappear before his lunch to head home, where he would go running with his greyhound, which was training for the both of them.

Den had given him a greyhound as a present, to train and with both Uncle and Father successful at training horses, he relished the challenge of the greyhound, particularly as this was something just for him to do. The dog had shown good skill, coursing at Altcar, near Ormskirk, and Den thought it might be something good for his younger son. David certainly got it fit; the two could be seen running across the meadows on a regular basis, with the greyhound on a lead. The first time David let it off the lead to see what it could do, it shot off at a hundred miles an hour, normally a good sign but when it would not return to his whistle, he became concerned. As he got closer to the area where he had last seen the dog, he could hear barking, loud barking — never good on a farm and even less so here, because the dog had four very frightened sheep bundled up against a fence. It took him all his might to move the dog away and free the sheep. Part of the experiment had worked — the dog was fast that was for sure, but he needed a better way to train it.

Good news for the training came in the shape of the "flapper days" held down at the Chester Greyhound track, now the site of the Greyhound Retail centre on Sealand Road. The principle of these days was that you paid a small amount to have the opportunity to put your dog in a proper starting box on the track. You could then see if it would chase the lure and start to learn to race like a greyhound before entering it to run in proper races. This appealed to David immediately. What could possibly go wrong, now that the dog could not get away? There was no livestock to upset and the dog was getting fitter and fitter, surely a coup on the track would only be weeks away.

His Uncle George was brilliant at delivering coups with his horses, his dad was getting the odd touch at the Bookies with the horses he trained, and now the youngest Pickering would become a great greyhound trainer. Not what five years at Rossall was all about, but I suppose you reap what you sow. The dog behaved impeccably on the way to the start and seemed a natural. He looked incredibly fit and as good a specimen as any other on show. David could see some of the other trainers eyeing up his dog once they knew George Owen's nephew was the trainer. It was with great expectation that David bundled the dog into the traps and in what seemed an eternity the lure finally got around in front of the boxes, the lids opened and — nothing. Nothing happened. His greyhound had turned around in the box and was looking for the way out, in the direction that he had been put in, literally facing the wrong way, and looking for David. He simply did not move. They tried a couple more times, but he just did not have an understanding of the game and so the first career change idea was well and truly nipped in the bud. David Pickering was not to be a Greyhound trainer.

Chapter 13
Investing in Life and People

After the failed Greyhound training career, it was back to the drawing board and back to Walmsley Henshall. With decent money in his pocket from pulling cars out of the Roodee and extra for driving milk deliveries across Chester on weekends for his father, the next of David's other possible career paths reared its head: the world of investments, stocks, and shares. In Watergate Street at the time, in the same way that you went into a bookie, there was a firm of Stockbrokers called Noble Pennington. In the early sixties the rules around compliance were vastly different to today. You could go into a stockbroker, look at the ticker tape, which displayed the, as near possible, real time share prices, that would then be displayed on the big boards, with their updated prices and as long as you could leave a 10–15% deposit you could buy a number of shares and the balance of payment for shares would be settled in twenty-eight days. This meant that you had twenty-eight days to pay the balance or sell the shares and either take the profit or pay for the loss. David liked the idea of buying shares, so every month he would buy £25 worth of shares and then save and work for his father to make the extra money to pay the balance of his shares. It was a fabulous discipline for one so young and he was a keeper of shares by and large, not a speculator who bought and sold quickly to make a fast buck. The first shares bought were Roots A, who were the forerunner of Leyland Motor Company, but many others followed.

During the years 1960–1965, David had joined the Chester City Club, where his father and brother were also members. He also joined the now defunct Palatine Club. He was playing snooker and billiards over lunch at either place regularly. These gentlemen's clubs would always have full size snooker tables, a place to play cards, a bar and lounge area and a willing steward who could organise food as well. At weekends, there was Rugby at Chester Rugby Club and Hockey with the Deeside Ramblers, social tennis and lots of socialising at weekends. There was always a party to go to, somewhere around the county. It could be at the Cheshire Young Farmers, where both brothers featured on the cover of their magazine in the Winter of 1960 or in one of the many farming family houses or perhaps a ball in one of the many halls that you found across the county back in the '60s. It was quite a social whirl.

David's friendship with Edward Walton was a strong one. They were at Hampton House together and they were regularly out at weekends in each other's company. It was at one such party, the eighteenth birthday party of John Shaw, that David met Sue Bateman and the two struck up a friendship immediately. Sue, born in Whitechapel, London, was technically a cockney, born as she was, within the sound of Bow bells. She was just seventeen and was boarding at the Mount School in York, a Quaker school, although it was not overly strict on religion. Sue's parents were from a medical background, with her father an Anaesthetist and her mother a Nurse. They lived in Loughton, near Epping Forest, Essex, and Sue was staying with John Shaw's sister, Liz, for the weekend of the party.

Sue was clearly impressed with her meeting with the dashing David Pickering. His family were well to do farmers, they owned and trained racehorses, the sons had their own cars and David was looking to become be a fully qualified Accountant. He was good looking, confident, and he seemed popular, maybe a little too popular for Sue's liking! She has her gaze set firmly on David and became aware, when talking to her friends, that when David is "dating" a girl he made a habit of presenting them with a silver rugby ball on a chain to be worn as a necklace. A nice gift and it's certain that Edward and The Walton family Jewellers were happy that David had a standing order with them for this item! Sue, however, saw more and more rugby balls and her thoughts of getting her own seemed overly ambitious.

Throughout the following years, they would meet up again at various parties and whilst no one can quite work out where and when things went from meeting at parties to them becoming an "item", it was not long before things became a little more serious and the meetings more frequent.

Not everything was parties and fun, the winter of 1962–63 was a particularly harsh one. There were six foot, and more, snow drifts across the UK. Travel was almost impossible, the Thames had ice flows and mini-Icebergs and of course the freezing conditions brought about huge problems on the farm. Fortunately, the loss of stock was exceptionally low because Den's cow sheds were performing well but that is where the good news finished. It was so cold everything was frozen, including the diesel. Machines would not work, what milk there was, was frozen in storage. Heating the average house was nigh on impossible, even the River Dee in Chester, froze over. Pickering's Dairies were struggling to supply their customers, even if they had the milk, they could barely get out to deliver, such were the problems on the roads. It was another extraordinary time to live through. But live through it the inhabitants of Rough Hill did. Like every other winter, this one passed, and the family set about repairing the damage and shoring up the farm just in case winter should arrive again with the same venom.

In the early 1960s, Sue Bateman had finished doing her A Levels and wanted to become a Nurse like her mother. She could not start Nursing until she was eighteen, so she enrolled on a Cordon Bleu cooking course in London for nine months and whilst this was a pleasant thing to do and she was mixing with those who are on the "Deb" circuit, the Nursing role was never far from her mind. After completing the course and turning eighteen, Sue enrolled as a nurse at Middlesex Hospital. Back in Chester, David's focus was clearly more to do with the advancement of pleasure than work, as a letter to all articled clerks in 1965, sent out by management, highlighted.

To all Articled Clerks

The activities of certain articled clerks during office hours has now exceeded all limits of tolerance from an office where it is accepted that they shall be treated as responsible individuals…….

Apparently, the office was not, and should never be, available for any social activities after working hours. It seemed that, for the articled clerks, gambling, drinking, and socialising was an indication that morale was good but work output less so. The management decided to put their foot down and whilst no direct blame is apportioned to David this was now curtailing his daily activities and he was not enjoying life in the same way.

On to more serious matters, David's articled accountancy exams were approaching at Caer Rhun Hall. He would sit them in September 1965 and his qualification, if successful, would be an important milestone. This he recognised as a major responsibility.

As well as his studies, David was a member of Chester Golf Club at Curzon Park, played Rugby at Chester Rugby Club and somehow found time for Hockey. Late in the winter of 1965, David was knocked unconscious whilst playing rugby and was forced to take time off to recover after a severe concussion. With the exams looming he decided that it was time to hang up the rugby boots and just stick to golf and hockey.

Assembly day for his articled clerk exams was set for the 18th of September 1965, and in true David style he passed with flying colours. No longer an articled clerk, but one ready for the challenges that may lay ahead as a fully qualified accountant. He was now the first professionally qualified Pickering and letters and telegrams came from relatives right across the UK. There was a growing feeling that Chester had now become too small for him and with bigger ambitions and qualification results in the bag, it was time for a fresh challenge and where better to find that challenge than London.

Chapter 14
London Calling

It is fair to say that if your family are making a good living as "gentlemen farmers", and you have an uncle who trains racehorses winning Gold Cups and Grand Nationals, that you are pretty well connected when it comes to Cheshire and that if you need something you either have the money to get it or you know someone who can get it for you. All that goes out the window as soon as you go to the big smoke, London. This move to London was going to be a major challenge for David and one that young people right across the UK were all doing at the same time, as the bright lights, parties and music of the swinging sixties become a huge attraction to head south.

David managed to get himself a job in London, working at Touche' Ross. A fine firm of accountants who did serious accounting work for serious companies. They were based at London Wall. Getting a job seemed relatively easy but finding somewhere to stay not so. David had to stand on his own two feet and while he had a handy portfolio of shares and worked some angles at Chester Racecourse, as well as a few successful bets, he was not flush with cash and finding accommodation in London was difficult. There simply was not enough housing for all of those who wanted to be in the capital. It was, after all, the Swinging Sixties and London was the place to be. Everyone wanted to either party there or work there and just as quickly as an advertisement was posted of available accommodation there were people on the doorstep in minutes taking up the offer.

David saw an advertisement in the paper one afternoon for a room to rent and share and as he arrived at the place on Camden Hill Road another person was already on the doorstep, clutching the same advertisement. It was Flat 3E, 4 Airlie Gardens, opposite the Windsor Castle Pub. The man he was met by on the steps was a chap called Jeremy Oates. The two eyed each other up, exchanged a few words and then agreed they would be flat mates. By today's standards another extraordinary occurrence. If you are a mother or father, think about your twenty-four-year-old son, leaving home and then sharing a room with someone they have never met before, no en-suite, a bath down the hall and a small wardrobe each to keep your clothes in. To say it was basic is an understatement. This is what people did in 1960s London and with little or no alternative the two simply got on and tried to make it work.

There was of course time to return home at weekends, play some golf at Curzon Park Golf Club and David was selected to join the Deeside Ramblers Hockey Club on their Easter tour to Llandudno. His commitment to the Hockey Club was difficult living in London but he was taken on as a playing member at the Crostyx Hockey Club back at the village of the Bateman family near Epping Forest, where he was spending significantly more time with Sue Bateman!

On the work front, the roommates got on well, Jeremy, and David were plotting their business plans and they hatched a couple of schemes that involved working together, that they hoped would make them good money in the commodities markets. Jeremy had just set up his own business. The eponymously named Jeremy Oates Ltd — Commodity Brokers. He had previously set up J. Oates and Partners, Import-Exports of 29 Princess Road NW1 but commodities were the favoured flavour of 1966. Jeremy had a little experience trading and was now ready to start trading commodities. David, as we know, had been buying and selling shares for some time and had his own little portfolio. It was this portfolio, used as collateral, that started to make things happen for the two of them as they worked the commodities markets.

Jeremy had a system to trade Copper and almost anything else for that matter but particularly copper. It involved being very disciplined and obeying a graph that he had put together. When the price hit various points on the graph, you bought the stock and when it hit other points, you sold the stock. It was fiendishly clever, or at least that was what the two of them thought and they were determined to make it work. They trusted the charts.

Both partners believed in the system and now they simply needed a broker to allow them to trade on margin, for the right size of stock to make it worthwhile. The chosen broker was Bassett Smith and Co, of Lime St, London. David lodged his entire share portfolio, then valued at in excess of £2500, something in the region of £40,000 in today's money, to act as security to allow Jeremy and he to trade. The problem with graphs and systems, is that they don't account for day-to-day blips. If there is a pandemic, for example, like in the UK in 2020, then your graph simply cannot account for that. With the significant trade of 25 tonnes of copper contracted under their names, they were shortly to hit a big bump in the road. A bump that but for the kindly partners at Basset Smith might have seen David's shares wiped out, as the big variation on the price of copper really caught them out. Bassets allowed them to make an immediate payment in cash to cover the margin shortage and to keep running the position, which in time recovered and they were able to realise a significant profit. But for Bassett's consideration and generosity it could have been all so different. They might have been wiped out.

A move from the Airlie Gardens flat to Allen St, W8, in slightly better accommodation, became possible after some successful trades and this made things a little more bearable. Living with the unkempt Jeremy was never easy. His appearance was of little importance to his day-to-day life and neither were his surroundings. David pointed out to him on one occasion that his trousers were filthy and needed dry cleaning. He took them off and put on another pair that were not much better and shamed as he was, duly headed to the dry cleaners. He seemed to be gone for an eternity and just as David was about to go looking for him, he appeared with not only the said pair of trousers cleaned but the ones he was wearing were also now immaculate. He explained that when he got there, they had a two for one offer so he removed the trousers he was wearing, offered up both garments to take advantage of the deal and sat in the dry cleaners in his underwear waiting for them to be finished. He really was quite proud of himself.

The same pride was not evident when Jeremy was arrested at Euston Station whilst waiting in a queue to get the train to Chester. Things had gone well on the commodities trading front and the two now had their own small business separate from Jeremy's own, which was called CF Commodities. David had asked Jeremy to take £500 out of the bank from their trading account, part of his profit, and bring it up to Chester, in cash. A lot of money to be carrying in those days, a figure ten-fold that would be about right now. Whilst waiting in the queue for tickets, Jeremy, with the £500 stuffed down his waistband, was preoccupied with the financial section of the paper and as the queue shuffled forward, he would pick up his "grip" and then move it on, without looking. Suddenly there was a small fracas, as a woman screamed and shouted for the police. A policeman duly arrived and grabbed Jeremy by the arm and led him off to a nearby interview room. It seemed he had absentmindedly picked up the young lady's case and was moving down the queue with it. He had to explain to the police how he had mistaken the lady's bag, for his own grip and quite why someone who looked like a tramp was carrying £500 in cash! Two trains later, he made his way up to Chester and delivered the money. The story had everyone in fits all weekend. That was Jeremy.

The postscript is that things did not work out too bad for Jeremy and his graphs. He bought a two-hundred-and-fifty-acre farm in Hampshire, which he told David was primarily down to some particularly successful cocoa trades. He farmed it until he couldn't make the money he thought it should. In recent times he set up a series of large secure warehouses on the farm that now don't house cows but very expensive cars for people who only visit London infrequently and want their car kept safe. He then has them delivered to their hotel or house when they are in the capital. Nice work if you can get it and he is yet another successful diversified farmer. The two remain firm friends to this day.

David's day-to-day business with Touche Ross was demanding. They were a serious force in accounting in the '60s and '70s and they expected results. For a young accountant trying to make his way in London, the Swinging Sixties were not so much as swinging, more rocking gently as you tried to fulfil the work quotas of your bosses. Sue was able to escape the Nurses' quarters occasionally. Matron would vet those who came to court her nurses, before allowing them to leave on a night out but that was all right, she approved of David. On a Thursday, where Sue had worked through the night for a week and was rostered off over the weekend, she would finish shift at eight a.m. on a Friday and then drive her car to have a couple of days with David, at Rough Hill in Chester.

Margaret, David's mother, is remembered fondly by Sue as she was extremely kind during these years. She would have a hot water bottle in Sue's bed waiting for her and then would put her to bed to sleep during the day to recover from her journey and the previous night's shift. Sue recharged after a sleep, would join David in the evening and the two of them would then head to whichever party happened to be on over the weekend after hockey or racing.

Chapter 15
A Race for Life

It was not always back to Chester at weekends. It was in June of 1966 that Den had one of his biggest wins as an owner. A highlight of any racehorse owner's time in racing is a winner at Royal Ascot on the flat. The Royal meeting only takes place for five days a year, it was a four-day meeting back in 1966. The blue riband Sprint race is called The Kings Stand. A flying, five-furlong race in which the horse's clock forty miles an hour up the straight. It is a far cry from Den's first real horse of quality, Grand Truce, of whom Den said, "I wish we could find a five-mile race for him" such was his stamina and staying power. Den's Ascot horse was called Roughlyn. Named after their farmhouse and the horse's sire Ballylinan. Roughlyn was being trained under the watchful gaze of Malpas based trainer Doug Francis and after a career that started with a best placed third as a two-year-old, he broke his maiden in 1964. He won five times as a 3yo in an amazing five-week spell and then showed his real class with a win in the listed Harewood race at York in 1965. It was after the York success that Doug and Den hatched their plan to run at the Royal meeting in 1966. In the spring of 1966, they put Roughlyn out at Redcar on the straight five furlongs, to get his "eye in", which he won with ease and then they entered the Kings Stand, set to be run on Day four of the 1966 Carnival. It was an ambitious plan for a home bred, up against some of the fastest horses, owned by some of the wealthiest people, in the country.

Roughlyn was one of ten runners and confidence amongst connections was high after a stunning win at Pontefract where he had all but equalled the track record. That was followed by an easy win in the Booths Gin at Sandown and then the Redcar win. Despite his success, and the raw speed he had shown, the Kings Stand was a Group 1 race and the experts doubted he had the class to win. They were wrong. He strolled in at a healthy 20/1, being delivered by his jockey right on the line, in what was described as a perfect ride.

But for the words of Horseracing legendary jockey, Lester Piggott, this might never have happened. Lester rode Roughlyn at two years of age and despite him only finishing third he told Doug Francis to put this one away for the winter, let him grow and strengthen up and you will have yourself a half decent sprinter. Doug did as he was told, and Lester was right. In today's world of horse ownership dominated by wealthy Arab Sheiks and American billionaires it's hard to believe that a small northern based owner could win this race but win he did. The sport of horse racing is always the richer when the "little man" triumphs. This was a collection of ordinary people who made something extraordinary happen and they dined at the top table of horse racing for one particularly important day.

It was a great success too for Mr Hugh Moss of Aston near Nantwich, Cheshire, for he was the farmer who had bred the horse. He sold it to Den for 250 guineas, with a clause that if he won a race another 150 guineas would be paid. He got the extra money and a decent breeder's prize for the Ascot success as well.

The other success story on the day was Roughlyn's Cheshire jockey, George Cadwaladr; he was the one who rode such a perfectly judged race and impressed all those who witnessed it. The Cadwaladr family were renowned in Cheshire for moving livestock around the UK with their haulage business and the Pickerings and Cadwaladrs had worked together for years. Den giving George the leg-up on Roughlyn seemed appropriate. George had ridden almost all Roughlyn's wins and The Kings Stand win was by far the biggest feather in his cap. It would propel him up amongst the elite jockeys who had ridden a winner at the Royal meeting and made the southern trainers with their huge strings sit up and take notice. Roughlyn would go on to win twelve times on eleven different racecourses and would win over £4000 in an all too brief career.

Den had numerous successes with his horses. Odd Man Out won 19 times and was placed thirty-one times over jumps, a phenomenal record for any horse. Tea Fiend won several times and of course that superb fourth in the National but it was doubtful any gave him as much pleasure as that super charged sixty seconds in front of the Queen at Ascot in June 1966. There is also no question that the 20/1 odds helped the bank balances of various members and friends of the Pickering family as well! One other thing was certain, David had inherited his addiction to the thoroughbred in a way that brother John hadn't.

Chapter 16
They think it's all over" — not yet

On reflection David's time working in London was not altogether what he wanted. It was a much more frenetic lifestyle than that to which he had become accustomed in Chester. The pressure to perform, day in day out, was ever present in the offices of Touche Ross. The work was far more demanding than in Chester, with large corporations paying for armies of accountants to sift through endless data. You were not a person, working within a business who cared about their staff, or even knew their names. You were simply a processor as part of a system. David had enjoyed too much his previous work opportunities where he could basically do what he wanted, when he wanted to do it, and the shackles of this London job simply did not allow him to be himself. London was a hugely different world.

Different world it was, but it was not without highlights. Sue and he were now seriously dating. She even confessed, bravely, in a letter in late 1966, to loving the fact that there were now "distinguished grey hairs" appearing on his head, although this statement came more as an apology rather than as a compliment. Other highlights of 1966 were, of course, that England won the World Cup and David managed to get tickets to see them play in their Quarter final game at Wembley. Under the incomparable Sir Bobby Moore, they beat Argentina 1–0 and progressed to the Semi Finals and the rest is history. Never a keen football fan, it was the sense of occasion that had the greatest impact as he could not recall the score later in life, convinced as he was, that England had lost in that game. It would have made winning the World Cup exceedingly difficult had they lost that Quarter Final!

He also got tickets to see British Heavyweight sensation, Henry Cooper, stage his second unsuccessful challenge for the world title against the enigmatic and greatest Heavyweight of all time, Cassius Clay. He would, of course, become Mohammed Ali. On the night, Ali showed everyone in attendance just why he was "The Greatest" by dismissing "Our "Enery" in just six rounds. Ali was so much more than just a boxer and the entertainment and stage presence of "The Greatest" was not wasted on David. Yet again it was the occasion rather than the result that impressed him most.

The event that had the most profound effect on the young David Pickering during his time in London was when he went to see the world's first modern day super star Evangelist, Billy Graham. To understand the coverage and respect this man commanded you need to realise that in 1966 in one televised broadcast around the world, it is estimated his preaching's were seen by over 2.5 billion people. Let us just focus on that for a second. There were only seven billion people in the world and he was seen by 40% of them, in today's world that is quite some market penetration. He fought against racism, he told of a better life for those who could use the teachings of Christ and he communicated about Christianity better than anyone had done for a long time and the crowds loved him.

While the Catholic Church, with its massive world following, demanded abstinence of almost all the pleasures of life, Billy Graham spoke of a Christ like existence that allowed human beings to, well, 'be human beings', if humans showed consideration and love for each other. In a world that was rapidly changing this was a special voice of reason. Recollections of the evening by David were not of a spiritual type. David and his family had always been church goers and he remembered fondly that his father, whilst not always at Church on Sundays, prayed every night. This habit, David has continued all his life and he feels it calms the day and repairs the mind. His memories of that night, though, were those of witnessing a stellar performance and awe at the way this man was able to bring so many people into his circle of influence. It was an unforgettable moment, but not for reasons that most would have thought, as he witnessed the whooping and wailing of the converted. No, this was for David, a lesson about marketing and communicating and the power of people believing in you. There is no doubt later in life these memories helped steer the process of David's choices and his desire to communicate and market the products for which he was responsible.

With the decision of a possible return to Chester weighing heavily on his mind at the end of 1966, David had a bigger proposition that he needed to get sorted before facing the work dilemma. He was contemplating a proposal of Marriage to Sue. He knew the family well and had stayed many times at the family home, "Araluen House" in Loughton, Essex. He seemed to get on well with Dr Donald Bateman and his wife Jane, Sue's father and mother, but asking for her hand in marriage was an unknown and he did not like unknowns. Surely, they would not turn down his request, would they?

David hatched a plan, one that he hoped would put the odds firmly in his favour and make the answer of 'No' from Sue's father almost impossible. It was a tactic he would use many times in the future, and it was all about timing. In early December he asked his family if he could invite Sue's parents to spend

Christmas at Rough Hill. With other siblings in the Bateman house, it was not altogether certain they would agree but they did. On a mid-December weekend, when Sue was staying in Chester, David and Sue took a drive in David's MG Midget, around the duke of Westminster's estate. Something you could do back then, an action that these days, with increased security, could result in you being arrested. Eaton Golf Course was on the estate and you could enter via Eccleston or the Wrexham Rd entrances. They arrived at twilight as the sun was setting. By that time of day, the Wrexham Road exit was closed, and they had arrived at that edge of the estate. With the way ahead blocked, they stopped there. It was fortunate the heater in the car worked as the temperature was below freezing. Perhaps it worked a little too well as it melted Sue's patent leather shoes but that was not the only thing that melted. With Eaton Hall as his backdrop on one side and the Golden Gates of the Estate on the other, surrounded by huge oaks and wild deer, David proposed. It was an idyllic setting.

Ignoring the fact that Sue is fairly certain David knew those gates would be locked, David secured the acceptance from Sue and he confirmed it with an engagement ring, courtesy of his good friend Edward Walton, where he assures us that a "small discount" was applied. Edward would inevitably take charge of the wedding ring as well, not just because of the family jewellers but also in his capacity as best man at the wedding.

That was part one of the equation sorted. Now the tricky bit. Firstly, to keep the news contained between the two of them and secondly so that David can ask Sue's father for her hand in marriage and get that all-important family permission. This is when timing is everything and his plan was in full operational mode. Surely no family would want to spoil Christmas by denying the happiness of their child to get married and certainly not when they are a guest in the beau's family house. A no from Donald would have put a real downer on Christmas! It was indeed a cunning plan!

Sue's family arrived at Rough Hill on Christmas Eve and on Christmas Day, after present giving, David asked Donald Bateman for his daughter's hand in marriage. Donald later revealed that his agreement was almost a formality and there were times where both he and Jane wondered if David would ever propose. Dr Bateman wrote a lovely letter to Den after Christmas where he thanked both Den and Margaret for their wonderful hospitality and expressed that both he and Jane could see how fond the family were of Sue and how happy that made them. He also expressed surprise that David was so unsure of what his answer to the question of marriage would be. Fifty-three years later that union is proof positive that everyone was right when they thought these two ideally matched.

It was difficult for Sue to go back to work in the new year of 1967. She had just enjoyed the most marvellous time at Rough Hill, and she was to be married. On returning to her hospital two other girls in her shift had also got engaged and life would be different for all of them in what was another whirlwind year. Sue changed job from Nursing to working as an Air Hostess (yes, that is what they were called then) for British European Airlines and was based out of Gatwick. David and she met up when her schedule allowed. Sue was now living in the ironically named "Paradise Cottage" in Horley. Those who have visited East Grinstead and the surrounds will understand the irony. She wrote to David regularly whilst travelling from exotic locations like the Taj Mahal Hotel in Bombay and the Missions Hotel in Denmark, from Singapore and Hong Kong and always the letters affirmed their love for each other. Her nursing background made her a first choice on many long-haul flights, including, the Airline believed, her ability to aid childbirth. On one flight a Chinese speaking woman had boarded at Gatwick, to return to Hong Kong, in a very advanced state of pregnancy. Sue spent the entire journey terrified the woman would go into labour and she would have to act as midwife in mid-flight. Given that she had not actually done much work in maternity as a nurse, this would have been somewhat of a challenge. It did not happen, however, and they arrived safely before the woman gave birth.

Whilst Sue was travelling the world, David was trying to work out how to extricate himself from London and get back to Chester, when he saw a job advertised to be a Management Accountant at Cabot Carbon Black, at Lees Lane, Ellesmere Port. This was a more practical use of his qualifications and it achieved all his current ambitions. A decent salary was on offer, a job with meaning, where people made something and an all-important return to Chester. Cabots produced carbon and then used that carbon initially in the process of making tyres and latterly as ink for the print industry. They were owned by the huge American conglomerate based in Boston and controlled by one of Americans most wealthy families the Cabot's. David applied for the job, was successful and in late 1967 he took up post.

Chapter 17
White, Black and Brown Collared Husband

Sue and David were married in October 1967 at Loughton Church in Essex, near Sue's family house. It was an exciting time leading up to the wedding. With both sets of friends living in different parts of the UK it was decided that a wedding and reception would take place in Sue's hometown with her family and friends attending on the day and then later another reception would be held at Rough Hill for all the Pickering family and friends. The latter party was very nearly cancelled as there was a severe outbreak of Foot-and-Mouth on the Shropshire/Wales border and fears were strong that should this disease spread the Pickerings could once again lose everything. Den and John instigated wash troughs with antiseptic baths across the farm, stringent hand washing, the sort of measures those of us living in the 2020s are becoming all too familiar with in a world of Covid-19. Anyone entering the farm sheds had to constantly dip their shoes in to these detergent baths and the prospect of 150 guests from across Cheshire and Shropshire visiting for the reception was a massive worry. With virus security at an all-time high they managed to stage the party for the assembled guests, everyone had a great time and Den and John managed to keep the herd relatively clear of the virus throughout the year.

After the wedding celebrations the newly married couple set off on what to many would have seemed a Movie star honeymoon. Not the Costa Del Sol for David and his bride, they flew off to the sunny, palm covered, sandy shores of Bermuda. It must have made quite an impact on David as many will have seen him later in life sporting a pair of tailored shorts and long socks, just like the Police officers and Gentlemen of this idyllic British enclave. For the newlyweds of course it had everything. Beautiful beaches, a wonderful English tradition, polite, well-educated people, who gave outstanding service and were extremely proud of their island. Bermuda is just ten miles from one end to the other and two miles wide and in essence the twenty square miles seems just a tiny dot in the Atlantic Sea, but it was the perfect place to spend two weeks and enjoy the start of married life.

New beginnings in every way greeted them upon their return. David had purchased, for about £3000, a big house, which was a former pub in the village of Llong on the outskirts of Mold. It was no more than three miles from Rough Hill and about a twenty-five-minute drive to his new office. Sue had resigned from BEA and taken up a nursing job at Meadowslea Hospital, Penyfford. The two set about immersing themselves in their respective jobs, relishing the challenge of setting up their new lives. David was keen to know everything about Cabot's and asked to be allowed to work on the factory floor to get to know the business better. There was no objection from management. The work clothes required for those working in this carbon industry was to wear black overalls, for obvious reasons. He had gone from white collar worker to black collar in one easy move.

David wanted to understand what it was like to work the night shift and the effect this had on workers, and during that period, both he and Sue worked nights in their respective jobs for a month. Sue to support David and David to appreciate and understand every aspect of the Cabot business. This self-imposed learning would become a principle of his involvement in businesses in years to come. Understand every part of what you are trying to do and find a way to make it better. It was what his father did, it's what his brother John was trying to do, and David would do the same.

Cabots were impressed. He had shown real commitment and word spread fast. Things were moving quickly in the late '60s in the world of accounting and Computers were going to be the future. IBM ran a special accountancy course to ready businesses for the new age and Cabots sent David to London for a month on the course. He was permitted to stay at the Carlton Towers Hotel in the centre of London and when he explained he could stay with in-laws instead, Cabot's allowed him to claim for the hotel rate daily but to stay at Sue's parents. This was a tidy earner for the newly-weds and helped tremendously with the cost of renovations on the house back home.

After a year of working at Cabots, so impressed were they with their new recruit, that they offered David the opportunity to join the main firm at their Headquarters in Boston. This came with a substantial increase in salary and of course a major move to live in America. He and Sue discussed the offer, but they remember that they never really, seriously, considered it to be an option. They just did not want to move so soon after the major upheaval of the last year and they could not see themselves living in America. Once they had decided not to take the significant career advancement by moving to America, the next move was an all-together easier one.

David took the decision to resign from Cabots and go back to the farm at Rough Hill. Den had handed over complete control of the Dairy to John, but his pig farming was proving to be problematic. Den was getting older now and did not want to keep working as hard as he had been. The introduction of the Swedish Landrace pigs had worked but there was always another problem and it was just so hands-on looking after animals that demanded so much more care than Cows to get the best out of them and make the business work. Den asked David if he would take control of the Pig business and see if he could make it more profitable. It was an offer he accepted. It is fair to say not everyone thought that it was a great idea. Both brothers believed the other was living the "life of Riley" but they, up until now, had stayed out of each other's way. Now the chemistry would be tested as they would be working on a day-to-day basis in the same environment. Not at loggerheads on decisions, as the two businesses were of course very separate, but on the family farm, sharing workers and machinery. David knew all about the dairy, he had driven deliveries of milk regularly, he had lived the life of a young farmer for some time before going to London but running the Pig business, now that was a steep learning curve, and one he was looking forward to.

Chapter 18
A Pig Farmer?

With three hundred years of farming heritage in the DNA of the Pickering family, perhaps it was no shock that just as David appeared to have escaped into society, away from the farm, to become a professional businessman, he would find the calling to get back into the family business, a strong one. David's brief journey into the big wide world was not without incident or indeed enjoyment but the challenge set by his father to take the pig farm and really run with it was one his ego could not refuse and he loved the opportunity to be his own boss. After all, how hard could it be? His father had run a dairy business, milked cows, trained horses, invested in a pub or two and looked after one thousand pigs; all he had to do was look after the pigs. The machinery was in place, the sales of the pigs was looked after by a syndicate and in Ray Diggory, his first lieutenant, he had a fine worker with real knowledge. This was not only a chance to use some of the skills he had learnt as an accountant but the opportunity to make a real difference to the business. Surely with a bit of fine tuning there was a good profit in this sector.

David's wife, Sue, had never wanted to leave the UK to go to America with Cabots when the opportunity arose. She was happy with her local nursing role; she was also now pregnant and expecting their first child, so the thought of uprooting everything and moving across the Atlantic was even less attractive. In truth, David's head was never in the game of moving either, so the decision to leave Cabots, where he was on a good salary at double the national wage average, was not really that difficult.

Den had planned well in the business for his family and adding another wage to the Rough Hill budget was not going to be too much of a problem, particularly if the "accountant" in the family, that being David, could identify the loss-making areas and make the necessary improvements. It also meant that Den could take things a "tad" easier. He was President of the Chester City Club; he lunched regularly with work colleagues and was enjoying doing a little less. For Den now, life was rather good. He had both his sons in the business, the future looked rosy. He could go shooting with colleagues in the season, he was a loader on the duke's estate which was a privileged position, played the odd game of golf, a few escapes to Anglesey, to his good friend Max Tatton's wonderful estate and the prospect of a grandchild and another marriage in the family made 1968 a particularly good year.

David's brother John had been courting Max Tatton's daughter, Josephine (Jo), for some time. Max had made a significant sum of money out of being amongst the first to important crimplene into the UK. This was being used in all the latest ready to wear and affordable fashions and in the '60s the UK couldn't get enough of it as Carnaby Street and its imitators provided all the latest fashion looks using these new fabrics. To say, in a farming parlance, Max made hay while the sun shone with Crimplene would be an understatement. One of the trappings of his success was a 1000-acre estate that he bought on Anglesey; it was the Dullas Estate, on the North Eastern side of the island. Both Jo and David's wife Sue got on very well, they had been sharing a bedroom whenever they came to stay at Rough Hill, so they knew each other and were good friends.

Everyone was confident it was only a matter of time before John and Jo were married and, so it was, Jo and John were married in 1968 and moved into the Rough Hill Farm main house. Den and Margaret moved to a newly built Bungalow on the premises. This was a particularly happy occasion for all the families.

In David's life Christmas has always been important. It started when he was at home with the traditional family Christmas, with a house full of people, lots of great food and exceptionally good company. Everyone got on well and Christmas was special. None more so than when David proposed to Sue back in 1966, but perhaps the Christmas of 1968 runs close. As the extended family sat around the huge table, about to feast on one of several geese that had been prepared, Sue, in an advanced state of pregnancy started to feel the pains that she knew could only be the start of labour. Her nursing background meant she was not easily panicked but, as the frequency of contractions increased, she knew the moment was coming and she had little control over the timing from here on in. When she explained her predicament across the lunch table, both David and Den asked if she might just be able to hang on, at least until after the main course! Ever so accommodating, this she duly did and then David raced her off to the Chester Royal Infirmary, where their first child Nicholas was born. Mother and baby well and possibly the best family Christmas ever, topping off a special year. Roll on 1969.

Rough Hill was, by now, a busy place, a thriving business if you looked at the accounts of 1968. Turnover exceeded £168,000. More and more milk was needed to supply the Dairy business, which was flourishing and the amount supplied by their own herd wasn't enough to meet demand. Contracts to supply were being established in and around Cheshire and churns of milk were being dispatched to bottlers and creameries across the county and into North Wales. There were also over one thousand pigs on site at any one time and the product David inherited was that Rough Hill Farm would take what are known as weaners — very young pigs of between 12–15kg. They would then keep those pigs until they were fat and more mature at about 65–70kg and then sell them as bacons in the market. It was an efficient process logistically but a little unpredictable where price was concerned.

All the mature pigs were sold to a company called Phythians of St Helens. Each Thursday or Friday there would be a telephone conversation between the two parties where a price for the pigs and the number that would be sold were agreed and then on Monday morning the Phythians truck would turn up and collect the pigs and take them away. It was a system that worked well but with so many middlemen in the equation there were a lot of mouths to feed along the way. When the price of pigs was good there was money to be made, when the market began to be flooded with imported pigs, as we found our way into Europe, the price dropped. It was becoming increasingly difficult to make a profit. This was the marketplace David inherited. Fluctuations in the price agreed each week, could vary by as much as 20% and with profit margins running at around 10–17% there were weeks when pigs were sold at a loss. Not good business.

The new head of Picks Pigs, as he had named the business, David Pickering, was determined to find answers and to try and smooth out the supply chain curves, not just for his own farm but for those he now represented. He had, in a short space of time, found his way to become Chairman of the Chester branch of the NFU. This was the start of David's representative work and he felt very strongly about the plight of the farmer. There had been no change in the way farmers were treated by central government since 1947 and, whilst up until now the subsidies applied to farmers had worked reasonably well, times were changing. The government of the day, earlier Harold MacMillan and latterly with Ted Heath, were working towards common market entry and with this came more and more cheaper European Imports and further price pressure on British produced agricultural products. While the Government subsidies, on which farmers relied heavily, had remained the same, the price farmers were getting for their livestock was under constant pressure and the margins for the farmer were squeezed, in a lot of cases below sustainability. It prompted the almost always optimistic Den to voice in a rare talk to Cheshire Young Farmers that he was…

"extremely depressed about our traditional farming in this area. We cannot go on indefinitely producing more and more for less and less... I cannot think of a worse investment than to buy a farm at say £150–200 an acre, stock it and try to make a profit out of producing milk". (Dens original speech note)

If it was hard for the average farmer to make a turn on their products, it was slightly easier for Picks Pigs because at the time, with so much milk being processed at the farm, David had a strong supply of the skim from the milk to feed his pigs. Up until the mid-seventies, to supply cream to the industry, the raw milk was taken to the factory, where they separated the cream from the milk, the waste product was the skimmed milk. We, as a nation, only drank full fat milk, so with all the cream from Rough Hill going to Bodfari Creamery in North Wales, the excess skim, which had no value to the dairy business, was used to fatten up the pigs, which they loved. In turn the "pig muck" was then collected and sprayed onto the fields, which was fabulous for growing grass, which then of course got eaten by the cows and so the cycle begins again. Highly efficient and organic.

The cow to pig to cow farming process, and its component

parts, was a bone of contention between the two brothers, who were always looking to improve margins in their respective businesses. John believed there was value to the skimmed milk as a pig feed and that David should be paying for it and David believed there was value in his pigs' bi-product, that fed John's grass fields and that he should be paying an appropriate price for that. Den the mediator intervened and suggested that net, net, they cancelled each other out and for the time being they let the matter rest without either charging the other for their products.

David was extremely hands-on with his pigs. Not only had he taken full responsibility for the finances of the pig business and usurped it from the farm estate, at least that's how John saw it; but he was also donning the overalls to care for his pigs. It was on one such day that he used up the first of his nine lives. He and Roy had a routine for loading the pigs on a Monday. They had created a corral for the pigs and at the end of the corral was a walkway that led on to the arriving truck. It was efficient and required little manual handling. It just required the herding of the pigs, from their stalls, into the corral, which was done with a series of pens that decreased in size. As the entrance to the bottleneck, just before they boarded the truck, became crowded, David noticed some heads of the pigs disappearing and with it his profit. He jumped into the middle of the pigs to find out what was going on, only to discover two of the slats on his floor above the waste channels had moved and created a huge hole, into which the pigs were falling and as more pigs got pushed in further to the pens, more were going down the hole. He halted the passage of the pigs and dived down into the trough, which was of course, filled with pig muck. He was dragging the pigs up to floor level by their ears where Ray would remove them the rest of the way out of the hole to safety. They saved all the pigs but the last to leave the hole was David, covered from head to toe in pig muck and with more than a few bruises. It could have been so much worse. Had Ray not stopped the small stampede he could have been buried under pigs and drowned in the slurry. Fortunately, too, there was no build-up of gases in the chambers below as this could have also been fatal. It was just one of the many areas in which farming can be dangerous. David would later reflect on how cleaning the inside of the skim milk tanks with pressure washers was also fraught with danger as again there could be gas build-ups in there which could prove fatal if not released properly.

Disaster averted, they fixed the slats and on returning home Sue promptly threw David's clothes out the bedroom window and on to the ground below. The clothes she declared to be beyond repair, had no place in the house and were, in fact, the worst smelling clothes ever. Being a farmer's wife, she had seen and smelt some pretty poor clothing.

For all its promise 1969 was a disappointing year. The farm turnover fell from £168k to £143k and much of this was down to the price squeezes caused by the imminent entry into Europe. Den needed to approach Martin's Bank to increase the farm overdraft and, like all his other negotiations, he was aggressive. The letters exchanged between Den and his bank manager showed a forthright tone from both parties. In the end Den won the argument and got the increase, although not before the bank, as usual, extracted their pound of flesh with increased rates for the "higher risk". It seems "small change" now, but they were arguing over a half a per cent increase in the rate charged and both parties were too proud to back down. Common sense prevailed, Den got his money with a quarter per cent extra over base and the farm had the working capital it needed to keep going during this set back.

Picks Pigs were also feeling the cold wind of economic hardship. The price of pigs had fallen, and David's new business was losing money. He needed to sell some of his stocks and shares to support the business and he needed some help from Sue as well. She had some shares, gifted from her father, in Merseyside Docks and Harbours (MDH) and when David explained the deficit in the business and how they needed to not only plug the hole but to expand, if this was going to work, Sue agreed to sell her shares and put the money in to Picks Pigs. Sue's father, Donald, was none too happy about this but he understood her commitment to her husband, and he believed in David's business skills. The irony was that Sue's two other siblings kept their shares in MDH and it was only a few years later that the company folded making the MDH shares worthless. From David's perspective, Sue and his combined investment and commitment to the business by both of them, was a statement of intent. David was proud of their capital raise and even prouder that his wife had seen fit to support him, not just emotionally but financially as well. The words of his father, Den, were ringing in his ears about the value of a good woman. Den had said many times to his sons that *"when you marry, pick a good partner because a farmer's wife is more a part of the outfit than she is in any other walk of life. If she happens to be a good looker, so much the better"*.

David not only had a "good looker" for a wife but one who also supported him in every aspect of their business. She was a young Mother, who made a happy house a home, and an escape from the daily pressures of farming; there could be no greater investment in team Pickering and one for which he would be forever grateful.

Chapter 19
Invest for Success and March for Glory

David had faced the problems of 1969 head-on and, with the liquidation of a few assets and some cash available, he had a plan for 1970. His theory was that he needed to streamline the business, get rid of the middlemen and take control of everything bar the selling operation of the pigs. If the margins were small, so be it, you just needed far greater turnover to get the profit you required and that meant an expansion of the current business. He would fight the problem head-on and show confidence in the industry.

It was a tempestuous start to 1970 and it would prove to be one of the most important years for the people of the UK, at every level. Change was coming and it was needed. It was not just David Pickering who was fighting back, the nation wanted more and was prepared to fight for it. This was about to be the time of change.

In February 1970, the front page of the Daily Express carried a picture of farmers storming the capital and trying to take over both the Houses of Parliament and 10 Downing Street, as they demanded a better deal for farmers and a fair deal in the upcoming price review talks. Pictured amongst the protesters was Chester's recently appointed NFU Chairman, David Pickering. No doubt this young rebel has a file in MI5 somewhere, after this protest, despite the fact it was a protest without serious incident. The protesters never did get to meet either Harold Wilson or Ted

Heath, but they made their point with banner slogans that read, *"Unless we have the cash you starve*" and *"A bankrupt countryside equals a bankrupt country"*. It was a clever protest, at the right time, in addition to being amongst the politest ever witnessed. The large crowds, barred from the Houses of Parliament by row upon row of police, even started chanting "more pay for police". Now there is a novel approach to protesting that might well have served Arthur Scargill better in years to come!

By April, David had negotiated to take the lease of Compton Hall Farm, in Higher Kinnerton. It had been run by his cousin Anthony Pickering. Anthony was ex-army, and it is fair to say his interest in farming was not always his priority as was shown when the milk tanker turned up one morning at his farm. The tanker driver could find no one around the farm, but he had been here before and he knew where the milk tank was, so, he connected the truck only to discover there was no milk in the tank. Some twenty minutes had elapsed and still no one to be seen on the farm. He then knocked on the farm door, no answer, waited a little longer and still no noise. He started throwing some small stones at the upstairs bedroom window. The next image was of a naked man opening the curtains most indignantly and shouting, "What the bloody hell do you want?!" The tanker driver replied, "Where's the milk?" To which Anthony curtly said, "Where the bloody hell do you think it is?" And promptly shut the curtain. No milk was collected that day.

Despite Anthony's lack of interest in farming generally, he was an accomplished mechanic and David, Den and John kept him on to work maintenance across all the farms, which he did for a long time. The acquisition of Crompton Hall Farm meant David now had eighty sows and he had his own new supply of weaners from these sows. It was not enough to get to the size of herd he needed but it was a good start. This was the way forward: independence from the constantly fluctuating price of weaners and a stock that he could rear in one area and then fatten later at Rough Hill. The first of his acquisitions was in play and he was convinced the figures would add up.

In May, with both mainstream political parties supporting an entry into the common market later in the year, the General election produced a somewhat unexpected result. Ted Heath's Conservatives were elected with a clear majority, gaining seventy-seven seats, and totalling 330 in number. It was a workable majority but, for those of us who have lived through Brexit, the language he used when assuring the House of just how he would proceed with an entry into Europe sounds incredibly familiar. It seemed the country was ready for the change and had bought into the prospects of better trading throughout Europe. To give a flavour of the time as Ted Heath tip-toed his way through the procedure, the following were his words on the eve of entry:

"If we can negotiate the right terms, we believe that it would be in the long-term interest of the British people for Britain to join the European Economic Community, and that it would make a major contribution to both the prosperity and the security of our country. The opportunities are immense. Economic growth and a higher standard of living would result from having a larger market.

But we must also recognise the obstacles. There would be short-term disadvantages in Britain going into the European Economic Community which must be weighed against the long-term benefits. Obviously, there is a price we would not be prepared to pay. Only when we negotiate will it be possible to determine whether the balance is a fair one, and in the interests of Britain.

Our sole commitment is to negotiate; no more, no less. As the negotiations proceed, we will report regularly through Parliament to the country.

A Conservative Government would not be prepared to recommend to Parliament, nor would Members of Parliament approve, a settlement which was unequal or unfair. In making this judgement, Ministers and Members will listen to the views of their constituents and have in mind, as is natural and legitimate, primarily the effect of entry upon the standard of living of the individual citizens whom they represent."

That was what the people of the UK believed back in 1970 and history shows they were right to back this stance. It was without doubt the most productive period, economically, in Britain's history. The increase in prosperity of both the nation and the individual is without peer. The wealth created between 1970 and 2000 saw a generation of those who would be turning to their pension funds from 2000 onwards as the wealthiest we will ever know.

With turnover increasing across all the Pickering Farm and Food businesses and optimism under a new Tory Government, 1970 was shaping up ok, but it was not without personal sadness. On the 12th of June 1970, Thomas Fox died at the distinguished age of ninety-five. This was quite an "innings" for a person who had worked on the farms all his life and was testimony to his disciplined lifestyle. He had, in no small part, been responsible for the Pickerings owning and keeping their farm when times were tough, he had been a mentor to Den, when as a young boy he was learning the ropes and he had personally seen four generations of Pickerings at Rough Hill. His was a funeral that brought many farming families across Cheshire together. He had touched so much of rural Cheshire in his time as Bailiff of the Grosvenor Estate and no one could remember a bad word said about him. Thomas Fox was buried in the Tallarn Church grounds in Wrexham. His legacy lived on throughout rural Cheshire. He was certainly one of the good guys.

Chapter 20
A Farm for Life

At home, moves were afoot for the young Pickering family. It was time for a change of house. David put Kitali, their former pub cottage that they had bought for £3000 in 1967, on the market and sold it for £6000. Not a bad return over the three years they owned it and the first of his big profitable deals as a married man. The place he found to move to is the family home to this day, some fifty years later. It is Grange Farm, Kinnerton, and he purchased it for just £16,000 in September of 1970. He convinced the bank to lend him the money, as his business was expanding, based on presenting a very astute case to his Bank Manager about the future profitability of Picks Pigs and how with increased stock numbers he would be even more profitable. He said he was optimistic about the move into Europe and that things for the farmer could only get better.

In October of this year Ted Heath, with the support of Georges Pompidou, the French leader, took the United Kingdom in to Europe and proudly proclaimed:

"Let's be very clear about it, this is a moment of decision that will not occur again for a very long time if ever... But tonight, when this House endorses this Motion, many millions of people right across the world will rejoice that we have taken our rightful place in a truly United Europe!"

It was a seminal moment and one that would see the country, as

Ted Heath promised, prosper in a way that few could have believed. It was a new period of hope for a country that was struggling with its identity and up until now had spent most of its time looking backwards at the war rather than forward to the brave new world. Now things felt different. There was optimism where there had been scepticism, belief where there had been doubt and ambition where there had been none. A new set of trading agreements and a level playing field for the country that included all of Europe was a good thing, wasn't it?

At Rough Hill, 1970 rounded off very well, Den was able to reduce the overdraft on the back of the farm revenue exceeding £175,000 for the year and in a back-handed compliment to David he said, "before you were here with your accountancy qualification, we lost money on the farm, now you're back, we still lose money, but the difference is you can tell us where we lost it". Whilst that wasn't entirely true, the farm was making money, but he was right, in that David could point out the non-performing areas and they could look at addressing them. Having looked at the many gifts given that Christmas to long-standing clients of the Dairy business, Den must have seemed like an early Father Christmas as he handed out Cognac, Pheasants, cheese, and wine, to a huge list of good customers in the lead up to Christmas 1970 but then he always knew how to spend money and he knew the things people liked. He would always reward loyalty and he was much admired for it, a trait David inherited early in his business life.

Chapter 21
The Real Work Begins

As 1971 approached so too did a new challenge for David. His pig business was running better, and he was making a difference. David was a significant help in the preparation of the company accounts. Den and John invited him to start doing some work on Pickering's Dairies and asked him to look at how they could expand this business. This was another challenge he was looking forward to. They had seen how he had grown the pig business through acquisition and some clever deal making and it was time to put those talents to even more use. David set about the task in his usual thorough manner. He started a process he would repeat for the next 50 years. In the traditional break between Christmas and New Year he would write an account of the successes and failures of the previous year and then plot his ambitions for the following year and how they could be achieved. Each year he would also compare the ambitions of the previous year with what was actually achieved, and this acted as a ledger that would drive him forward year after year. His own personal checks, balances, on the job learning and a programme to achieve success.

The first task for David at Pickering's Dairies, was to examine every aspect of the business from grass grown to potted yoghurt on the shop shelf, cows milked to cream on the strawberries. He spent most of 1971 understanding the business and keeping an eye on his own expanding Pig operation. That expansion was not limited to the farm activities either, it also included the inhabitants of Grange Farm, for Sue was pregnant with their second child and on 25th March their first daughter, Angela was born.

There were now two children under two at Grange Farm and for Sue looking after a full-time farmer and young children it was particularly demanding. Much later in the year the family took their first holiday, a trip to Menorca, Cala'n Porter. It had been two and a half years of solid work without a break and David would reflect later that whilst it may well impress everyone with your dedication to your job, in reality, it is counter-productive to go so long without a break. The mind needs some downtime to process what you have been doing and make sensible decisions going forward. Coming back from holiday and feeling incredibly refreshed and eager to set about his tasks he would vow to never let that happen again. A decent break and some small weekend escapes would become part of his working life from now on.

Chapter 22
Mergers, Acquisitions and What's in a Name?

January 1972 was another key date for the 29-year-old David Pickering. His father proposed him to become a "Name" for Lloyds of London. For those not familiar with this process, Lloyds of London are the Worlds No1 Insurance underwriters. In essence, insurance companies take huge parcels of risk covering many, many different scenarios in similar fields, including oil tankers, small country housing estates, shopping centres, airlines and just about any insurable debt, to Lloyds. Lloyds then offer out to tender the insurance of that business with different accounts and behind every one of those different accounts are a series of assigned liabilities, and the responsibility for those liabilities is covered by named individuals. These groups of people will, if their fund is hit with claims, stump up the insurance money to the client. If they have few claims, then a pro-rata proportion of the policy premium is paid to the names. In essence it is like betting against disaster striking and of course the broader your spread of insured "things" in theory the less you are exposed to any one risk. In good years, the returns for investors can be very good, much higher than the stock market. In bad years of wars, earthquakes and tsunamis, a name can be wiped out. Den had been a Lloyds name since 1959, when he paid £2300 to enter this high risk, high return world. To date, events across the globe had been kind to him. Den had made significant profits and now he was proposing his sons.

To qualify as a name in 1972 you had to prove you had at least £60,000 in assets and, with his pig business going well, the shares he retained, his share of Pickerings Dairies, his new house and Rough Hill Farm, David met the criteria easily. Whilst there was significant kudos in becoming a Lloyds name and quite often great returns it would be three years before you received your first cheque, if one was due. It was all terribly civil as well. Each year in January the Lloyds appointed representative would turn up and invite you to lunch at the Grosvenor Hotel in Chester, where good food and much wine would be consumed. In 1972 our Man from Lloyds collected a cheque from David and handed over, pro rata, last year's share of the profits to Den. They say there is nothing like being a Lloyds name for the want of getting the morning papers and scouring world affairs to see how your finances could be affected. Most of us can only imagine! The headlines take on an entirely different feel when you wonder if that oil tanker that has sunk, or shopping centre on fire, is part of your insured risk. David was about to experience that responsibility.

By April of 1972 David had put most of 1971's planning for both his business and the Farm business into effect. The first was in his own business of Pigs. He bought Fron Farm, near Mold for £12,500 and this took his pig population to beyond three thousand. He now had sows in three different places producing weaners for him, which was his breeding operation and the fattening was still happening at Rough Hill. He had also invested in the welfare of his young pigs with the addition of big fans to circulate air and even warmer facilities for the winter with double skinned roofs and much less draft. Cold pigs do not put on weight easily. A happy warm pig was a healthy pig and a healthy pig put on weight more quickly and created more profit. In the same way as Den had profited with his Dairy herd by creating slatted floors and draft free barns, David was applying similar tactics with his pigs.

Not content with the responsibilities of Fatherhood and a new business he also found both time and money to buy a 10% stake in a company called Dee Electronics. They were, as the name suggests, a Deeside business that manufactured electronic panels and controls. David would later admit that, over the years, continually investing in this business and the associated technology would cost him £200,000 but, in 1971, Electronics seemed to be the future and he wanted to be a part of it.

On the dairy front, David had recommended that Pickering's buy Bodfari Creamery. Up until this point, Pickering's produced the cream, that they then sold to Bodfari, who packaged the cream and yoghurt and distributed it to the shops. David could see that if they could purchase Bodfari for a fair price it made sense to own the entire operation. An early "farm to fork" model. They offered a reasonable price and after some negotiation, the owners Hugh Davies and Geoff Butterworth agreed to the sale and they also agreed to stay on to run the business. This was a significant acquisition by team Pickering, and it was just the start.

There was just one major acquisition to come in 1972 and that was a farm called Maes-Y-Grug, the farm of Rex and Jean Uttley. They agreed to sell their pig business and David's pig empire grew even bigger. It had been one heck of a year in the Pickerings' M&A department and it sent out signs to the rest of Cheshire and North Wales that the new team of brothers meant business. Den was still in the office and oversaw proceedings, but he very much left the day-to-day running now to his boys. The last piece of the 1972 jigsaw was for Den to make David a full partner in Pickerings Dairies, which he did. David's hard work was recognised and rewarded. He had now made himself an integral part of the business and it was flourishing. It must have been a satisfying moment for Den. To have both of his boys now jointly responsible for the business and them taking control and showing all the ambition he had when he was their age. He was happy to take a back seat. His sixty a day cigarette habit was taking its toll. He did not fancy getting about as much as he had and these days much preferred a glass of red wine to discuss business over a long lunch than getting out on the farm. He had paid his dues and now was the time to sit back and put his feet up.

With all the acquisitions and new responsibilities in the business David took 1973 very much as a year of consolidation. Picks Pigs and Pickering's Dairies had taken on more debt as they expanded, and they really needed to deliver in terms of both turnover and profitability. They had invested in stock, machinery, and people and now all the component parts needed to contribute to making this a successful business.

David was still able to turn out regularly at Deeside ramblers for some Hockey, where, off the pitch, he was now Treasurer; it is what happens when they know you are an accountant. He also found time, as a new father of two, for some frames of snooker at the City Club where he was "racking up" quite a bit of gold type on the honour's boards (he holds the record to date for the most amount of gold type on the boards). There was plenty of work to be done as Chairman of the Chester branch of the NFU and he was quickly appointed the County delegate and the Chair of the West Midlands branch of the National Dairymen's Association. David believed that "if you want something doing ask a busy man "and he obviously liked to stay busy. In a conversation years later with his brother he would opine, when asked why he got so involved in so many different things, that he felt he needed the challenge, and he was reacting to the lack of opportunity initially within the family business. He was making up for lost time now.

If 1973 was a year of consolidation, then by 1974 the Pickerings were back on the acquisition trail. The first in their cross hairs was Kendricks Dairy. Bob Kendrick was a lovely man who bought milk from Pickerings, bottled, and delivered it. Up until now, he himself was out every morning with his horse-drawn cart, delivering across Mold. It was rumoured that a woman leant out of the upstairs window one morning and shouted, "Bob, have you got the time?" To which he replied, "Yes, but I will need someone to hold the horse!" Bob was a colourful character who employed Big Hilda in the office to do the accounts and look after matters of finance. She was so named because she was called Hilda and… she was big. This was yet another deal where the Pickerings could get two margins for their milk and it increased turnover yet again.

David, though, was not finished yet. Finally, came the purchase of the remaining parts of Bodfari, the Farmhouse and Continental Cheese division. This meant both Hugh and Geoff could now retire and leave the business completely, although they did retain some shares in the business. It was another good year, and with acquisitions and mergers, the company was now turning over £648,000. This was amazing growth in such a short time and things were following David's blueprint for growth. On a personal note, this was the third year of his qualifying period for a payment by Lloyds of London and to his knowledge none of his syndicates had been hit by any major disasters. So, at the end of 1974 over a nice lunch at the Grosvenor, he received a cheque for £21,000 for three years of profits with Lloyds. When you consider the average annual wage in 1974 was £2000 and that on top of his Lloyds cheque the two boys received a dividend from the family business of £5,000, as well as their wages which were listed as £4000, yes, 1974 was indeed a good year.

The first acquisition in 1975 was Fishers Milk, another small milk business with its own distribution. It was much like Kendricks and it meant that Pickering's Dairies now had milk rounds supplying to households from Mold, all the way back to Chester. They could now source milk and retail it direct, rather than rely on wholesale prices, their cream was going to Bodfari, where they were again retailing and of course David's pig business was using as much skim milk as they could create to feed his pigs. It was becoming a noticeably big business with tentacles reaching out across North Wales and Cheshire. This year also saw David add to his unpaid roles, as he became the Chairman of the Chester and North Wales Accountancy Students, as well as being appointed to the National Dairymen's main board and the National Dairymen's Processors Council. There was barely a midweek night that he did not have one meeting or another.

The purchase of Siglen farm near Cuckoo's Nest, in 1975, signified a further expansion. This called for the creation of a business which they named Todays Egg and Poultry Company Ltd. The move into chickens and eggs was a further signal that the Pickering brothers wanted to be all things farming and they had both the money to purchase and the knowhow to make the businesses productive and profitable.

Chapter 23
The Pendulum Rarely Remains Still

Just as things were really moving forward in the business, tragedy struck. On the 22nd of September 1975, John Dennis Pickering (Den) died suddenly in his bed from a massive heart attack. He and Margaret had enjoyed a meal with friends, in North Wales, and retired late that evening. At about two a.m., Margaret awoke with a start as Den complained of severe pains in his arm and chest and, within minutes, he was dead. Margaret ran to the house to get John but there was nothing he or the paramedics, who arrived swiftly, could do. His lifestyle of smoking too much, an increase in weight and enjoying his semi-retirement had put too severe a burden on his heart and he simply could not survive this attack. By the time the medics arrived, Den was dead. John called David at Grange Farm. It was almost four a.m. and David knew it was not good news. John told him what had happened, and David asked if he wanted him to come to the farm. John, in the pragmatic way farmers deal with death, said there really was not any point, there was nothing David could do as his father was dead and they should meet up later in the day to discuss arrangements for his funeral, which they did.

It was a big funeral; Den was extremely popular, a larger-than-life character, as this book tells, and his life touched many others throughout the close-knit Cheshire farming community, all of whom wanted to attend his funeral to pay their respects. Den was a worker, an optimist, a gambler, and an achiever. He had a simple philosophy on life and lived by it. He had summed it up best when he spoke to the Cheshire Young Farmers some years earlier:

"My advice to you is.... Do your job to the very best of your ability. Work hard and play hard but don't play before you have worked."

He had dealt with both disaster and success in equal measures and he had moulded, with the help of his loving wife Margaret, two sons who were now totally in charge of this important family business. Den said during his life, that:

"*When you have a family, give them the best possible education you can afford — no one can take that advantage from them.*"

And now his investment in his family was paying dividends. He would have few regrets and certainly did not die wondering, "What if?" He pushed the boundaries as far as was possible and challenged himself time and again to succeed where others had failed. He was an innovator on his farm; he had travelled where necessary to learn his trade. He had imported animals from two different continents, had owned and trained racehorses, dined at the best tables and eaten and drunk the best foods. His opinion was sought after by many and he had always conducted himself as a gentleman should. Farming today described his farm perfectly "*Rough Hill Farm — the best of tradition coupled with the spirit of experiment*". He would have been proud of that quote. Most precious to him always, was that he had the love and support of a good wife, who was a wonderful mother to his children. Whilst his life was shorter than it should have been, he certainly crammed a lot in to those sixty-three years and he had shaped a farming dynasty. Spare a thought also for Den's wife, Margaret, who lost her mother as well as her husband during 1975. That is a lot to deal with for anyone.

At the time of his death, Den would have known that Pickering's Farms were on for another record year. It seemed all the acquisitions were working, and the extra profit margins were flowing through to the bank account. When the accounts were done for 1975, they showed turnover had risen to an amazing £933,000. This was a year-on-year increase of a stunning 43%. Most importantly the gross profit had also increased year-on-year by 30% and both David and John were able to take a dividend payment of £15,000 each, up from £5,000 in 1974. If, as Mahler suggested, "*History is the transmission of the fire and not a worship of Ashes*", then it had indeed been passed on by Den and it was burning bright at Rough Hill. The Pickering brothers were doing nicely and whilst they were delighted with their efforts of the previous year both were aware that three hundred years of family farming at Rough Hill now rested firmly on their young shoulders. They had an obligation to keep things working and to make the most of this amazing asset that had been left in their charge.

Chapter 24
The Brothers Make Hay

From the time David left London and then Cabots, just over a decade ago, it had been one deal after another in order to grow the business and make their significant assets work harder. That was the task he set himself and one that brother John was happy to go along with. The partnership worked as the two personalities complemented each other. David had the ideas of how they could get bigger and John acted as the balance to ensure they did not grow too fast, too quickly. Not every deal was right, as the next years would show, but there was no doubting it was exciting. David's greatest source of frustration was his ongoing battle with the Milk Marketing Board (MMB). The process which worked across the entire milk producing members of the UK was indeed a complicated one and, in David's eyes, an unfair one. In essence all milk was ordered to be sold to the MMB at an agreed price, known as a quota. The MMB then sold this unprocessed milk to the various milk processors and adjusted the price back to the milk producers, based around another complicated formula, once the component prices of the milk were realised. If that doesn't make sense to you, so be it, you will never need to know how it worked, suffice to say it was complicated. One person it did make sense to was David Pickering, who found the loophole. If you processed your own milk on site, that being that you separated the cream from the skim and you also bottled milk for delivery, then you could pay a levy to the MMB for using your own milk.

Importantly, this levy was a lot less than the enhanced profit margin you got by retailing your own milk, which meant your milk margin was greater than if you sold it to the MMB. This system worked well for Pickering Dairies and, with David's many contacts across farming, through his now active representative roles as Chairman of both the Cheshire and North Wales National Dairyman's Association, it was not long before Pete Samuels, at Decoy farm, was happy to commit his milk to the Pickerings and so too was Sir Donald Wilson from Old Field Farm. The only problem was that the official margin and levy to be charged was retrospective so occasionally Pickerings would pay both Sir Donald and Pete Samuels too much, something they would only be aware of when the MMB set the previous quarter's levy. It was on one such occasion that David was given the job of recouping an overpayment from Sir Donald. Sir Donald viewed the young "whipper snapper" in front of him with disdain for him daring to ask for money. David showed him the figures and why it was correct and whilst a cheque was forthcoming David was, not to mix our farming metaphors too far, seen as the black sheep of the family from that day on. The relationship continued but John was very much the contact as far as Sir Donald was concerned, despite the fact it was David's ingenuity that was making more money for all of them.

In 1976 it was a time to review the various businesses and see how they were all performing. One that did not make it through muster with a clean bill of health was Crompton Hall. This was the first of the pig business acquisitions and David was not convinced it could do any better so, as the lease came up for renewal, he rightly allowed it to lapse. Anthony Pickering, the operator who found that this "farming lark" very much got in the way of his other activities, was a far better mechanic than he was farmer, either of dairy or pigs, and the Crompton Hall weaner supplier was simply too expensive to justify continuing.

Sue was also pregnant again and an audit on the home front revealed that the children numbers would double from two to four when she was ready to give birth, as twins were on the way. For a good while it looked like Christmas day would be replicated as the heavily pregnant Sue sat at the dining-room table, but the twinges were just two babies fighting for room and on the 6th of January 1977 the twins, Stuart and Belinda, were born.

A holiday at 'Portobello House, on the Dullas Estate on Anglesey, the family home of the Tatton's was a well-deserved break for the now, six-member Pickering family. All have fond memories of beach holidays, sandcastles, and an escape from the relentlessness of farming, seven days a week, twenty-four hours a day. It also gave David some time out to consider his various investments and come back with new plans.

David was made a fellow of the Chartered Accountants institute during 1977 and with his accountancy principles firmly in mind he decided to close Sychdyn Farm and hand the lease back to the Uttleys. Like Crompton farm the figures just were not adding up and so cutting your losses is always the right decision and inevitably, as Rod Stewart sort of said in his hit single, "the first cut is the cheapest". David strongly believed that, "too often in life we hang on to our losers in the hope they will get better and we take a profit in our winners far too quickly, when in reality it should always be the other way around".

One thing that was performing well was Bodfari creamery and the brothers took the decision to buy the remaining shares from Geoff Waterworth and Hugh Davies. David and John had big plans for this business, and they wanted to own a lot more of it. It was a calculated and bold move at a time when they were keen to use profits from within the business to keep growing their turnover. Following hot on the heels of this deal was the purchase of the Cadwaldr Milk round. It was all well and good having more and more milk available but to take advantage of the MMB loophole you needed a lot of retail and this added significantly to their area with Cadwaladrs having great support across urban Chester.

Now that both Hugh and Geoff were out of the Bodfari business it made sense to bring the creamery closer to home. This required significant investment in new machinery, which was undertaken so that the creamery business could operate from Rough Hill. This made management that much easier and of course got rid of pointless road miles sending the cream down to Denbigh when it could now be done at home under the watchful eyes of the Pickerings. Rough Hill was now a particularly bustling place and it would get even busier as 1977 rounded out. A good year but not a great year was how David remembered it. Turnover was up dramatically and had now gone through £2 million, not all of it was profitable as was shown by the closure of Sychdyn farm. David was also starting to question just how the pig business, for all the work and investment, was ever going to make decent money. The fluctuations in price achieved for the stock were still too great and the margins just too slim; when it worked it was good but it just didn't work well often enough. He was torn and not entirely sure how to get out even if he decided he should.

Chapter 25
Keep Believing and Back yourself — Always

There is no doubting that faith was a big part of what had got David Pickering to this point. The faith in his ability to spot a good deal, to read the figures put in front of him and to believe that he and John could run things better than the people they were buying them from. It was also a major part of David's personal life as well. Whilst his father had rarely gone to church save for High Days and Holy Days, he had been someone who said his prayers every night and was unashamed to admit it in front of those who knew. He felt it relaxed him and gave him the calm he was looking for before sleeping. It was something adopted by David and he took it a little further, often seeking out Churches in his younger days when he was away from Chester, for the calm of a Sunday service. As he and Sue were settled at Grange Farm, so too did they settle on, the aptly named, Hope Church as their local place of prayer. It was a tiny Church of England parish in the village of Hope, just three miles from Grange Farm. The Pickering Family attendance on a Sunday, as well as for the family Christenings meant they were well known to the Congregation and it was a lovely start to 1978 as David was made Church Warden, something of which he was particularly proud.

A problem that did need solving was that demand was so high for the Pickering products that they needed even more milk and Pete Samuels of nearby Decoy Farm was persuaded by David to come on board as a Producer/Retailer, committing all of his milk to Pickering's, where he would enjoy the extra margin possible for his entire milk herd. He was nervous about abandoning the MMB, who currently got about half of his production, and fearful of reprisals, but David and John seemed to be doing well, so he took the gamble.

With all this extra milk secured there was more investment required at Pickerings in the shape of a bottling plant on site. Pickerings had previously needed to ship the milk to the Cadwaladrs bottling plant on the other side of Chester but, with the purchase of an expensive, but good, second-hand bottling facility, it was yet more in-house expertise and more profit margin for Rough Hill.

If 1978 was a pause for breath and a chance to make some money, then '79 was anything but. It started with the appointment of Bob Blears as an in-house accountant. It simply wasn't possible, with the level of business being achieved, for David to keep an eye on every account, look for new opportunities and peruse the figures of every aspect, from farming to manufacturing and retailing. Bob provided that back up and a vital role in the preparation of accounts, something, by his own admission, David really did not enjoy. One of the first decisions that Bob provided information on was the failing Fron Farm at Mold. This was closed by June of '79 and sold the following year for £45,000. A decent profit in terms of the land sale but losses accumulated over the years ate into that profit quickly. At best the whole operation had been break even.

Chapter 26
The Politics of Farming, Living, and falling foul of the Law

The first of the 1979 acquisitions was Minafon Creamery on Anglesey. This got "right up the nose" of Northern Dairies, who prided themselves as having Anglesey and North Wales "sown up". Minafon added nicely to the Bodfari portfolio and gave a further good outlet for cream across the many herds now delivering raw milk to Rough Hill. David was also appointed Vice Chairman of the Milk Processors Council of the UK, which required twice monthly meetings in London but was again a vital source of information for David as to what was best practice across the UK. David was never slow to adopt a new idea and these meetings were a rich supply of what was and, most importantly, was not working.

He also found time to join the newly formed Chester Small Business Bureau, which he thought was a good idea to bring the businesses of Chester together. It was formed by the Chester Conservative Association and it gave David his first exposure to Politics as he then joined the Chester Conservative Party in October 1979.

A three-week marketing course put on by the Worshipful Company of Farmers, a Guild of London group, was held at Wye College in Kent and David, ever thirsty for more knowledge, was invited and accepted. His belief was that with his farming business now being very much an end-to-end business, from farm to fork, he would need all the skills available to market his products, both wholesaling and retailing. David described this as "one of the most formative events of his life". Twenty people attended and apart from the immense knowledge imparted to the twenty who attended, twelve still meet up every year at a dinner somewhere in the UK. They have become lifelong friends, shared successes and failures and enjoyed each other's company over four decades.

It was shortly after this sabbatical that David, Pete Samuels, and Gerald Mallinson would create Lyndale Farm Products. There was already a successful chicken business operating out of Lyndale Farm near Pulford and the proposal in front of the threesome was a simple one. They would raise Guinea Fowl. In Guinea Fowl, they had found a marketplace that did not have a regular, affordable supply and that seemed the perfect place to start. Top-end deli's wanted Guinea fowl, so too did restaurants and pubs. It seemed everyone wanted this moist, slightly gamy bird and so with prices holding up well in the market it was just a matter of bringing the economies of scale in to play by increasing the breeding capacity and this would be a winner. That was the theory at least. It was not long before trouble beckoned. The problem was that Guinea Fowl simply don't take well to domestication and artificial insemination. The cost of rearing chicks and the mortality rate during their life was just awful; couple that with three bouts of Foul Pest and the figures were appalling. When they closed the business years later, total losses were in the region of £250,000 and that was after putting in just £5,000 each to start things off. Not every good idea works, of that there can be no doubt and Guinea Fowl remains a classic case of the laws of nature that must be obeyed.

In March, David was awakened in the middle of the night to

the smell of acrid smoke. He dressed quickly and realised the smoke was coming from the Pig sheds. He fully expected to hear the anguished cries of pigs squealing but was met by an eerie silence. It was only when he opened the doors, with the fire brigade approaching, that he realised the pigs had all been asphyxiated by the smoke, in their sleep, which explained why it was so quiet. The Fire brigade put the flames out and brought the fire under control quite quickly. By early morning, in an ironic twist, Sue had got up to serve the firemen coffee and bacon sandwiches for their breakfast. Perhaps the most expensive bacon sandwiches made for some time as the final numbers totalled more than two hundred pigs lost!

Another Directorship beckoned as North Western Farmers (NWF) of whom David was Vice Chairman, appointed him to become a director of their transport business, Grocotts. Whilst this was very much an overseeing role, it did give David vital intel on who was moving animals around the county, where they were heading and who was struggling to pay their bills and might be open to the right offer, as the Pickerings expansion plans were far from over.

The sale of Fron Farm went through and with £45,000 burning a hole in his pocket David installed an anhydrous milk plant, whose job it was to create even more skimmed milk, which was by now proving to be popular in the shops. Whereas at one time the skim was used as a waste product to feed the pigs and fatten them up, now the great British public were realising the need for a slightly less fat heavy diet and milk was the next item to hit the diet headlines. With a market now established for skimmed milk and, therefore a value, the pig diet changed to one of feed only and the milk was now generating income in three areas. Whole milk, skimmed milk and cream and the Pickering lads were doing all of it on site and with all the extra margins and levies possible.

If there is a recurring theme in the notes and diaries of David Pickering it is that he is at his most dangerous to himself when he is not busy and/or has money in the bank. They say the easiest person to sell to is a salesman, as they always want to believe in what they are being told by one of their own and in this case the salesman being sold to was David Pickering. Armed with cash after another successful year and a healthy dividend payment, David decided to invest in Intergraph Personnel Services. It was the right time to be investing in recruitment companies and £15,000 for 50% of the business seemed a fair deal. It was not as bad as the Guinea Fowl business and it ran for a couple of years before folding. Clearly David's investment helped them stay afloat for a while, but it was destined to fail, with poor management and even poorer administration. We will put this one into the Good Samaritan category of investment, rather than the speculative. It was not the first and it certainly was not the last.

Chapter 27
The Importance of Contacts

During July of 1979 the NWF opened their new mill facility and what would become a major transport hub on the road between Tarporley and Nantwich. It was a big investment and, as regional Director, David was asked to attend the opening, where Minister for Agriculture, Peter Walker, performed the official opening. This was, for David, one of the first brushes with a high-ranking Politician and there is no doubt that it sparked interest in the field of politics. David's pedigree for the Conservatives was without peer. He was now the head of their new Business Forum in Chester, had joined the party locally and was just about to be elected to the committee of the ultimate Chester old boy's network, the Chester City Club. Notes from the family holiday in August show that, far from being impressed by the Minister, it made David think how he had something to offer the party and that perhaps a career in politics would be an important part of his future. However, those thoughts were put on the back burner when he returned to work, as his hunch on Anglesey had played out well. Northern Dairies were annoyed that the Pickerings had stolen Minafon Creamery from under their noses and they came knocking to do a deal. David extracted an extremely good one. In return for Minafon, Northern Dairies would deliver 800 gallons of milk a day to Denbigh for processing and delivery. This was a significant quota to pick up and made the Minafon sale extremely profitable.

Despite the nagging doubt in David's mind about the profitability of the pig business it was in late 1980 that he invested in new Pig and Sow Boxes at £10,000 for each box. These would make moving and dealing with the pigs that much more efficient, cleaner, and easier to work with and so the decision to invest seemed a logical one, particularly as investment of this type before the year end lowered the tax burden. With that investment, the building of a new office area at Rough Hill and the implementation of the first computer in the business, it was yet another hugely important year.

On the personal side of things, David also invested in humans, as he joined Action Aid, whose job, with donations on a monthly basis, was to care and educate young children in parts of Africa where governments were trying to pull young lives, blighted by civil war, back together. David made a series of commitments from 1980 and continued to support these children for many years. This was a milestone, as one of his first charitable commitments; many more would follow.

His good friend Jeremy Oates took his eponymously named company public in 1980 and whilst those shares never set the world on fire it was a sign of how both former partners, and still good buddies, had moved on in life. A visit to Henley Regatta in the height of summer was the ultimate social occasion for David and Sue, with a stay at Wallingford a nice distraction as well. For those who have not been, this is the grand finale of Rowing. The Cheltenham Racing Festival of the water and where the big universities and clubs vie to become National Champions. In the summer on the social circuit, there is Wimbledon, Royal Ascot Races, Glyndebourne, Last Night of the Proms and Henley. All things that should all be experienced by any person born or visiting Britain, at least once in your life. David and Sue could tick this one off their list.

The investment of £30k each by David and John, into a farm at Burwardsley owned by Mike Hanson, was how 1981 started. It was called Cawley Farm and Mike was struggling to make it pay. David and John structured a deal with him which ensured greater margins for everyone and of course that all important supply of more raw milk for the Rough Hill processing machine. Comments in David's diary show the concern at this stage for the Guinea Fowl operation, just one word is written — Appalling. On a brighter note, the youngest members of Grange Farm, the twins, would start at The Firs in September and now Sue had all her children at school.

The family holiday included a stay at Hotel San Louis on the Island of Menorca. A twenty-minute drive from Mahon, it was ideally located and very scenic. Menorca is the quietest of the Balearic Islands and it proved to be a great getaway. The children loved the beaches and pools of the hotel whilst Mum and Dad could relax in what is still known as a safe family holiday destination.

Chapter 28
The Canadian Mounties Always Get Their Man

In a mildly less busy year David decided to retrace just some of the footsteps of his father, Den. Back in the late '30s Den and Gorstella farm owner, Bill Chadwick, had, under the guidance of the enigmatic Baron, gone to Canada to buy cattle. It was something that worked incredibly well. Not only did they make their own herds stronger with the introduction of Canadian Holsteins, but they achieved phenomenal sale prices for the other animals that they sold at auction. It did not all go according to plan though. To buy abroad at the time, you needed to get permission to buy other currencies and Den managed to get the Treasury to agree to his request. The problem was there just weren't as many cattle for sale at the right price and at least half of his Canadian dollars remained unspent. Rather than bring them back and suffer two exchange rate penalties he decided to seek some investment advice. He had, like his son later in life, £500 burning a hole in his pocket and he decided he would import Canadian Fir Trees. Having gotten extremely excited about the prospect of setting up a fir tree farm back in the UK he then discovered that UK Agriculture would not allow him to bring the trees into the UK. To the credit of the vendors, they allowed him to have his money back and rather than repatriate it to the UK, he had the money sent to a firm of stockbrokers in Toronto and asked a man he had never met, Marshall Stearns, to invest the money for him. Thirty-four years later David was to meet Marshall in Toronto and trace both the investment and the history of just how Deacon Hodgson Inc, Marshall's firm, had looked after those funds.

The trip to Canada started with an aborted visit to say goodbye to Nick at Rossall School. He was poorly with a particularly virulent cold and his carers suggested they keep it brief and without much contact. The idea was to visit Nick and then head to Manchester Airport to catch a Ward Air flight. David had got the return flight on the Tri Star for £200 and admitted to being particularly teary as he said goodbye to Sue, Angela and the twins at Manchester.

On arrival in Toronto, Marshall had booked him in to the Royal York Hotel and this seventy-two-year-old man, whom David had never met, went out of his way to include David in his family life, with dinners and lunches at his home, introductions to the family and places of interest. They visited Niagara Falls, they had lunch at his exclusive clubs and as ex-President of the Toronto Stock Exchange, Marshall was able to take him onto the exchange floor and meet with the current traders. It was an extraordinary commitment by one who had little contact with the Pickering family and David was particularly impressed and grateful.

When they got down to discussions about the investment Marshall explained how, as a junior in the firm, he had been allotted this small sum to personally invest on Den's behalf. He sat on it for quite some time until he found the first investment. His first purchase was one thousand Newmac Oil Shares at 60 cents. In 1978 the shares were split two for one and one thousand were sold — at $15. With the $15,000 he purchased four hundred Texacogulf for $2500 which in 1981 were valued at $12,500 and one thousand Kaici Resources for $10,000, which were now valued at $22,000. By late 1981 the total portfolio was valued at over $100,000. He had done a remarkable job of looking after Den's original investment of that there was no doubt. David could not believe the figure.

On leaving Toronto, David gave Marshall a Silver Salver, with a Chester hallmark on it. He had spent £200 buying it from his good friend and jeweller, Edward Walton, and in a typical act of honesty, declared the item at the customs desk as he entered Canada, only to be hit with a £50 duty on the said salver. That aside, it was a lovely memento and one treasured by Marshall. In true David style, he considered buying property in and around Toronto and even went and visited a farm owned by two sisters of sixty plus who were looking to sell. The prospect was sold to him by the realtor, on the basis that they had already dropped the price per acre from $3000 to $2000 and that in a couple of years, with the new motorway coming so near and the prospect of planning permission for houses, this would be worth upwards of $10,000 an acre. Ironically, it was the significant losses through Lloyds of London that year and the need to come up with his first cheque by January of '82 that would prevent David from yet another investment in something of which he knew little. That is not to say it would not have worked out. He decided not to look at what had happened to the land in the years that followed. It may just have been the one that got away!

Chapter 29
Lloyds and Other Syndicates — What Cost?

Up until January of 1982, every year since 1972 the Lloyds of London man made his way up to Chester to see the Pickering brothers and a couple of other Lloyds names. He took them out to lunch at the Grosvenor Hotel in the city and handed over cheques of various sizes, representing the returns of the various syndicates. It had been a fruitful experience for the young David Pickering and his ten-year returns totalled more than £55,000. This year was to be different. This year he needed to hand over a cheque for £13,672. In 2020 that would look more like £100,000 and, whilst he had it, no one likes to hand out money. That was the nature of the beast. They had enjoyed a good run and it still represented a great ten-year return on his investment. When you consider that the amount David covered was £150,000 liability, it could, of course, have been a whole lot worse.

The Lloyds meeting was anything but the perfect start to the year, but with eldest son Nick now at Rossall School and daughter Angela starting at The Queen's School in Chester, there was a lot of optimism, after what had been another stellar year at Rough Hill. Turnover exceeded £5 million, there were articles in the local papers about Pickering Dairies and their meteoric rise and David and John now employed over one hundred people within their various enterprises. Pickering Dairies had invested heavily in the latest technology to produce their dairy products and it was paying off. David's marketing skills were also coming to the fore with well placed advertisements across the Cheshire and North Wales region. He was building a brand and his below the line marketing was effective. Their milk and cream had a longer shelf life than many others that had travelled great distances to be sold in supermarkets across Cheshire, North Wales and Merseyside and customers could taste the difference. A local product, made with care and attention to detail, available locally, was how Pickerings sold their dairy products, and they were sending it out by the truckload, daily.

The Horse Racing bug was never far from Den Pickering and with David it was no exception. David gathered a group of local Chester business owners and collectively they formed a small syndicate to buy a horse. Syndicates are quite a common occurrence now in the racing world, but back then it was ahead of its time. The idea being that, for a small sum, you each owned a fraction of a horse and that way horseracing became more affordable. It appealed to David's friends and the horse they bought was called Personality Plus. It was trained by Doug Francis. Doug had great success for David's father and in the spring of 1982 this 2yo, broke his maiden, a term that refers to a horse winning its first race and not an unfortunate event. The syndicate recorded their first success. As David explained much later in his horse owning life. "Owning Racehorses is months of misery followed by moments of Magic". Aptly put, but for these owners, joy had come early in the racing cycle.

Locally, the Reverend Ken Williams was appointed to Hope Church, as the previous incumbent, Rector Cooke had retired, and David struck up an enduring relationship with Ken. David was the Church Warden, and they would lean on each other as one dealt with the ebbs and flows of business and family, whilst the other contemplated on just how to keep a failing congregation and deteriorating asset going, against the odds. The latter was a challenge that David enjoyed immensely. One where he was able to bring much of his local influence and business acumen to bear.

In June of '82, Sue and David achieved another of those tick list of things to do, if you are British, when John Heath and Randal Hibbert of Walker Smith and Way, invited some clients, including David and Sue, to attend Royal Ascot with them. It is never a cheap day out at Royal Ascot and solicitors are not renowned for throwing their money around, so this invitation gives you a reasonable idea of the amount of legal work the Pickerings were generating with their business purchases, asset sales, partnership creations and employment requirements. John Heath, whilst thankful for the business, could see this was only going to accelerate over time and he needed to keep the brothers happy. Sadly, David could not repeat his father's achievement with Roughlyn back in 1966 when he won the Kings Stand, with a Royal Ascot winner. Personality Plus was not up to that class, but it was a terrific day out regardless, with the highlight, as always, the Queen arriving at the track as she does at two p.m., for every day of this wonderful racing festival. This was something she continued to do, unbroken until the Covid-19 pandemic of 2020 where racing was held behind closed doors for the first time and without Her Majesty in attendance.

Taking stock of the various positions outside Pickering Dairies, at the end of 1982, David was still Chairman of the Chester Branch of the NFU, he was also a Non-Exec Director of the NFU at a national level, Chairman of the Processors Council of the National Dairyman's Association in London and Director of Grocotts Haulage, on behalf of the NFU. He was also Chairman of the Chester Small Business Bureau and on the Conservative Committee. He had invested in Intergraph

Personnel Services, set up a new Guinea Fowl operation, and had this year agreed to become a member of the Chester District Health Authority, where he Chaired the Finance sub-committee and teamed up for the first time with Neil Large. They would become lifelong friends. Neil described meeting David in an email: "*I was a little in awe of him with his business skills and reputation in Chester*"; but as he got to know him over the years, he realised that the aura was not the real person. He also quickly identified what was clearly one of David's other great skills:

"I learnt that David had a subtle skill in getting other people to organise things in a way that it just crept up on them (including myself) and you were then left with the task. David enjoys involving people and gets enormous pleasure seeing other people enjoy themselves and develop with the opportunities he has created. The number of events both business and social, he has personally instigated and has subtly or not so subtly got others to arrange, are endless. He is actually, despite his public business face, a very sincere and humble man who has put a lot of his personal time and investment in supporting both people and organisations (charitable and non-charitable) in and around Chester".

Late in 1982, David also accepted the role as Director of Chester Football Club. He had long believed that cities and towns needed successful sporting clubs for people to both play at and support and he felt this was a sleeping giant that needed his special brand of guidance and help. Readers who follow Chester City may well recognise that not everything David touched turned to gold but dissimilar to those who simply moan — he at least tried to do something about the club. It seems that some things simply cannot be fixed and nearly forty years later Chester FC continues to lurch from one financial disaster to another and in a downward spiral in terms of leagues.

As if he was not busy enough, he then accepted the role as Chairman of The Queen's School Parent Association in early 1983. His daughter Angela was a scholar and he felt he owed the school a little of his time. Not that there was a lot left!

Chapter 30
The Hunger That Knows No Bounds

David's personal demand to do more surfaced again and flush, as he was, with 'a few bob' after a good previous year, David decided to invest in Carmic Electrical. It was a fledgling business that specialised in a new type of floor lighting. It had the ability to illuminate steps with its strip lighting flexibility and they had already secured their first deal for the nightclub that was under the Midland Hotel in Manchester. Nowadays we see this strip lighting everywhere but in 1982–3 it was innovative and was clearly destined for big things. David's good friend Anthony Diggle told him about the business and David decided to back it with £20,000 for a 50% share. Again, he did not get much of a run for his money with Carmic. It was a good idea, of that there is no doubt, but the manufacturers did not protect their distributors and within months these products were everywhere with every supplier under-cutting the other and destroying any chance of making a profit. A combination of over-supply, tiny margins and perhaps a less than enthusiastic workforce, saw the money run out very quickly and Carmic Electrical did not last through 1983. The only consolation for David was that he did get the loss of his investment to use against his own taxes.

More tax relief would follow in 1983 as the shareholders decided to close the Guinea Fowl business and David would add a further £250,000 in losses to his tax return. It had been an utter disaster. Yet again what appeared to be a strong business case, where demand was assured, simply did not pan out. There is a reason why we do not see Guinea Fowl farms across the UK and despite the best of intentions, the latest technology and knowhow, these innovators could not make it work.

A quick stocktake of David's investments outside the Pickerings Farms would make you think, that with all the failures and losses now close to half a million pounds, an amount more like £2 million today, that his appetite to invest in other businesses might now be dimmed. Not so, we are just warming up, Ladies and Gentlemen.

With the disappointment of these investments, a scaled down holiday to a static Caravan at San Rafael in the Spanish Balearic Islands was the break that this year refreshed the mind and body. This Ibiza hideaway is beautiful and these holidays pre-date the wild rave scene of the late '90s. It was the ideal getaway with stunning scenery and lovely, hospitable people and David and Sue always cherished their family time away. This was no exception.

As 1984 started David was determined to build an even bigger business at Rough Hill and the appointment of Gordon Steinke as General Manager of Pickering's Dairy was the first part of unlocking that puzzle. David's philosophy was a simple one. Appoint people over-qualified for their position and then give them the authority and ability to grow your business to match their abilities. Gordon had a peerless pedigree and had already achieved more than what was being asked of him at Rough Hill. Pickering Dairies and Bodfari were groaning as they grew, and Gordon's appointment was an important one. There were, firstly, the huge interactions between product and logistics, then the immense number of staff involved, who all needed guidance and without the correct procedures, things could come unstuck. Gordon was a stickler for detail, he set fabulous work standards that he had created in his previous employment and he would create a structure that could really benefit the business. Over the next decade, the Pickerings would continue to grow under Gordon and he was definitely the right appointment at the right time.

For both David and brother John, Gordon's arrival was timely, and it meant that David could once again get away from the day-to-day running of the business to work out the next move. In addition, he continued to manage his incredible workload of commitments outside the office. His mind was clearly put at ease, as, socially, he enjoyed his best year on the green baize at the City Club winning both the billiards and snooker tournaments that year. He is an immensely competitive man and there really was no such thing as a "friendly game", you either played to win or you did not play. It was the thrill of the challenge that excited him, and David found that on the hockey pitch, the golf course, the tennis courts, in a hand of bridge or even on the snooker table. It was just the way he was made. Magnanimous in victory and gracious in defeat, but always competitive.

Chapter 31
A Step in the Wrong Direction

Impressed as he was with Canada when he visited back in 1981, David decided in July they would return as a family for a week's break. They booked "La Chateau, Montobello Hotel" in Quebec from the 23rd to the 30th of July, with the children in a triple room next to Mum and Dad. Set on the Ottawa River about fifty miles west of Montreal, the Chateau boasts the title of being the largest log cabin construction in the world. The holiday was organised by local Chester company LG Travel. Those who go back far enough in Chester will remember them being based in what was then Mercia Square and now would be the second floor of WH Smiths. This courtyard area opened out, off the walls, behind the Cathedral and housed such wonderful businesses as Pierre Griffs, Chester's first wine bar and the Pump House, an all you could eat buffet style pub. They both had outside eating areas, in what was a regular sun trap for late afternoon drinking. The holiday destination was chosen on the recommendation of Chester travel stalwart and LG Travel owner, Drew Foster. He would later, with partner Geoff Moss, go on to own Caribbean Connection, out of which would spring, as the partners split, International Travel Connection and Elegant Resorts. These two businesses, based in Chester, were two of the top three accounts ever held with British Airways. They, and Pickering's Dairies, had humble beginnings and that small wine bar created some mammoth businesses during its all too brief life. Regretfully Drew Foster, a wonderful

Chester character, is no longer with us and the Chester travel scene poorer for his loss.

Back in the UK, later in the year, Sue's father, and mother, were staying at Grange farm and in the simplest of accidents her father, Donald, tripped on three steps when leaving the kitchen and broke his leg. As a doctor, he was familiar with both the treatment required and the healing process and he argued that during his life, as a pipe smoker, the damage to his body was minimal by comparison with cigarette smoking. It was only when the leg failed to heal quickly that he realised that belief may well have been wrong; the leg simply would not mend. Further extreme complications after four months saw the necessity for the leg to be amputated. The leg still had not healed and worse: the spread of the problem meant he was in danger of risking his life. He made the decision, relatively easily, to have the necessary operation to remove the leg, in order to save his life. It was a sad start to 1985 for Donald and all the family.

Cawley Lodge Farm was also under pressure and brother John wanted out, so David took over his share of that business to ensure Mike Hanson could stay operating this herd for them. David admitted it was probably the wrong decision, but he thought Mike was working hard and deserved the continued support. It would not be the last time he would carry on and support an ailing company when others decided they had seen enough. Those decisions were often at odds with his financial opinion, but he believed in people and thought those who worked hard deserved his support. This was one such case.

Chapter 32
A Journey of a Thousand Miles Starts with Just One Step

Having been the Captain of the Deeside Ramblers Hockey fourth team during most of the '80s David's personal fitness was good. He had always been lean, and from the early days when he was training his greyhound he had run and kept fit. He decided that in 1985 he would challenge himself to run a Marathon and where better than to run the New York Marathon. He and his friend Ken Probert trained hard as they wanted to run a time of around four hours. For those not familiar with this kind of physical test the training requires that you run about thirty to forty miles a week for at least eight to ten weeks in the build-up to the event, longer where possible. You run between eight and ten miles at a time, three times a week and once a week run twelve to fifteen miles, all so that you can complete the gruelling 26 miles 385 yards of this famous race. The training alone is very demanding but very necessary.

These days Marathons are a dime a dozen, with every city and town running their own version of the classic race but back then there weren't very many and men/women weren't entirely sure that everyone could run this distance, let alone do it dressed as the Pink Panther carrying a tray of cocktails or wearing a deep-sea diver's outfit. The times have changed. The greats like Abebe Bikila, the incredible Ethiopian athlete, could win marathon gold medals running bare foot around the streets and hills of Rome, but many had seen the distressed faces of runners who had "hit the wall" in the last two to three miles and run like punch drunk boxers until, with wobbly legs, they collapsed to the ground. This was a brave bid by these two and they were amongst the running pioneers to travel abroad to take part.

Having been accepted to run in the race they chose the Chester Hospital Scanner Appeal to raise funds for, as well as the Police Force Supporting the Deaf Society. In the week leading up to the scheduled day of departure poor Ken got injured and simply could not run. At the last minute, Mike Williams, another friend, said he would take Ken's place, having done absolutely no training at all! All Mike's friends agreed this would indeed be a test for him. On arrival in New York things were edgy on the streets. The city was totally under the control of the Mafia mobs during the 1980s and in fact the night before the two arrived to check in at their hotel, two people had been murdered just around the corner in what was described as a gangland massacre. This was an almost daily occurrence as tit for tat assassinations took place by rival gangs right across Manhattan.

As edgy as it was, David felt the need to "feel" the streets and try to understand the city a little more. How better than a walk around, take in the smells and see the real city of New York that so many had raved about. He came across a small crowd gathered around three African American guys, two huge and one smaller. The smaller was performing the oldest magic trick in the book, the game of the three coconut shells with a $10 note underneath one of them. David watched mesmerised for a while and saw them take note after note off unsuspecting tourists. He wanted to have a go and thought he had spotted the trick. If he was right, he would of course get his $10 back and another $10 from their hard-earned profit. His money went under the shell and after a period he made his choice. As luck would have it, he was right, and it was at about this time that he learnt another valuable lesson. It was one thing being right in business, it is quite another getting paid. As he looked at the faces of the two larger guys, he made the decision that rather than reach in and take his ill-gotten booty $10 was a fair price to pay for this bit of entertainment and that he would simply retire with grace back to his hotel room safe in the knowledge it had only cost him $10 and he was not about to taste the hospital food on 42nd street. A wise decision indeed.

The day of the Marathon arrived, and our two runners headed for the start line. As the starting gun sounded David and Mike set off, but as they crossed the first bridge on their way out of Manhattan, there are twenty-one in total, Mike disappeared, off down a side street. David carried on without him. Twenty-five miles later, up, out of the subway station, Mike reappeared and re-joined the race to cross the line with David in four hours and two minutes. Whilst David missed his four-hour time by the smallest of margins, he had run it alone, without a pacemaker; it was a brilliant first marathon attempt. Given Mike's lack of preparation, the plan had always been for Mike to ride the subway to rejoin the race later and it worked perfectly. No one was the wiser as to Mike's tactics and David crossed the line feeling elated. It was a personal triumph of note. The two "came clean" about Mike's role but everyone was happy to pay their sponsorship contribution to the very worthwhile causes and the charities benefitted substantially. It wasn't the last time, that because of David's fund-raising efforts, that local Chester Charities receive a much-needed shot in the arm.

Chapter 33
Planting the Seeds

Both 1984 and '85 had been kind with Lloyds of London, paying £25,000 back to David, a sum that more than recouped the losses of '82. David was now a little concerned he was underwriting greater and greater amounts each year. His personal liability was now over £300,000 and whilst he had the assets to prove that level of surety, it was not always liquid and his morning reading of the papers became that much more focused, with so much money at risk. No reward without risk was always his motto and so onwards he would go for yet another year of underwriting.

Peter Hughes, the Chester based Barrister decided to step down as Chairman of the Chester Conservatives and now, thanks to his various roles across the city, there was virtually no conservative member who did not know the name David Pickering. For that reason, he was a popular choice to become Chairman of the Chester Conservative Party. The Conservatives had held Chester since 1974, thanks to the efforts of local MP, Sir Peter Morrison and few had bad words to say about him, at that time. He had entrenched himself in Margaret Thatcher's Government, after being amongst the first to urge her to stand as leader and she had rewarded that loyalty. He became not only Deputy Leader of the Party in 1986, but he was also Minister of State for Employment. Chester and the local Tories did indeed have friends in high places. In the 1983 election he held a nine thousand majority and Chester was considered a safe seat — but he could not go on forever — could he? David most definitely had his eyes on standing in, should Morrison decide to resign, and he was in the perfect place to pounce as Chairman of the local party, if and when it happened. In the meantime, he would keep doing what he was doing and keep the party faithful wined and dined. The political plot was thickening.

David got word that New Hall Farm, at Higher Kinnerton was struggling and with two hundred acres and a decent herd there was the chance to add even more milk to the quota, so he made Noel Morris an offer to stay on as tenant and bought that farm to add to their portfolio. At about the same time, son Nicholas decided he wanted to attend Reaseheath Agricultural College to learn all there was about Farming so that at some stage he could play a major role at Rough Hill. David encouraged this move and Nick left Rossall to attend the Nantwich centre of Agricultural excellence.

For some years, the newly built, Christleton Country Club, on the outskirts of the beautiful and quintessentially British village of Christleton, had been the home of the Cheshire Young Farmers. It was an adventurous project when it was first built and it was a building that David knew well. It had a gym, it had meeting and conference rooms and a fabulous setting; the downside was it was out of Chester but most importantly it was for sale. The price was, in the eyes of David Pickering, very reasonable at £200,000, so he decided that this should form part of his personal business "empire" and so another set of conveyancing documents hit the desks of Walker Smith and Way. (For those who wish to correct the author by stating there is no "and" in WSW, may we advise, this was before the Chester based firm of solicitors had paid £30,000 for their rebranding, which involved the removal of the word "and", from their title. Money well spent I am sure you all agree.)

Before the year was out The Wilson Brothers transport business had been added to the list of companies now owned by the Pickerings. This was a business they had been using extensively and it made sense, as the biggest customers, to make the owners an offer and add this to make an end-to-end business solution. In this regard they were ahead of their time and one of the reasons why turnover and profit kept growing in tandem.

By the end of 1986 David was left very satisfied with his year's' work. He rewarded himself and the family with a trip to Vilamoura, in Portugal. It is a fabulous purpose-built harbour for boats, surrounded by three superb golf courses and great beaches. He had also splashed out on a trip for himself and Sue on the Orient Express to Venice, ticking off one of the great Romantic aims in life, and as he wrote down his list of accomplishments in the annual personal stocktake between Christmas and New Year, it was a mixed bag of losses on outside interests with further strong gains for Pickering Dairies and associated businesses. A chance discussion with one of the other big Cheshire farming families would make the next year an even more important one.

Chapter 34
The Birth of Bodfari

In what proved to be an impressive year financially, the Pickering Family took a holiday to Chandris Dassia in Corfu. At the time it was a Club Mediterraneo complex and had all the amenities a young family with active parents could want. A stunning beachside hotel with a huge teardrop pool that overlooked the sea and a perfect place for David to weigh up just what he had achieved in the previous year. The answer was that in everything but his personal investments, things were going rather well. The farms and foods were really producing; Bodfari Group would announce turnover for 1986 doubling to £104 million and a 300% increase in profits to £1.7 million. Yes, there were a few extra mouths to feed around the board room table but in anyone's language that was a stunning year and proof that the decision to make the company an end-to-end business and grow through acquisition was indeed the right course of action.

John Pickering loved his shooting, something he inherited from his father, not so David. David inherited his father's fascination for horses. John, through his shooting, had been for some time good friends with the Chantler family. They were one of Cheshire's other big dairy farming families. In fact, they too had an end-to-end solution and were also taking advantage of the MMB loophole by having their own dairy provision at Stretton, on the other side of the county. John Pickering and Peter Chantler had been on many shoots together; it was an activity, that whilst he occasionally took part, just did not really appeal to David — it was John's thing. During 1987 the subject came up, between the two shooting friends about using their combined strength in the Dairy business and with it the idea of a merger was discussed. When John approached David with the proposal, David immediately saw the merit and so for about four to five months they went back and forward between the Chantlers and Pickerings, working out the relative value of each business to ensure an equitable merger. In the end, common sense prevailed, and a 50/50 merger was agreed, with a new company name, Bodfari Foods. The documents were signed later that year and the merger came into full effect. They were now an enormously powerful Dairy entity in the Northwest.

The new company employed 150 people and was, "strategically located in the largest milk fields in the UK, if not the world", according to a piece written by David at the time. They also had a contactable population of ten million people within one hundred miles and there had been rapid retail growth in the sale of non-returnable milk containers. The clever part of this partnership was that it did not include the farm interests of either family. So, whilst they both sold their milk to the new company, Bodfari Foods, their personal milk production was not part of the company business. That would prove vital in time. This new partnership was perfectly placed, both in time and location, to supply some noticeably big clients. In a short period, they had secured Morrison's, Kwik Save, Iceland and Gateway, throughout the Northwest and North Wales and were selling as much skimmed milk as they could gather. They also now had a plentiful supply of cream for the Bodfari Creamery division to work with as well.

The other pressing matter for the nation, during 1987, was a general election. Not all of society was enamoured with the work of Margaret Thatcher and there was quite a push back for her ruthless handling of the miners. This was reflected in the general election where Chester's MP, Peter Morrison, had his majority reduced by 50% to just 4855. It still saw the Conservatives win but the warning signs were there, both locally and nationally; do not take the electorate for granted. As the Chester Party Chairman, David was simply pleased they had won another election and he and Peter Morrison rightly praised the work of the local party and celebrated well in to the night and next morning after the election results were delivered at Chester Town Hall.

A sale of Wilson Transport to Wincanton produced more cash for the business. The new team wanted to concentrate more on milk production and processing and less on logistics, so it made sense to sell and it was a profitable deal. David was keen to move further into, as he saw it, electronics, and a meeting with Brian Early, the owner of Sumlock Computing, saw him invest further into this business. Brian had good contacts with IBM, the undisputed world leaders in computing, and he needed some help running the business. In David's mind his earlier investment in Dee Electronics and now Sumlock was one in the same industry and he thought the two companies may be able to work together. Jim Robinson was doing a good job at Dee Electronics but like all small businesses he needed more money and David provided another £60,000 for Jim, in the hope he and Brian Early would work well together and benefit both businesses. He had found David Williams to oversee his interests in both Dee and Sumlock on his behalf and he was convinced that if David Williams could get Brian and Jim working together, they would benefit from savings.

He was wrong. They simply had little synergy. David Williams was not the leader that David Pickering thought he was, and David Pickering really was not able to, nor was inclined to, give Brian the time he needed to help run the Sumlock business. David had bigger wars to fight in the dairy business and they were now well and truly warming up, so he allowed the two businesses to just coexist and drain more money from his account.

The combined buying power of Bodfari Foods and the huge supply of milk that this newly merged company had was something that simply could not stay off the radar of the Milk Marketing Board. They were angry with the Pickerings and Chantlers for exploiting the loophole around Skimmed milk but up until now it was not a huge deal. Now they were furious with the merged company, the sheer volume and their continued defiance and exploitation of the skimmed milk margins, as well as the huge number of dairy farmers who were now supplying this new company was intolerable. The threatening letters started to flow from MMB headquarters and soon solicitors were involved on both sides.

David's audit of his pig business did not make much better reading than the threats from the Milk Marketing Board. He had worked out he was losing £2000 a month on his pig business but he was confident that by raising the pig numbers next year, to fifteen thousand, he would return the business to profit by 1989. He had a blueprint to profit in the shape of some investments on Anglesey and he would buy two more pig farms in quick succession.

As 1988 started, David was unhappy with how North Western Farmers (NWF) was being run. He had issues with the Managing Director, and he was making some waves with the

Chairman as well. In what was an arrogant and audacious action he launched a takeover bid for NWF. The shares in this agricultural collective were valued at £6 by the board. David thought this a heady figure but to get control he would need to go higher. The bid was £8 and, thankfully for the Bodfari team, it was rejected. They would have overpaid for the entity and he would later reflect they simply did not have the expertise to run a conglomerate the size of the expanded group, if they had been successful. This, however, alienated him from the other Directors of NWF and later in the year, when a vote for returning Directors was held, with fewer directors proposed as part of a cost saving policy, unsurprisingly, David was not elected. Effectively he had been sacked. Not for the first time and not the last. He had ruffled too many feathers both at board level and in his actions as a farmer and it was time to move on.

In the late winter things were also tricky at Deeside Ramblers Hockey club. As the season 1987/88 closed out it became apparent the clubhouse and changerooms were in dire need of repair. This project saw David at his best. He pulled together fellow players, Pete Samuel, John Heath and others and said they all needed to put in £500 each. They also needed to find ten other people to put in £50 each, from either current or ex-players. In two months, they raised £11,000 and the repairs were done. Mission accomplished. If only all his fundraising could be so quick and easy to resolve.

Chapter 35
The Figures Do Not Lie.

Closer to home David was still the Church Warden and at Conservative Party HQ, Chester, there was a shock: they would lose Frances Mowatt as their Agent. The job of an agent is more or less the Marketing Manager for the party and the MP or candidate. These people are invaluable; they organise press conferences, they create literature for party members to ingest or to pass on to the electorate and in short, they make the candidate electable.

Frances was particularly good at her job, but it is possible with the benefit of hindsight, that she had heard rumblings from central office about the conduct of the Chester MP, Sir Peter Morrison. Conduct that would much later run to an investigation and she may well have believed it was time to move on. David was sorry to see her leave and recognised hers were a difficult set of shoes to fill. Vanessa Wilson was the chosen replacement and whilst her reign was cut short by ill health, she would die from cancer within two years, she was incredibly capable, thorough, and trustworthy in her position. As David's own political aspirations grew, he decided that the role of Governor of Lache Park infants was a good place to help and he took on this role in 1988 as well as all the other offices he held.

The addition of the Bodwina Piggery on Anglesey meant capacity was approaching the fifteen thousand-pig mark and whilst he had dramatically reduced the £2000 a month loss, he still didn't seem to be able to make it pay. This was proving a tough nut to crack. Back at Rough Hill the appointment of Malcolm Alcott as CEO of Bodfari Foods was not universally celebrated. Peter's son, Simon Chantler, had wanted the job and that atmosphere made Malcolm's task that much more difficult. Malcolm was clearly very capable and was doing a good job under the circumstances. He understood the business and they were producing results but his was never an easy office to control even with David as Chairman to support him and calm the family waters.

David's personal businesses now numbered seven, and he needed help. He appointed Jane Dewhurst as his secretary to organise his diary, type up the myriad notes from the endless meetings he attended and to have accessible, at a moment's notice, the relevant information that would solve whatever today's problem was. This she did with unerring accuracy and diligence. High on the list of problems was how to make money at the Christleton Country Club, of which he was the new owner, having paid £200,000 for the business. The idea of a golf driving range was proffered and meant the investment of quite a few thousand pounds. It was a good driving range and had it been built just five years later, as the game of golf exploded, with literally hundreds of thousands of new players, it may well have worked. At that time, however, it was just another cash drain on the Pickering wallet and in time the nets would come down and the balls would remain buried in the sodden turf over winter. Yet again proving that having a good idea is just part of the answer; the right timing and the right people delivering it are equally as important.

Chapter 36
Having Fun Fundraising

Despite the incredible number of meetings and businesses David was dealing with daily, he still managed to find time to embark on a particularly ambitious fund-raising activity for the Countess of Chester Scanner Appeal and Hope Church. He was still on the board of the local Health Authority and buoyed by the £4500 he raised when he ran the New York Marathon he decided the time was right to ride a bike from Land's' End to John O'Groats. A gruelling 925 miles by road. A route which takes cyclists anywhere from twelve to twenty days. For those not familiar with this route, it starts at the very tip of Cornwall at a house called The First and Last House, so called because, depending on which end you start, it is one or the other. It finishes at the very tip of Scotland at a place named after the former ferryman, a Dutchman called Jan De Groot. Nowadays, Sir Ian Botham has done numerous fundraisings on this route and even Speedo Mick covered a huge distance in winter wearing just his Speedo's but back in 1988 these feats were rarely attempted and, in this regard, David was a pioneer yet again, just as he was in his visit to New York.

As you might expect the journey was not without incident. His planning was meticulous. Good friend and owner of Trevalyn Estate, David Birkett Evans, sorted a Range Rover and caravan as the support vehicle in which there was room for the two Davids and another support person who would change during the journey as work commitments required. He added to this list, cycle shorts, helmet, bike, important spares for the bike, tool kit, water bottles, overnight stop agenda and OS maps. The start date was the 18th of September and he set the target of September 30th as the finish date. He was giving himself just thirteen days to cover the 925 miles.

The training involved riding a minimum of one hundred miles per week and at that distance per week he was comfortable, but this trip was a whole new ball game. He would have to cover just over seventy miles a day, every day, for two weeks. Not only was the physical target demanding but so was the financial one. David wanted to raise £2000 for the church and £14,000 for the scanner. The build-up involved a lot of training, and a lot of arm-twisting to find sponsors. These included farmers across the county and just about anyone David came in to contact with across his network of committees and institutions. The press was incredibly supportive and most people in and around Chester were aware of the man they nicknamed "Mr Chester" and his fund-raising bike trip.

It did not start well. Not only was there heavy wind and rain but on the second night, in what could only be described as incredible irony for one of Cheshire's leading dairymen, one of the inhabitants of the caravan from the support party spilt milk from the fridge all over the floor of the van during the day and didn't tell anyone until later that night. The smell of stale milk was appalling, so bad in fact they had to abandon the caravan. No use crying over it!

Plan B, however, worked better and the Farmers of the NFU offered beds for the night on farms that bordered their route. The farming fraternity pulled together and made it work. On route north David duly arrived in Chester, the halfway point, at

Christleton Country Club, to a hero's welcome and with press in attendance the pot was growing; he had surpassed his £16,000 target and was on course for £18,000 if he could make John O'Groats on time. The days were gruelling as he headed north, with strong winds, big hills in the Lake District and long barren roads with little protection from the elements. It was a lot tougher than he thought it would be.

He was getting behind in his schedule and it was getting harder, not easier to keep going, day after day. By the time it got to the 29th of September he was still 135 miles from John O'Groats. It was going to have to be a punishing last day. Despite the daunting task ahead he was significantly buoyed by the news that Chester had really got behind him and the total was now sitting at £25,000 but only if he could complete the task. On the 30th of September, wracked with pain, David set off on the last leg at seven a.m., knowing he would need every minute of the daylight hours, which were significantly shorter in the far north of Scotland, to peddle his way to success. Peddle he did, as at just on seven p.m., in the fading light he rolled into John O'Groats and toasted a mammoth fund-raising success with a glass of Champagne at Jan De Groots house.

It was incredibly satisfying, knowing he had set the stiffest of challenges and conquered all the demons. No headphones with iTunes playing while riding, just the solace of think time in the saddle, mile after mile. A triumph of determination and physical endurance and the pleasure of knowing the money you were raising would make a significant difference to both charities. Later that year, with David's help, the Scanner appeal would reach its £750,000 target and work would start to deliver a wonderful healthcare addition for the people of Chester. The reward for his efforts was some well-earned recuperation time in a villa on the island of Rhodes. The muscles were sore and some Greek sun and swimming was just the tonic.

There was a family shock to follow when eldest son Nicholas decided that having qualified at Reaseheath he would go to Australia to work for a while and, with family relations in Perth, Sue and David packed him off to sunnier climes. David sent him with a two-way ticket and enough money to last six months, after that he would have to stand on his own two feet. One month after arriving the phone rang at Grange Farm with Nicholas keen to return home. He simply was not enjoying Australia. His father and mother persuaded him to stay a little longer and give it a chance, which he did but after three months he decided Australia was not for him and he returned home.

Among all the comings and goings, there was a nice family break late in the year to visit Sue's Uncle, Norman Bateman, at his villa on the upmarket estate of Sotogrande, in the heart of Andalucia, Southern Spain. A wonderful escape. A huge, gated village with a superb golf course, its own private beach and restaurants on site. It made this another perfect venue to unwind and enjoy some winter sun. By now, David was working on his golf game, as it became more and more a part of the social scene at corporate level, so the chance of some practice in the Golden triangle of golf, as it was known, was one not to miss.

As 1989 started David had a liability of £350,000 at Lloyds and apart from the scare a few years earlier it had remained a very profitable investment. If it is working, why wouldn't you want more of it? He now had significant assets to put up and no small amount of money coming in from dividends and salary from the successful Bodfari business, so it was natural to make those assets work harder with Lloyds, who, in all but one year, were doing a sterling job.

To bring about a more cohesive company David had been appointed Chairman of Bodfari. It was obvious that, despite the appointment of an independent CEO, both families still went about their business disregarding board decisions and it made their CEO, Malcom Alcott's job almost untenable. David would remark in some personal notes that:

"*the board is not controlled or organised well enough, it is still made up of two families — and it shows*".

He also found dealing with John difficult. John commented that David had a short fuse and David believed the same was true of John. David also believed,

"*that our board has four entrepreneurs and one Executive, who simply doesn't know who to take instruction from, which makes it extremely unbalanced*".

Perhaps this was just the teething problems of a growing business but David sympathised with Malcolm as he couldn't get his fellow board members to do what they should. It is symptomatic of family businesses right across the world. Those businesses tend to work much better as dictatorships, at Bodfari they were trying to combine not one but two families. In time Simon Chantler would usurp Malcolm as CEO and with the Pickering's having David as a Chairman and the Chantler's having Simon as the CEO, the politics of this family business would work significantly better.

Chapter 37
Counting Sheep and Hearing the Bells

After the long and successful bike ride of the previous year it was no surprise that the family holiday incorporated bikes into the agenda with the hiring of a fabulous canal barge that started in Montpelier in France and worked its way up the tree-lined rivers. Each day they would get on bikes and follow the Canal barge up the towpath and then meet the barge at the end of the day to bed down for the night. The countryside was breath-taking, the food wonderful and the cycling simply great fun for all abilities. Whilst David loved it there is no record of how universally accepted this was for the rest of the family!

On the fund-raising front things did not go quite as well at the Conservatives Masked Ball Annual fundraiser, where the Chairman, David, was convinced by his committee that in an effort to make more money the gathered crowd would be just as happy with Bangers and Mash for their main course in order to keep the cost down. To say they got it wrong would be an understatement and in fact the masked ball aspect only served as ammunition for the dissatisfied who believed that the food provision was more akin to highway robbery. They would not make that mistake again. Perhaps this was just a portent of things to come for the Conservative Party.

At Hope Church, the recently appointed Warden made, what to some, was a controversial decision. David decided to bring sheep into the Church grounds, hoping to keep both the costs of upkeep of the Church Grounds and the grass down. Most of the congregation calmed down after a while. Later in the year Sue Pickering was appointed Captain of the Bells. Just like her husband, Sue was accumulating quite a CV and not even David could add to his CV, a commission in campanology.

A pressing matter was the replacement of one of the stained-glass windows at the Church and David agreed to pick up the tab. He instructed the stained-glass maker to incorporate both Sheep and Bells into the design to commemorate this year. He was never one to back away from a decision. The glass blower did just that and the window is still in place today, as are the sheep, who, despite occasionally escaping and needing some fence repair, are both practical and symbolic of Hope Church, being, as they were, present at the birth of Jesus under the command of their shepherds. It was hard to argue David's logic on this one and he had the full support of his Vicar.

Poor health was a significant feature of the year, with Jo Pickering, John's wife, being diagnosed with Myalgic encephalomyelitis or ME, a chronic muscle fatigue illness that is both debilitating and notoriously hard to treat. She was, for the most part, bed ridden and barely had enough energy to venture out at all. In addition, David was also rendered immobile. He was running down the wing at Hockey and was momentarily convinced he had been shot in the back of his ankle. He stopped in pain, unable to move. In fact, he had ruptured his Achilles tendon and an extremely long period of recovery would see him having to work hard with his physio to just get back to normal. The recovery was slow but within three months he was back playing regular tennis with his partners, Roger Hargreaves, Brian Johnston, and Edward Walton. It did, however, require the end of his days as a Hockey winger at Deeside.

Another omnipresent Chester stalwart died in this year, Dennis Diamond. He and John Heath were the most frequent contacts at family solicitor Walker Smith and Way. He had been on almost as many committees across Chester as David and had been the driving force behind Chester Rugby Club. His illness and death came as a shock to the many who knew him, and his funeral was of course very well attended by the great and good of Chester.

On a more positive note, Sue's work, and efforts at the Hospice of the Good Shepherd as both a volunteer and fundraiser for Crossroads, the charity that provides welcome breaks for full time carers, was really given a welcome shot in the arm when Princess Diana paid them a visit to open the new centre facilities. The Princess was the talk of the town for quite some time after. Through her visit David and Sue were able to shine a significant light on to the Hospice and some thirty years later its work is without peer. Princess Diana would be delighted to know this was one visit that really did make a huge difference to a charity that makes a significant difference to people's quality of life at their most vulnerable time. All charities are special but this one has been Chester's stand out Charity since its inception.

As the new academic year started Angela Pickering went to study Home Economics at Cardiff University. It seemed the perfect appliance of science, given that she was raised on the type of farm that collectively produced more than 60% of the daily proteins consumed on the kitchen tables of Great Britain. Her attendance at university was only after the family had visited the beautiful region of Vancouver in Canada. This time on his revisit, David decided upon the west coast of Canada on the recommendation of David Birkett-Evans. Birkett-Evans was importing leather goods from that part of the world and had introduced David to Noel Roddick who was based at Whistler. More known for its snow skiing in winter, there was none in late summer, but the beauty of the place was stunning and everyone enjoyed the clean fresh air and the amazing mountains and lakes.

Chapter 38
The Hamster's Wheel — If in Doubt Just Turn and Go the Other Way!

As the end of the year approached it was time for the Pickering stocktake and David was less than happy. The Bodfari businesses were doing well and he had significant shares in the them, but his pig business was still losing money. He had invested more money in Sumlock and Dee Electronics and they appeared to be going nowhere. The Christleton Country Club was also losing money and his big fear was that at any moment Lloyds might come calling for up to £350,000 if there was a significant loss anywhere in their portfolio. He felt like his life was on a knife edge and that things could go either way at any time. Was this how it was meant to be?

On paper it had, according to his figures, been a particularly good ten years. He was worth about £800,000 in 1979 and a decade later he was worth almost £3 million when you added up the value of his shares in the family business. The problem was he had a £900,000 overdraft — yes, that is right, a personal overdraft of £900,000 and interest rates approaching 15%. Just to service the debt you need to pay £11,250 a month in interest. This was a concerning time for both him and his bank manager. No matter how much money he made, at best he was just standing still and at worst going backwards. There was a very real chance he could go bankrupt if things continued in this vein.

David was experiencing anxiety attacks in the middle of the

night. For those not familiar, these take the shape of waking, normally between two a.m. and four a.m., where you go through every scenario in your head of what might happen and how you might solve a massive problem. You do the figures time and again and as you do this your body temperature feels like it is well over 100 degrees, you sweat and shake but when you touch your skin it feels cold. You know that if you want to solve the problems you need sleep, but you simply cannot relax. It is at these times that your faith is tested, both of God, if you are that way inclined, which David most definitely was and in your own ability to come out of this without damaging your family and you in the process. For David, the fight was on. He simply had to pull back and slim down his investments, narrow his cost base and reduce that overdraft. Hard decisions would have to be made in the year ahead. It is a credit to him that almost no one in his immediate circle, bar Sue, knew the extent of the problems he was facing. He vowed to sort them out and carry the burden by himself.

Fortunately, there were no demands from Lloyds this January and whilst the cheque David received was only sufficient to pay about three months interest on his overdraft, it did buy some breathing space while he considered his next moves. First to go was Sumlock; it had been an expensive mistake at over £250,000 in losses but it was time to cut the cord. As bad as David felt about liquidating his first business, his bank manager said that he needed to protect himself and his family. While this business continued to trade at a loss, he would never be free of debt and that could be his undoing. He needed to act for the greater good and this business did not work. He also closed the pig business at Rough Hill. This too was not making money, and the pigs were in the way of the core business that was positively booming. Bodfari now needed the space and David needed to lighten his financial load; this was a "no brainer".

David's farming figures also showed that the previous decade had been the warmest on record and long term even more warm weather was predicted. This was good for grass growth in the UK. With its abundant rainfall and fertile soil, that in turn was great for the milk industry. Cows seemed to have a lot going for them, less so pigs. Perhaps the Good Lord was trying to tell David something? It was too late to stop the addition of the Anglesey pig business, but this was pretty sound by itself and was capable of making money, so that survived the clear out, for the time being.

An indication of the lack of funds became apparent in this year's holiday destinations. The first was a camping trip to Lac Du Juanay, in France. Whilst it was perfectly adequate, it was a far cry from holidays of the recent past. The second escape was to Rita and Probo Bernie's apartment in Tuscany. Whilst this was beautiful, it was at "mates' rates" which helped. The Bernie's were an Italian family and Probo, David's friend. The family owned a car dealership in Queensferry. Rumour has it, Probo's father had befriended Lester Piggot over the years and each year, when Lester came up to ride at the Chester meeting, the garage would provide Lester with that year's latest Jaguar to drive for the following year. One can only imagine it wasn't a one-way arrangement and that from time-to-time Lester may well have been able to point the fanatical punter that was Probo's father in the direction of a winner or two. Sheer speculation on our part of course. Suffice to say the Tuscan escape was superb and enjoyed by the Pickering family.

Chapter 39
You Reap what you Sow

David had stopped some of the financial bleeding, in terms of his loss-making businesses, but it still did not solve the cash problem. He did, however, feel significantly more positive and in his role as Chairman of the Conservatives, he, with Peter Morrison, created a charity for the party called Polcha. The name was a way of linking Politics and Charity. The challenge was to make useful money for a chosen charity from their various contacts. The idea they came up with was that prominent Chester business men and women would pay a fee to come to London, experience the Palace of Westminster, then dine and stay at a top London hotel, where Peter would organise a top flight speaker to talk to the group in a very informal way. It was a nice idea and it started well, with maximum attendances. They made £10,000 for charity in the first year. This was all part of David's new decade pledge to make 10% of his annual salary for Charity each year. He certainly exceeded that this year.

With a few less businesses to draw his attention, David decided to take up golf more seriously and as the recently appointed President of the City Club, following in the footsteps of his father, he had no problems at all in getting the necessary nominations and support to join the Old Eaton Golf Course. Amazingly, in these days of "hyper security" for the rich and famous, this golf course was actually on the Duke of Westminster's estate. It was a superb parkland course, where deer roamed across the course all year and only the great and good could aspire to join the club. David started playing and was awarded a handicap of twenty-five. He would work hard, with lessons from the then professional, to reduce this handicap over the years and would find an immense amount of pleasure on the course. It filled the void left after his hockey retirement was forced due to the achilles tear.

One of the twins, Stuart, started school at Ellesmere College during the year and the other, his sister Belinda, was destined for Wrekin. Both fine schools with excellent amenities and providing a quality education. Den, David's father, would have approved of the investment in the family schooling and there was the bonus that they were not terribly far from Chester. So, with Bodfari well and truly firing on all cylinders, it seemed like things were going to work out just fine after his panic attacks earlier in the year. It looked like David was turning things around. That was until his worst fear came to light. Lloyds advised him that one of the funds he was covering was hit particularly hard by a series of incidents and that he was going to have to find £100,000 to cover his proportion of the debt when the time came in January. He was of course crest fallen. Whilst he had assets, these were not easy to liquidate and there was no way his bank manager was going in any deeper than the £900,000 he already owed on overdraft. It was after days of soul searching that he suddenly remembered the investment that he was now in charge of in Canada and the trip to Toronto a few years earlier to meet Marshall Stern. At least this could be worth something to help the cause and as much as it would hurt him to sell something left by his father, surely Den, the gambler, would appreciate this would be a good use of the investment.

David tentatively made the call to Marshall. He chatted for

a while, not wanting to look too desperate and not thinking it would amount to much. After what he thought was a polite time, he asked Marshall the all-important question. What was the current value of the portfolio, if indeed there still was one? When Marshall replied, he could not believe his ears. When converting from Canadian dollars and taking out appropriate fees, the net balance was a total of just more than £100,000 and it was almost liquid. He explained his predicament to Marshall, who then made the arrangements to liquidate the positions and repatriate the money. It was almost like getting help from the grave. The commitment to Lloyds was covered and he was profoundly grateful. Another lucky escape.

Chapter 40
To be MP or Not to Be

With his Lloyds losses covered by the Canadian investments it was another cracking year at Bodfari. Growth was again greater than 30%, profits were up, and good dividends paid to the four major shareholders. David was back from the brink of disaster. He was determined to never be in that situation again. Having steadied the ship, he could make plans and one of those was to attempt to become the Parliamentary Candidate for Chester. It very much looked like an opening was becoming available and that, the recently knighted, Sir Peter Morrison would not stand for the seat of Chester at the next election. Rumours were rife and David saw this as an opportunity to unite the party and secure the seat for the Tories.

It seemed that when Frances Mowat left the Conservative Party two years earlier, that Chester was awash with rumours about the behaviour of their MP, the soon to be knighted Peter Morrison, and that she may well have been jumping ship at just the right time. Subsequent Chester Labour MP and political opponent, Christine Russell, was particularly vocal, as one might expect. In her then role as Agent for the Labour Party and Prospective Parliamentary Candidate (PPC) David Rowlands, she was hardly impartial, but she told an enquiry that Chester was:

"*awash with rumours about Peter Morrison's private life — his alcoholism and penchant for young men — from the early 1980s onwards*"

A further quote from the enquiry reveals even more damning statements as this excerpt shows:

"*Ms Russell told us that the rumours were widespread not only within the political community but also throughout Chester. She said the allegations were being made by police officers and Conservative councillors. When she asked them what they were doing about the rumours, the response would be "he's being protected", which she thought meant they had tried to substantiate the rumours or had not bothered as it would be a pointless exercise. She told us that Conservative councillors would say he was "being protected from on high*", in other words by the upper echelons of the Conservative Party."

Ms Mowatt denied Ms Russell's account of Chester in her enquiry interview, saying Chester was not awash with rumour and she was unaware of any sexual deviances that involved Sir Peter.

David Pickering's recollection, as one who spent significant time with Sir Peter, both in Chester and London, was that he did not witness any behaviour unbecoming of the MP for Chester. David said that Peter had been particularly kind to include both he and Sue, wherever possible, from the time David was appointed as the Chairman of the Conservative Party. He remembers fondly being invited to Sir Peter's house on the island of Arran, where the two of them were treated to wonderful hospitality by Sir Peter. Yes, he had heard the rumours and he had certainly had a goodly drink or two over the years with a man he called his friend, but he found the allegations terribly difficult to substantiate. However, allegations they were and particularly damaging ones.

As the voices of discontent grew louder from outside the party it was time for Central Government to act and Sir Peter decided to stand down as Chester MP at the next election and allow the party to find a new candidate. He said he had done all that was possible in politics and now was the time to start making some money. Many did not believe his reasons and the enquiry that followed his death did a lot to damage his hard-fought reputation as a loyal and trusted servant of Mrs Thatcher's government.

The transcripts of the enquiry that followed Morrison's death were damming. Graham Nicholls, lifelong Trade Union and Labour Party member, was insistent that not only was Sir Peter a homosexual but that he had been involved in an incident concerning a fifteen-year-old boy at Crewe Station and that he was known for throwing parties for young boys in London. As Sir Peter stood down, Nicholls and others were convinced that there had been a Conservative Party cover-up, involving the local police, an agreement not to publish by the local papers and a gagging order on all politicians of both sides. David Pickering was unaware of any such deal and, if there was one, he felt certain he would have been involved in it.

The story also suggested that Ms Mowatt had brokered a deal with the then Labour Candidate, now deceased, David Rowlands, not to push this matter further, on the assurance that Sir Peter would not stand at the next election. Ms Mowatt strongly refuted any meeting took place or that any deal was brokered. Christine Russell could not recall, in her testimony, any deal or meeting but was aware of a call by Ms Mowatt asking to speak to David Rowlands. Ms Mowatt denied this call ever happened.

In her testimony Ms Russell denied any agreed cover-up, adding that in her role as agent the political mileage that would have been gained by allowing the story to reach the press, would have been considerable and it would have been in their interest, as a party, to see the story run. Despite this testimony Mr Nicholls was adamant there was not only a police cover-up but that both the Chester Chronicle and the Wrexham Leader had quashed the story at the request of "higher powers". Mr Lucas, the Wrexham Leader editor, strongly denied he had withheld this story, saying that no evidence had been produced to him and he would have run the story to make Sir Peter accountable, if it had.

The end of the enquiry, which concluded in 2019, suggested that whilst there is no official record of Sir Peter having been guilty of any offence at Crewe Station or on British Rail property, that in today's society these allegations would have been thoroughly investigated. It is probable that in an atmosphere of ignorance of Child abuse during the 1980s that all parties concerned decided not to ask the relevant questions. Was Sir Peter Morrison gay? Was he troubled by the concealment of those feelings in an atmosphere that was already baying for "gay outings"? Should the original allegations against him have been better investigated? The enquiry concluded that they should have.

Where was the Chester Conservative Party Chairman in all of this? If not oblivious to it then pragmatic. He believed, that with the lack of any evidence and from the denials by Sir Peter, that this was aggressive campaigning of the nastiest sort in politics and while he sympathised with Sir Peter needing to resign, given his poor health, he did not fight it nor suspect any cover-ups at any level. Sir Peter's drinking was heavy and the workload as Minister and MP extreme and it had certainly taken its toll. It was time for Chester to move on and time for David Pickering to throw his hat in to the political ring.

The process of achieving the nomination for the right to stand as a Prospective Parliamentary Candidate for Chester is not an easy one. It requires central party endorsement after having sat an arduous two-day course at Conservative Party HQ in London. You then need two substantial references from qualified people and then finally, when a short list is drawn up, you need to convince fellow members that you are the right person to represent them.

One would have imagined that the application of David Pickering would have looked extremely impressive. He was first and foremost the current Chairman of the Conservative Party, you do not get that title without being respected by the local members. He was also a successful businessman. He had raised significant funds for charities over several years. The press referred to him as "Mr Chester" having been Director, Chairman, President, etc, etc of almost every important Chester institution. The family had lived and worked in Chester for three hundred years and it was doubtful that there could be any candidate, on paper, more qualified than he, to serve the constituency of Chester. Surely, he was a "shoe in" not only to be nominated but to win the seat at the next election and become MP of Chester.

As David's religion had shown him over years, God's hand moves in mysterious ways. He was most definitely the most qualified Chester candidate to represent the Conservative Party, but he had not reckoned on the importance of a "safe seat" and that was what Chester was deemed to be by Tory HQ. What happens with safe seats is that Central Parties send out people they think are the next bright stars who currently do not have a seat and push them in to that electorate, which because of loyal voters means they can get their favoured candidate an easy seat as an MP. In truly theatrical style, enter Gyles Brandreth. He of the funny sweaters, charismatic personality, quick wit, and consummate command of the English language. In other words — the perfect candidate, that is bar one thing, which no one at Tory HQ cared too much about, he was not from, nor did he live, in Chester.

To say local heads were turned would be an understatement and in the various interviews and debates that took place leading up to the nomination being announced it was obvious that both the personality and sheer political "nouse" Gyles possessed meant he had become the overwhelming favourite to get the job. And so it proved, as Chester Conservatives nominated Gyles Brandreth to stand as the MP for Chester, and for him to be elected at the upcoming 1992 election.

David was extremely disappointed, but he did understand fully why it had happened. In years to come he would take that turn of events in a particularly positive way. He was confident, with hindsight, that had he been elected and become an MP it would have come at a very heavy personal cost. He saw up close how marriages suffered with being away from home, the heavy drinking culture that existed and the complete lack of personal freedom to pursue other interests. While at the time he thought he was the perfect candidate to represent Chester, in retrospect he feels had had yet another lucky escape.

There is no concealing that directly after the vote, in favour of Gyles Brandreth, he did feel betrayed by his party but there was, also, no doubting the new kid's' credentials. David would now need to be seen to be, and to actually be, supporting Gyles in the upcoming election, if the party were to remain united and to triumph. To add insult to injury he also failed to become the

Chairman of the National Farmers Union but again on reflection it was another good miss, despite two such rejections in such a short time denting his confidence.

At the 1992 election, the unthinkable almost happened. The safe Tory seat of Chester was almost lost to Labour. Gyles Brandreth was the duly elected member but with a much slimmer majority. It was now down to just one thousand votes. David Rowlands, a quiet man with little to shout about and much maligned by Gyles in his book *Breaking the Code,* almost wrested the seat away from the Tories. It was a sign of things to come and one not heeded by the Conservative Party.

Chapter 41
Counting Your Chickens or Guinea Fowl

The year had not started well but a break with Nick and Sarah Bateman, brother and sister-in-law, in a lovely cottage in Salcombe, South Devon, was a nice battery recharger. David's mood was to improve immeasurably with the news from Bodfari HQ that Northern Foods had made an approach to buy Bodfari Foods, the recently created partnership between the Pickerings and the Chantlers. Bodfari was currently buying 40 million litres annually from farmers across Cheshire and North Wales and was an attractive target. Northern foods were acquisitive and had plenty of cash and since 1987 Bodfari Foods had shown 30% compound annual growth. They were a great success story and Northern Foods wanted them.

With 25% of the company and a £900,000 personal overdraft David was keen to support any deal that brought in cash but Simon Chantler, the Bodfari MD and chief negotiator, was keen to exact as much as possible out of the deal. When it was finally done, Northern Foods had agreed to buy Bodfari Foods for £25.5 million. The really clever part of the deal was that it did not include either of the Pickerings or Chantlers individual milk supply and Northern Foods were happy for both families to supply them with skimmed milk from their herds. It was win-—win. After the dust settled from the sale, the Pickerings and Chantlers decided again to work together and called this new business, using their existing milk supplies — "Pickchant".

David was elated. This deal had earnt him just over £5 million. In the space of little more than a year he had gone from being virtually bankrupt and rejected by the Conservative Party and North West Farmers to becoming a millionaire. Not only did he have the money from the sale, but they also had a new business, Pickchant, which was not altogether different from their old business. It was quite some turnaround.

Despite his rejection by the Conservatives and Sir Peter's failing health, David continued his Polcha efforts with what would be one final event at the Stafford Hotel. In attendance were Rodney Witter, Cheshire High Sheriff, and Lord Hailsham, the Lord Chancellor. They would talk to an assembled group from Cheshire. Polcha raised another £20,000 this year and the annual dinner for the Hospice, called the Moonlight Ball, which was staged at M&S HQ raised a record £17,000. David had continued to achieve his annual goal for Charities amongst a backdrop of very trying business deals.

It was also a big year for Sue Pickering. She was now the Chair of Crossroads, the charity that helps families of terminally ill patients. She was also the Patient Care Coordinator at The Hospice of the Good Shepherd, a role that took on a tremendous importance for all those who needed help but was particularly, emotionally, draining for her. In addition to these positions, she had her role as Captain of the Bells at Hope Church. As the name implies, she oversaw the bell ringers and the timetable for bell ringing. Sue was continuing to echo her husband's efforts with charitable work, and she was making a significant difference to the groups she served.

Further developments at the Church involved the Church Warden stumping up for even more fencing as his sheep, who were doing a good job of grass cutting, were constantly finding ways to escape, literally, to greener pastures.

In the office David's excellent secretary, Jane Dewhurst, said she would have to leave work. Her health was getting worse and she lost her battle with cancer by late 1992. She was a significant loss. The further loss of Guy Dodd, David's Uncle, and Peter Barker, one of his accountants, made it a desperate time. The year was made significantly worse when David called on former nanny, Mae Guest, to see how she was. This was something he did with regularity. She was quite old now and, while in reasonable health, she was at an age where she needed support. David knocked at the door and found no answer. After repeated attempts to raise her he became concerned, until finally he grabbed a brick, smashed the window, and found Mae in a desperately bad way unable to get up from her bed. He called the ambulance. She was taken to hospital but unfortunately died a few days later. Mae had been with him since birth and had been like a second mother to him. It was a bitter blow and David decided to take some time out and think for a while.

This he did with three other friends, as they walked the hills and mountains of Scotland, basing themselves at Fort William. The pace of walking helps the brain relax and the clear air and stunning scenery connects you with nature and the elements in a way that those of a spiritual persuasion speak very highly. David was no exception and in years to come he would resort to this manner of "retreat" time and again.

Chapter 42
Solving the Racing Conundrum

One of the direct consequences of this time to think in Scotland was a decision to join Chester Racecourse Chairman Bobby McAlpine in his Racehorse Breeding Operation at Tilstone Lodge Stud. Bobby always liked the idea of others sharing in the cost and David seemed an ideal partner. David paid £70,000 for 50% of the Stud business.

Bobby had been a senior officer at McAlpines, the road and construction building company, a firm his father Jimmy McAlpine had started in the late 1920s. With the explosion of motorways across the globe, the company had done very well and despite one or two hiccups along the way Bobby had enjoyed a good time at the family firm. He was now winding down from the business. Bobby, having owned one or two highly successful horses and with a healthy list of contacts, had decided that breeding horses was the way forward and he welcomed David as his partner.

Bobby's Tilstone Lodge is an impressive family home just outside Tarporley and was ideal for the stabling of horses. Setting up your own stud was also commercially very efficient as your interest in horse racing now became tax deductible, given that raising racing horses and improving their value to sell on, was now a business and not a hobby. With David's family background it was no wonder that, with what he thought was £5 million in his pocket, he was keen to get involved. The idea of offsetting initial racing losses against his significant tax bill was not wasted on the accountancy part of his brain either!

Bobby McAlpine also boasted a true and strong friendship with the pre-eminent Racehorse owner of the day, Robert Sangster. His Golden Fleece had won the Epsom Derby in 1982 and his familiar green and blue colours were seen on racecourses across the world. Bobby also had a long friendship with legendary trainer, Barry Hills, who had trained champions at every level and stayed at Tilstone Lodge for many years when he attended the annual Chester May Festival of racing. These were good friends to have and David knew that, through Tilstone Lodge Stud, they were now well connected in the racing industry. Surely success would naturally follow as it had for his dad and uncle.

Part of the Tilstone Lodge Stud brood mare stock was Bobby's most successful horse, Cormorant Wood, and her daughter Cormorant Creek. The mother had won the Group 1 Champion Stakes in 1983 and the following year the Group 1 Lockinge. She was as classy a mare as it was possible to own and her daughter had shown, if not the same prowess, certainly a high level of ability. David's ambitions for Tilstone Lodge were rightly high.

It was a mixed bag that David's new PA, Pam Leach, inherited. There were still the minutes from various schools, charities, political parties, and farm related associations, to prepare and file, there were meetings to be chaired and papers required for Pickchant of course. David's Pig farms were still big business, and he was still a partner in two other farms across the county. Pam had a lot to get her head around and even more to stay on top of. David was not one to sit still for long.

In 1992 there were a series of personal and family

milestones, as quite often happens in life. David would celebrate his fiftieth birthday. Daughter Angela was now finished at Cardiff University and celebrated her twenty-first birthday. Sue's mother and father celebrated their fiftieth wedding anniversary and, with just half the number of years but no small achievement, Sue and David celebrated their twenty-fifth Wedding Anniversary. That was a lot of parties and a lot of good family time. The only note of sadness was the death of Norman Bateman, Sue's Uncle, who died in Spain, at Sotogrande where he lived.

Chapter 43
Time is Money — So Keep Peddling

In his personal notes for 1992 David titled the page, "Spend, Spend, Spend", and as this year unfolds it is easy to see why. Sometimes, no matter how hard you try, you just cannot stop the bleeding. It was one event after another and yet another catering bill, or travel arrangements to be paid for but it was all for the family, so you just chalk it down to experience. Problem was, it was not just family matters that were emptying the purse.

On a positive note, David's son Nicholas was "thrown in at the deep end" at Grange Farm, when he was asked to run the business at home, just as David had been by his father all those years ago and, with the help of Graham Edwards, he was doing fine.

The biggest spend of the year was David's time, as he decided to raise funds for Chester Cathedral, who were celebrating their nine hundredth year. He wanted to mark it with something special and he had just the thing. David would highlight this event with a bike ride from Rome to Chester, all 1600 miles of it, across three countries. He would meet the Pope at the Vatican City, tell him of this challenge to commemorate this amazing nine-hundred-year birthday and present communiques from the Bishop and Dean of Chester, then set off back to Chester on his bike, all the while raising money for the Cathedral Appeal.

The training was, once again, incredibly time consuming, as

it was not just the ride from the 2nd of September until 30th September that had to be accounted for. This new cycling challenge required much more training than his UK jaunt and more planning, but he was determined to do it. It was to be his fiftieth birthday present to himself. What it turned out to be was 1600 gruelling miles in four weeks. A punishing 400 miles a week. Not exactly everyone's idea of a perfect fiftieth birthday present, but as this story has shown David Pickering is not an ordinary person.

Training was not only long and hard but was fraught with problems. Somehow, whilst doing all this riding he had to put some weight on so that he would have bodily supplies to draw on when using so much energy, every day on the way back from Rome. That meant lots more eating and a carbohydrate heavy diet. During training things did not always go to plan either. There was a dog sticking 'its head of out of a window of a passing car, barking at him as he was riding and scaring him almost into a ditch as they went past. Lambs at the side of the road were a worry as he climbed Snowden, with a steep descent on one side. What would happen if they spooked and ran him off the road over the cliff edge? He knew only too well the unpredictability of sheep. He was soaked to the skin continuously on a ride back from Anglesey which was bad, a tooth dropped out in the Lake District at Cockermouth and he had a brush with the law for riding through the Conway tunnel, which is forbidden for bikes. These, plus the inevitable flat tyres and near misses by trucks, all featured in training. If it was this tricky in the UK, what was it going to be like on the continent, where most drivers, particularly in Italy — are mad!

'Mad' was a word many offered as an explanation as to why David was attempting this marathon task. His family, while supportive, were more than a little worried. The chance of an accident is always high on a bike, even if you are fit and able, but after continuous days of riding and oxygen depletion through the high hill climbs, your chances of crashing increase exponentially. This challenge was not for the faint-hearted.

The list of supplies he would need and must carry with him was much bigger this time with extra shoes, shirts, shorts, glucose tablets, Mars Bars, spare tyres, maps, suntan cream, first aid kit, puncture kit, and ID, just some of the items he was going to need.

The plan was that David would always have two helpers on hand and these helpers would work on a rota basis, with different people coming out at different times, to act as support crew. His journey would take him up the West Coast of Italy, then down the east coast of France along the French Riviera, through Cannes, up through the Lyon Valley to Caen, in Northern France, where he would catch a ferry to Portsmouth and from there, through Oxford, the Midlands and home to Chester. His target this time, to raise £30,000.

The arrival at the Leonardo Da Vinci Hotel in Rome, after a flight from Manchester, went smoothly. David exercised his legs for two days riding around the city and learning the roads and how they operated before setting off on an initial road familiarisation. The first practice on the 30th didn't go smoothly. He rode on two stretches of motorway which was strictly illegal and brought about a cacophony of car horns, before working out how to get off and back on to A roads. Then he got his panier caught in the back wheel breaking five spokes and buckling the wheel, all within ten miles of Rome. If you can do that sort of damage in ten miles, what could he do the next 1590. Fortunately, he was able to fix the problem, which was not made easier by his inability to speak Italian, although it did require him putting in a new wheel with less gears than his original one as the bike shop didn't have a perfect replacement. He would have to make do until one could be brought from the UK.

Repairs done and on Tuesday 1st of September, with messages from the Bishop of Chester, the Dean, and the Lord Mayor, he arrived at St Peter's Cathedral at the Vatican to deliver a gift from Chester to the Pope. The Pope was not in situ as he was recovering from an operation but his assistant, the Prefecture, assured David, the Pope would receive these messages and blessed his journey to Chester whilst presenting David with a set of coins to commemorate the nine hundred years of Chester Cathedral. A wonderful gesture from the Vatican and David would ride with these coins on his person, back to Chester.

At eleven a.m. David set off for Tarquinia, some eighty miles away, to meet Mike and Probo, who you may recall was an Italian speaker and who had booked the evening's accommodation. It all went according to plan and confidence was high. From Tarquinia they all headed towards the coast, the support crew by car and David on his bike, on the N1, bound for Castiglioncello. He covered a staggering 102 miles on day two and as good as that sounded David quickly discovered that one hundred miles was too far in one day because the recovery time necessary is too great to achieve big distances again the following day. Valuable lesson — do not get carried away, you need to pace yourself. The following two days were arduous with hill climbs and a crash into a gutter that caused superficial wounds that needed treating but he made it to Probo's family flat in Chiavari by the 6th.

Over the next few days, the route would include Santa Pargherita and Portofino as he headed towards San Remo. At the French border there was a support crew change. Sue and her friend Ann Ladd arrived. They brought good news and bad news. The good news was they had a new back wheel. The one David got in Rome was functional but not helping in the hills. The new back wheel had the right number of gears and would make riding a little easier. The bad news was David's mother, Margaret, who was living in the bungalow at Rough Hill, had experienced a fire and the house had burnt down. She was unhurt but very shaken. With the fire and the worry of her son riding across Europe, it was not an easy time for her and David was rightly worried about her.

As David set off from San Remo the route took him through Nice, Monte Carlo and Cannes before heading inland through the picturesque, but extremely hot, valley of Lambesc. It was decided that a small diversion to Avignon to see the Palace of the Popes was in order. This was the former escape of the last French Pope back in the 12th century and was a place of huge historical value. It would have been wrong to come so near and not see this majestic Palace. David agreed it was time and effort well spent. He then travelled along the Rhone River heading towards Montelimar and further on to Roanne across hills over 3800 ft. It was hard cycling but stunning views, wonderful flora and fauna and a beautiful silence. With so few cars on the roads, he was really able to enjoy the ride and think, just like he had in Scotland when walking.

At Roanne, Sue and Anne returned home and were replaced by Edward Walton and David Birkett-Evans. If the previous seven hundred miles had been tough, the next part of the journey was incredibly hard work. Flat, boring scenery, with acre after acre of straw fields, high temperatures and a feeling of getting nowhere. It was physically challenging but the real problem here was the challenge of the mind. How to stay motivated and believe you were getting somewhere. It seemed endless. Moral was low and Edward and David being in the wrong hotel and bar for their scheduled evening rendezvous meant a ten-mile retracing for David at a time when his limbs were aching and he was feeling oh, so tired. Suffice to say he was not in the best of humour when he eventually found the two of them enjoying a cold beer, after they had realised they were in the wrong place.

David fought on to Caen and arrived in good time to catch the ferry and get a much-needed day's rest into his legs before heading back to the UK. As the ferry took off on Sunday morning at four thirty a.m. he was headed for Portsmouth and back home to Blighty. For the first time he really felt that now he was going to make it, something he had not dared to think of until this moment. News of the fundraising also raised his spirits when he discovered that he had exceeded £30,000 and was close to £35,000 and rising. That made it even more important he keep to his schedule. He desperately did not want to fail on this task when he was so close to realising his goal.

As the ferry docked at Portsmouth, he set off for his first pit stop, a mere twenty-five miles away at Petersfield, in Hampshire. It should have been a "doddle". This was where lifelong friend Jeremy Oates and his wife Margaret lived on their farm and he had planned to stay the night and was looking forward to it.

Being a farmer, you would have thought David might have realised the impending problem when he saw that Hampshire's farmers had been out cutting their hedges. He got not one but two punctures on the way to Jeremy's and having run out of puncture repairs he had to walk the last few miles or risk further damage to his bike. As he approached the farm lane, Jeremy was at the entrance looking for him. David was some three hours late and Jeremy had been concerned. For David, Jeremy was a welcome sight, in more ways than one. The two hadn't seen each other for some years and with only having cycled twenty-five miles that day, David was refreshed enough to enjoy both dinner and some very nice red wine.

The following day he set off for Lambourne, one of the three great racehorse training establishments in the UK. Acre upon Acre of grass gallops and home to the stables of Barry Hills, chosen trainer of some of David's horses, and significantly far enough north for him to have an overnight stay. He was also looking forward to seeing these "state of the art" stables and understanding more about Barry's training methods. It proved to be a highly informative stop even though Barry had been called away. Despite his absence David was well catered for and appreciated their efforts to accommodate him at South Bank.

Having witnessed the beauty of Lambourne and its surrounds and seen his horses work up the gallop he set off for Coventry Cathedral. There had always been a close liaison between Coventry and Chester Cathedral and so when he arrived at Coventry, after a longer than anticipated, ninety-five-mile ride, he was greeted by the Deputy Dean and Bursar of Coventry. His stop could not be a long one, as nice as it was to be shown around and fed and watered; he had a tight timetable to achieve his goal. Pleasantries exchanged there was still twenty-five miles to ride to get to his overnight stay with friends in Sutton Coldfield. This had been an exhausting 120-mile day. He was, however, determined to arrive in Chester at the pre-arranged time and it had to be done, although he knew he could not go on for much longer. He felt painfully thin and had lost a serious amount of weight. His days in the saddle were taking their toll but the finish line was in sight.

The following morning, he set off on the final journey of this epic adventure. As the gates of Grange Farm appeared, he reflected on twenty-nine days of cycling, 1637 miles travelled, the pain, the immense pleasure of nature and the surroundings across three countries and now the prospect of a hot bath in his own house and, in time, to sleep in his own bed, maybe for two whole days! He had one more important thing to do and that was "spruce up" and pedal the final eight miles to Chester Cathedral and complete the 1645-mile journey.

To David this felt like the Yellow Jersey ride into Paris for the leader on the last day of the Tour De France. He was riding on pure adrenalin. He had conquered the journey and was elated with having raised £43,000, almost 50% more than he had hoped. As he rolled into Abbey Square on his faithful Raleigh Diablo, he was more than a little emotional.

There was a huge crowd headed by the Dean, the Very Reverend Stephen Smalley and various members of the press, where he presented them with the nine-hundred-year commemoration coins from the Vatican. David was told by the Dean that he had received an official communique from the Pope wishing him luck and safe journey and that the Dean would send news of his safe arrival and delivery of the coins back to the Vatican. It rounded off a phenomenal and life changing experience. David had conquered the hardest challenge he could have possibly imagined and found out that the levels of his own personal endurance could be pushed beyond that of which he thought he was capable. He had challenged himself both physically and mentally and he had won, he had also raised a staggering £43,000 for the Cathedral — but had it come at a very real personal cost?

Chapter 44
Pickchant and the Courts

As good as the bike ride was, to take a month out when your business interests spread so far and so wide, can be a cause of great concern. Fortunately, David had good people running Pickchant, shortly to be renamed Bodfari Producers and David's comment about this business at the end of '92 was a simple one, "phenomenal!" He opined that Jack Howarth was doing a good job of running things on the production side, but he was wary of falling prices for 1993 and how these might affect margins.

His own lack of day-to-day management of his pigs though was costly as both businesses were still losing money and he seemed incapable of addressing the problem, preferring instead to just write another cheque to plug the financial hole and hope it got better.

Obviously, things had improved significantly on the finance front after the Northern Foods pay out, so no more camping trips; this time it was a wonderful hotel on the lovely Greek Island of Kos and a villa break on the Algarve at Sarges, which meant two nice family holidays this year. David was determined to enjoy himself and with going racing from time to time, playing golf and working at his handicap, he was.

Simon Chantler, now in charge, was doing a good job at Pickchant and they did change the name to Bodfari Producers during this year. The two families came in for a bit of harsh press later in the year as despite assurances that Northern Foods would keep all employees post the purchase, a little more than nine months later they decided to close Stretton Dairy, with the loss of 180 jobs. Headlines in the local paper screamed, "Jobs disaster at Bodfari". Obviously the Chantlers had no control over this, as it was no longer their business, but it didn't reflect well on the former Bodfari team. Like most publicity though, it blew over and David, as he always did, fronted the press for the company and explained the situation.

Simon Chantler and Alec Pickering had moved to Belgium, both for tax reasons, as they had both benefitted substantially from the sale of the business and to better understand the AMF business throughout Europe. AMF stands for Anhydrous Milk Fat. They were convinced that AMF was the way forward. You may recall in earlier years David had bought a machine that took full fat milk and separated the AMF from the skimmed milk. Once you have this product you can sell it to virtually any dairy product manufacturer. It is much easier to store, lasts longer, up to twelve months when stored correctly and is at the base of so many mass-produced products from chocolate bars, like the Mars Bars which sustained David on his bike, to mayonnaise, ice cream, soups, diary spreads and many, many more. It was the early days of adoption of this product and the realisation of its versatility by the food trade generally. Whilst in Brussels, Simon and Alec became aware of a UK business, based in Burnham in Buckinghamshire, run by Norman Oldmeadow, that was also doing quite a lot of AMF business throughout Europe. They proposed a deal to Norman to merge with Bodfari Producers and after a short courting period Meadowfoods became another arm of the business for the two families. It would prove to be yet another sound business deal.

Meanwhile David was keen to increase the amount of milk that Bodfari Producers would have available for the future and he needed to defend his actions against the MMB at Farmers Union meetings across the county. If not the Chief Executive of Bodfari, David was most certainly the face of the company and he talked to and argued with farmers at forums on a regular basis, most times convincing them that Bodfari was working for them and with them. In a feature article within the Farmers Weekly he explained the company decision to both fight the MMB and sell to Northern Foods:

"*The logic for us is that we are a group of producers having a go, adding value, cooperating, and making a profit. You could say we are greedy and if you say making money makes us greedy then yes, we are*" and he told the National Farmers Union in Nantwich. "*people like us should be allowed to take an initiative. There's something wrong if we are not allowed to do that*" and to farmers, directly, he said — "*do you want to be in the risk business or just dairy farmers producing milk".*

It was clear what he and Bodfari wanted to be: they wanted to oversee their own destiny and be free to make the best decisions around profitability and working practices for their business. How many more dairy farmers would be brave enough to look at alternative supply routes? That was the question that was rumbling through the dairy industry at the time.

David's fight was with the MMB, not with farmers, as he proclaimed in May to the Farmer's Weekly paper:

"I Hope the MMB survives and that what we are doing will hopefully prick the MMB into becoming a better organisation" — "We have an injunction against us and we are dealing with it"—

This was the moment he explained to the assembled masses about the aggressive action being taken by the MMB. Bodfari Producers were being threatened with legal action by the MMB and the penalty of £8 million in fines if an impending court case should go against them. It was no joking matter. The personal liability for David was conservatively £1.5 million.

Chapter 45
Fight or Flight?

The saying, "it never rains but pours' was never more apt than right now in David's life because to add insult to injury and, with David now underwriting Lloyds Insurers to the tune of £500,000, Lloyds were under siege. Asbestos claims were going through the roof, and they were being back dated. One of his Funds, Gooda-Walker was looking at claims totalling 1000 per cent of premiums received, other funds were at 750% of claims and David was yet again exposed, substantially. This was another incredibly difficult time with anxiety levels sky high and sleepless nights aplenty.

Things were not much better on the horseracing front either. A half share in Cliffalda resulted in the horse breaking down on its one and only start and Cormorant Bay, progeny of Cormorant Wood, the Group 1 winning mare, was nowhere near the level of ability everyone hoped for. Dee Raft was beaten a short head before developing sinus trouble and both Northern Bluff and Bironi suffered from slow horse disease — this is almost terminal for a racehorse for obvious reasons and sadly incurable. These two would go on to become expensive giveaway ponies for children and live an incredibly happy life away from the racecourse, having cost their breeders upwards of £12,000 each.

However, David extolled in his notes that his first year in the Stud business had been *"a great experience and good fun"*.

It is amazing how £5.5 million can disappear so quickly. By

the time you have paid tax liabilities totalling over £1.5 million, lost a million or so on MMB back levies, paid out another £1.5 million to Lloyds, supported some ailing businesses, invested in a few other projects, paid off your £900,000 overdraft, bought 50% of a stud and invested £80,000 in horses; then suddenly, your £5.5 million is gone. This had not happened yet, as there was significant litigation in at least two of these debts, before the losses are realised but these are the prospects that have emerged in 1992 and they might all become due in 1993. Clearly David intended to fight and it might be a while before he has to pay but contingencies now have to be made.

There are two sayings that dominated his mind during this period of reflection and that David kept as a reference over the coming years. The first was from Robert Hiscox, fellow Lloyds of London name and now the owner of the highly successful Hiscox Insurance; David and his paths would cross again in the future. Of their respective losses at Lloyds, Hiscox was convinced there would be better days and he penned to fellow names as he tried to rally the troops:

"As the great man said, when the storm rages the small birds take cover but the eagle soars". Which are you going to be?

And the other was the slightly different story and possibly more apt, of Mark Twain's cat, who was described by Mark as being a cat who regularly sat on the Aga to get warm, only to discover after a time he burnt his backside and had to jump down, yet when he got cold again, he would jump straight back on the Aga to repeat the process and burn himself once more. As an observer, the cat story and the dichotomy faced by the feline was perhaps a metaphor for David's life and described his current predicament to a tee, but it was the first quote from Robert Hiscox that he would adopt as his way to fight his problems and that mantra has stayed with him to this day. He got aggressive and went in harder.

As 1993 approached, David was in the process of negotiating some very heavy financial hits and fighting them with everything he had but he was determined to fulfil another of his ambitions; this time it was to become a director of a public quoted company. In other words, a company quoted on the London Stock Exchange. Now, the only way to achieve that is to accumulate enough shares in a quoted company and then to be able to demand a seat on the board.

The process was simple enough: buy loads of shares and make your intentions known. The problem was picking a company where you could get enough shares without having to pay a huge sum of money and a massive premium and of course find one where, if you got a seat, you could add something to the board's existing skill set. In other words, benefit the business you have invested in. David chose S Daniels, makers of the Covent Garden Soups. It seemed perfectly logical and his brokers agreed.

Here was a company who was involved in food production, as was David, doing something that people liked and appearing to do it well. David duly invested, over time almost £1 million and accumulated a significant percentage. He owned 1,168,300 shares which represented 14% of the company and he requested a seat on the board. David had met CEO Paul Daniels several times socially and he could not understand why, given he had been a main board director of so many businesses and just seen his company acquired for £25 million, the company weren't pleased to welcome him. However, eventually they acquiesced, and David became a main board Director of a listed company, another ambition fulfilled. This one had not been a cheap one to realise but as long as the company traded well, then his shares would appreciate in value and things would work extremely well. He would have achieved becoming a director of a quoted Company and he would make a profit on the deal. Perfect.

Be careful what you wish for — you just might get it, words never truer than in the case of S Daniels and Covent Garden Soup. David found the infighting within the group difficult and his heart sank when he decided to visit the production plant at Horrills Dairy. If there was one thing David knew about it was Dairy production. It was extremely poor at Horrills. Bodfari Processing had significantly better systems, had invested well in machinery and people and S Daniels had done none of this and were not about to let some "hick" from the North tell them how to modernise and save themselves. Over time this investment would cost David £500,000 as the share price went down and he eventually liquidated his position and went away to lick his wounds. Mark Twain's cat retires from the Aga again — bottom burnt!

Chapter 46
H'away the Lads — C'mon Chester

Back in Chester, the Gowey Councillor, John Bramhall, had suffered a severe heart attack and needed to stand down which necessitated a by-election and David was convinced to stand for the Conservatives, which he did and he was duly elected to the Cheshire County Council as a Councillor for the Ward of Gowey. In 1993, the City of Chester had a council, and the County had a council. Unitary councils for Cheshire East and West would not come until some years later. This involvement, at a county level, gave David a unique understanding of Cheshire and enhanced his retinue of contacts even further.

Next on the agenda was the long running saga of Chester FC. Having, earlier in his life, been a Director of Chester FC, David was aware of the problems at the club and so, as he expected would happen, the club was yet again in severe financial difficulty. David made an offer to buy the club for £1. To the uninitiated and to many of the fans, this seemed rather rude but for those who understood the machinations of company law he was prepared to buy the club for the single £1 because with its current debts standing in excess of £250,000, if the Club was to continue to trade, David would have to take on those debts personally and invest further into the club to get it back on its feet and trading profitably. His commitment if they agreed was more like £500,000 than just the £1 offered. It was an almighty undertaking and one that many have failed at before and after.

Perhaps he didn't package it correctly, maybe he needed a bit better communication to the fans at the time. That is not how the Chester faithful saw it and his offer was rejected outright. It was a seminal mistake by the club as they lurched from one disaster to another, one set of owners to another, full of false promises and even in 2020 their future, despite the fact they are playing in much lower tiers of football, is less than secure.

History often repeats itself and in 2020 Chester FC have just turned down the investment of £1 million by Chester businessman, Stuart Murphy, in real terms probably about the same amount David was promising back in 1993. Having turned Mr Murphy down the club have struggled with fan donations to raise £120,000 to stay afloat and their future is less sure than ever.

Not getting Chester FC was probably a blessing in disguise as making hard business decisions and trying to answer to a passionate fan base do not go hand in hand, so it was best to move on and leave football as something David never conquered.

Next on the agenda was the purchase of the Dene Hotel. During the big bike ride across Europe, Bill Wood had helped as manager at the Christleton Country Club and he had been in charge at the Dene Hotel. Bill was convinced this was a sound business, in need of a bit of investment to bring it back to profitability. The asking price was £950,000 but, in a buyers' market with interest rates still high, the vendors agreed a sale at £750,000. It was, on paper, a good deal and David was now a hotel owner as well as a Country Club, four farms and various other businesses across Cheshire. Enough? Nowhere near yet.

The purchase from the Receiver, of BD Technology, was another addition to the Pickering Portfolio. Jim Robinson, the man running Dee Electronics for David was convinced this one could work and introduced the business to run side by side with

Dee. Jim was the intended CEO of both companies. The plan was to amalgamate BD with Dee Electronics, but Jim needed to get BD running well before he could do that and that is where the problem started. Splitting your time between two concerns, as David well knew, can sometimes be to the detriment of the one you have working well, particularly if you could not bring them both under one roof. This proved to be quite a challenge.

There was also another significant investment in Horses during 1993. Dee Raft won at Lingfield, Chester and Doncaster during the season and was then sold for £20,000, a good return on a home bred. Dime Bag won at Newmarket in April and was installed as favourite for the Chester Cup, something of which her two owners were immensely proud and expectant. The Chester Cup is a trip over 2 miles 2 furlongs and the feature race of the May Festival. The horse ran badly at Chester in the Cup, which was disappointing for all concerned as there was a lot of local support at the betting ring. She was not the first to struggle with the tight turns of this unique track and whilst that could account for some of her problems, more worryingly, the stud and racing clubs No1 trainer, Barry Hills, had a virus in his yard that affected the horses and accordingly they ran poorly this year. It can take a full season for a yard to get healthy again, just like the old farming days with foot-and-mouth, so David understood these problems better than most, but it was an expensive year, with significant losses and little prize money because of this issue.

With the profit from the Dee Raft sale, a horse called Greek Gold was bought, on the advice of Bloodstock Agent, David Minton, out of the Sir Michael Stoute Yard. Greek Gold was owned by the very wealthy Weinstock family, but they would sell this one horse, for £30,000. The horse would prove disappointing and sold on for £8,000, realising a £22,000 loss. Easy come, easy go.

Further disappointment followed when, out of the eight mares on the Tilstone Lodge Stud, only five were in foal, and there was even more bad news, when River Jet attempted to give birth to twins. This is a rarity in the equine world and one that hardly ever works out and in this case it didn't either. One foal dead on delivery and the other dead shortly thereafter. David would describe this racing year as:

"an interesting year but I went into it with my eyes open".

It seems the fun that he described in 1992 has dried up as the losses mounted and he was not delighted with the way things are going.

Meanwhile at Lloyds, David's losses are showing at greater than £1 million and still growing. Lloyds offered to settle at £449,000 but David's advice from the action committees is to not pay yet as there is still more negotiating to be done. Despite all the problems he further heeds the advice of Robert Hiscox and increases his exposure from £2 million to £3 million for 1994 and decides to represent himself to the Lloyds adjusters to see if he can mitigate the offer of £449,000 further.

For Bodfari Producers things were really getting interesting as well. The litigation was in full swing and the war with the MMB intense with solicitor's letters being fired back and forward. News of the war was definitely frightening some of the Bodfari suppliers. This was a dilemma that needed to be "nipped in the bud". Without a supply of raw milk, they had very little product, and whilst the Chantler and Pickering herds would always be able to supply some milk, it was nowhere near enough for the order books, which were full for the AMF product.

David and his partners invited three hundred farmers for lunch at their new offices to show them the commitment to milk and processing. They wanted their customers to see their investment of £1.5 million in "state of the art" machinery and processing equipment and to show that despite the problems, they were going nowhere, hopefully giving confidence to the dairymen. That year over six hundred Christmas Cards were sent to thank milk contributors and make sure Bodfari was ever present in their thoughts and to reassure them that things were under control. The owners explained that Bodfari Producers was in effect an important Cooperative and they were trying desperately to calm their suppliers and steady the ship. Bodfari also sent out seven hundred contracts to prospective suppliers with whom in the past they had a supply of milk. The big question was how many would sign up to continue supply. It would make for a very uncertain Christmas.

David's year-end notes suggest that with interest rates down to 5.5% that the economy is doing all right, so there was reason for optimism and he fully expected property to be a big winner. He was well placed to enjoy that ride if it happened, as he owned Grange Farm, New Hall, Siglen Farm, Cawley Lodge and the two pig properties in Anglesey, as well as the Dene Hotel and the Christleton Country Club. It was just the nagging doubt about the milk contracts and the MMB negotiations that were unnerving him most, that and of course Lloyds.

David's son Stuart had finished at Ellesmere College and started working at Llysfari, so there were now two family members working in the pig business and Belinda stayed on to do her A Levels at Wrekin after achieving good grades in her GCSE's. Daughter Angie did eight months of work at accountants, Morris and Co in Chester, but like her father never really took to the day-to-day work of an accountant and went back to Cardiff for a Teacher training course. David's mother's house was rebuilt after the fire and she had moved back in, so with the family in good health and his finances okay, if not precarious, David felt satisfied. The MMB litigation and the

Lloyds losses, however, were never far from his thoughts as they had the ability to rock the boat in a major way.

After attending a Henley Management Course, David is taken by the Chinese word Kaizen — the literal meaning of which is — Change for the Better. This word had been explained to him as a culture that adopts the art of continuous change. He decides to adopt this in his philosophy of business going forward. Be brave, adopt change for the better and keep moving forward. It describes perfectly were he wants to be and how he wants to act, and he would use it in the marketing of his businesses throughout the coming year.

If 1992 and 1993 had been helter-skelter, both personally and financially, 1994 was a year for reflection. The ongoing row with the Milk Marketing Board was in full rage. David had realised, after two years of pushing the accelerator flat to the floor, that he could not go on this way much longer. He had a massive Capital Gains Tax bill of £600,000 to pay for the sale of shares in Northern Foods, these were the shares that had been gifted in lieu of cash through the sale of Bodfari Foods. He had sold his shares, which realised a profit, to pay for more and more of the debts on loss making businesses, horses, and investments, but the gains were taxable. An attempt to "bed and breakfast" the shares, a deal that sees you sell the shares in late March before the year end at a loss and then rebuy them at the lower price in the new tax year, had backfired, as they went up in price and added a further £25,000 to the CGT bill and all the time the pigs were still losing money. One bright note, if it can be described that way, was that through his own representation he managed a further £100,000 reduction on the Lloyds bill, bringing it down to a mere £349,000. He would have twelve months to make this payment, as well as the tax bill and the clock was ticking.

Chapter 47
Where Has It All Gone?

David was neglecting the day-to-day running of his own businesses in favour of the things he liked doing and convincing himself that the fundraisings, the Councillor Duties and his own personal image was more important than seeing to the accounts and welfare of the businesses he had invested in. In some cases, that was not a problem. Bodfari Producers, Simon Chantler and brother John, were doing a great job of the micro-management of this business but there was a huge fear, with rapid changes at the MMB in the pipeline, that their ability to get continuous supply would be severely curtailed. David was heavily dependent on the continued survival of this business and if it folded through fines levied and a ruling on supply through the courts, be that UK or European, then there was a very real chance he could be bankrupt within a year. It was a chilling reminder of the risks he had taken and the consequences of the downsides if he got it wrong. After the huge windfall of the Bodfari sale and the successes of Bodfari Producers, again, he was just one wrong decision away from being bankrupt and losing everything.

David needed a clear out of his personal businesses and to do some serious soul searching. He had allowed himself to be taken advantage of through lack of control at Cawley Lodge, by Mike Hanson. He had also shown a lack of willingness to address the personal issues of his tenants on one of his other farms, who were going through a marital break-up, which was hampering production, and making those places inefficient and the "damn" price of pigs kept going down. Another frank letter of concern from NatWest Bank Manager, John Rawcliffe, stung him into action, the basis of which was, start tidying up your affairs or risk ruin. You are an accountant; start providing proper quarterly accounts and start caring about these businesses or there could be worse to follow. The NatWest Manager did not know how close to coming true his prophecy was and David needed to act now to make things right.

First and foremost was how to lighten the load. The sale of Christleton Country Club was imperative. With some good, attendant publicity, which would not have been possible without his high profile in the community, a sale was agreed that created around £150,000 in cash. It had been a small profit on the deal but at least he had something to show for it and he no longer had loan repayments to make to the bank for this property. David calculated that left him another £400,000 to find before January 1995. Everything was up for consideration. New Hall looked most likely to go and he doubted Siglen or Grange would ever be profitable, so they were on the table as well.

The date approached for the MMB Court Case in London. It was a heady affair with the future of the archaic system, against which David had fought for so long, at stake, as well as a personal loss of about £2.5 million if things went very wrong. To Andrew Chadwick of Gorstella Farm and many like him, who had supplied Bodfari over the years, this was a vital moment as he recalled when he was asked to testify in court. What if the Pickering's and Chantler's called on him to help pay the fines? His account of his days in court set the mood of the time perfectly.

"The arbitration took place in Fleet Street over two weeks. I

attended for one week. The central table was occupied by the Arbitrator, Lord Acker and two QC's. On one side were "our" QC's David Vaughn and David Anderson and our solicitors, and indeed my solicitor for this, Roland Dawson. On the other side were the RMMB QCs led by Ken Rokison and also with Freshfields solicitor.

Behind Lord Acker and his QCs were three sets of files and as one side or another referred to a file, say D4, they would all swing round in their chairs and collect D4 page 100. Then E3 page 80 might be referred to and they would swing around again and replace D4 with E3. Much talk among the lawyers, not about the case itself but about legal matters and especially charging rates, took place in the "Gents loo"!

Having said all that, from the little I knew, it was very fairly and professionally conducted. At one point there was a discussion as to timing. After two weeks Ken Rokison had to leave — to go to Hong Kong, I think. Could therefore, we start earlier so as to be certain of finishing on time? No apparently not, because Ken Rokison's son was starring at the time, in Just William *on the television and had to be taken to school!*

The cross examinations were very thorough and detailed and extensive. The MMB's own solicitor requested an adjournment to give himself a break.

When it was my turn, I was nervous and slept very little the night before. My cross examination lasted four hours but with a lunch break in between where I was not allowed to talk to anyone. I went for a walk to St Paul's on my own. When the cross examination resumed Lord Acker asked if I had gone to seek inspiration.

At the end of four hours, I was exhausted and being Friday I was very glad I was going home that night. I had no idea how the arbitrators were viewing it and indeed there was another week to go.

The judgement came quite a time later — we lost. I was shocked when John Pickering rang me. He was calm and said he would send me the summary — 50 pages. I read it and it seemed even handed but then at the end came down on the side of the RMMB.

I understand Bodfari continued to negotiate with the RMMB but I never knew the final outcome. Whatever it was they bore it and never came to me with complaint or anything else. I still admire that."

They did indeed continue to fight, this time in the European Courts. David's courting of the European MP Lyndon Harrison helped to a certain degree to mitigate their problems but David, John and Simon lost the appeal case in the European Court and were ordered to pay significant penalties. David's share was £1 million; it could have been a lot more. While they lost the ruling on the back levies owed, they did at least secure the right to continue to trade under the new Milk Marque operation which meant suppliers of milk to Bodfari could do so without fear.

The Milk Marketing Board, after so many years of acrimony, collapsed in November and was replaced by the Milk Marque, so in effect David had won, as they were still trading and the MMB was gone forever. It was disappointing to have to pay the fine but the future of Bodfari was now without doubt, as legally they could now trade.

David got to work very quickly marketing the company and in addition to offering all their suppliers an extra penny per litre than that which was being offered by the Milk Marque, Bodfari would also offer shares to everyone who signed up to commit their annual milk quota, which would then allow them to participate in the success. It was a masterstroke and a terrific success. In a short space of time, they had signed up a commitment to 120 million litres a year. The Bodfari supply was well and truly assured now. The appointment of Damian McDonald as Financial Controller was a good one as well, something David had insisted on and was paying dividends already, as he could now accurately forecast both minimum and maximum returns for Bodfari and the bank liked what they saw. This was now, again, a profitable business with a big future, free of litigation. David was confident in the Executive at Bodfari, who were very capable, and this business was now being run extremely well. The shoring up of your financial foundations is vital if you are to survive or flourish and this was now on a very firm footing. It gave his bank manager confidence to support David's personal position knowing that his chief source of revenue was in good shape.

Despite his continued personal financial problems David carried on with his commitment to the Hospice Annual Ball as Chairman and that year was another record year with £25,000 profit and, just for good measure, he accepted the role as Chairman of the Cathedral Appeal to raise £2.5 million. Some might argue this was yet another significant distraction that might well take up time he could ill-afford. One thing that was certain was that, faced with problems, he was particularly good at striking a deal, working through the problem, and getting a solution. He wrestled with the dilemmas he had faced over the years in a note that he penned by hand at five a.m. one morning towards the end of the year, he argued,

"you shouldn't have to get yourself into difficulty in order to find out how good you are by getting out of them".

It was not good for his health, with sleepless nights and anxiety at an all-time high and it certainly was not good for his bank balance. Surely it would be easier to manage his affairs on a daily basis more efficiently, and keep things moving towards his targets. His own assessment was that his macro-management and strategic awareness was excellent but his ability to micro-manage his many projects was poor. If things were going to change then 1995 would have to be the start of it. He had got lucky with the MMB, Lloyds and their new deal and the commitment of supply of milk to Bodfari Producers. Now was the time to show his mettle, show a little more patience and a little less ego. He *"had taken far too many risks and been reckless with his time and money"*; all his words from his diary notes. Now would he be able to change and adapt?

As 1995 got underway the proposed merger of Meadow Foods with Bodfari Producers was being discussed and taking up a lot of think time for David. Regular meetings meant he was able to concentrate more on these businesses and work out how they could make a better business by combining both. The senior partners all agreed that this was the best way forward and during the year the companies became one. It was yet another important move. This brought about further investment in a new plant at Chester and an agreement that Meadow Foods would act as the sales agent for Bodfari Producers. The Bodfari turnover for 1995 would reach £50 million and make a profit of £594,000. On a modest valuation that made the business worth, again, between £15 and £20 million and with David owning circa 15% of the new business his annual income with dividends was approaching £150,000 and he needed every penny of it. Further good news followed as Bodfari was nominated for a prestigious ADAS Food and Drink Award. Recognition at a national level of their exceptional business.

Chapter 48
The Luck You Have is the Luck You Make

A winter break skiing at Les Gets in France with the Cheshire's, John and Elizabeth, and meeting up with Sue's lifelong pen friend from Grenoble, Marielle, made for a great start to the year. Sue and Marielle had been exchanging letters as pen friends since they were fourteen and this chance meetup was joyous for them. It followed for many years as they returned annually to ski and to meet with Marielle.

It also looked like the gamble of increasing his exposure at Lloyds to £3 million was paying off as the annual dividends accrued looked as though they just might be enough to clear his £349,000 debt without him having to reach into his pockets too deeply. Had he been brave or reckless? Who knows. He had increased his exposure at a time when he could ill-afford to but it had worked. Some might say lucky, but David believed you make your own luck, and these gambles were working. He did need to give himself a talking to about not increasing his exposure at Lloyds any further and not to get greedy! Surely £3 million exposure was enough for anyone.

His time management though was still a struggle. The Cathedral Appeal was high profile but incredibly demanding and he did not want to fail. What he desperately needed was more help and that would be the focus of his attention. He needed to find people who were good at what they do and get them to assist him for the greater good.

There was a bright family moment in July when son Nick married his wife, Claire. It was a super event with the Reverend Gerald Griffiths in fine voice and daughters Belinda and Angie playing the piano and flute. It was a very proud moment for Sue and David where the wine and the speeches flowed freely, and you could escape from the pressures of daily life for a while.

On the racing front there was modest success, Dime Bag, after a modest four wins from nineteen runs, was retired to stud and although the Cormorant Wood line of progeny was not producing the quality that either David or Bobby McAlpine would have wanted, they had the odd winner to keep things going. One bright spot was when the Dean of Chester accompanied David to Chester Racecourse for the inaugural Sunday Family Funday meeting. David had sponsored a race for the Cathedral to raise awareness of their fundraising. The Bishop of Chester was very against Sunday activities, other than church going and the very Reverend Stephen Smalley, Dean of Chester, was very keen to move with the times and liked the idea of being involved in racing. The Daily Telegraph captured a beaming Dean Smalley, sat next to Racecourse Chairman Bobby McAlpine's wife, Angela, as the Cathedral Stakes set off. John Roberts, a member of the Lord's Day Observance Society was quoted in the *Telegraph a*s saying that the bishop, who had taken a well-timed break away on this day, was "absolutely livid". John Alexander of the Keep Sunday Special Group, saw it as "contributing to the moral decay of society". Whatever their view it was all wonderful publicity for the Cathedral.

Whilst the Dean and Bishop did disagree, the race, which was paid for by the Racecourse, highlighted the plight of the Church and their need to raise £2.5 million for restoration. It was a Marketing triumph for David Pickering. Dean Smalley was quoted as saying that his designs to raise this money from racecourse attendees was much the same as the bookmakers and they shared similar ambitions on the day. The bishop said to the Dean over breakfast in the week preceding the race, that whilst he disagreed with the Race, his advice to Dean Smalley was "You run the city, Stephen and I will run the Diocese". Whatever the ecclesiastical outcome, the exposure to a national audience about the plight of the Cathedral boosted the donations substantially. David's gamble had yet again paid off. Racing coming to the aid of the Church, now who would have thought that?

It is amazing, that despite getting rid of the "macro-problems" of his tax bill, the MMB debt and the Lloyds payment David had still managed to avoid dealing with his more minor problems closer to home. He still had not done anything about Cawley Lodge, BD Technology was losing substantial money and he had reasoned away the Pig business losses in his mind because he had two sons working in these businesses and he felt they needed his support. So much for 1995's resolution to sort all of these things out. Would they come back to bite him as they had before? Time would tell.

There was, however, time to play golf and he had got his handicap down to nineteen, with an ambition to take another two shots off by the following year. He also managed to learn something important in this year, which was the ability to say "No". He reasoned, when asked, that he simply had too much on to undertake any new projects and for the first time and he stuck to it. No one could argue with him on this.

Apart from an ambition to reduce his golf handicap further David said, in his end of 1995 notes, that he was determined to get a better team around him to help with the fundraising and his personal businesses and to grind away at the businesses that were not working. It is almost like: we have heard it all before!

Chapter 49
Opportunities, Challenges and Solutions.

In 1996, the year started well. The annual Deeside Ramblers Hockey Trip saw the team take to the slopes of Sëlva — Sëlva is a commune in the Val Gardena in South Tyrol, northern Italy, and is the highest village in the Dolomites. These annual jaunts were extremely popular, with some hard skiing and even harder drinking filling in much of the "off piste" activities. The Hockey Club let their hair down with a little more exuberance this time as they were celebrating the installation of their new all-weather pitch. Evidence of the high jinks was apparent when David released a picture to the club, taken while away, of room-mate Noel Barraclough "resting" on his bed, wearing only, a particularly large and unpleasant pair of underpants. Noel still blushes to this day at the thought of the photograph and him being caught at such an unflattering moment.

There had been a lot of fundraising to get this pitch in place and the bid writing to the lottery fund was very time consuming, so everyone thought a drink or two well deserved whilst they were away. They definitely had the one they came for and as Noel described in a note as he reflected on their time together; their skiing trips were "weeks of belly laughs and camaraderie with relatively minor challenges and some of the best times of my life".

On his return to the office David was installed as Chairman of Bodfari Limited, the parent body to both Bodfari Producers and Meadow Foods. The more testing part, politically, was the appointment of both Simon Chantler and Norman Oldmeadow, who would be joint Managing Directors and John Pickering a director of the business, the latter proving to be less prickly as John was never too worried about status or position, as long as everyone just did what he said! David then introduced former Hillsdown Holdings Chief Executive, David Newton, to the Bodfari board, where he was appointed as Director. With his usual succession planning, it was David's ambition that Newton succeed him, as Chairman once he had learnt the business. There were no objections to this plan.

David Newton was easy to tempt into the fold as Bodfari had been an incredibly successful business over the years and in particular the newly formed group in the last two years. Bodfari were already supplying in excess of 50% of the UK's entire AMF consumption and were on most food companies' radars. Their client list was sparkling as well, featuring Cadbury's, Mars, Nestle' and Walls. For David Newton this was an ideal time to be involved and his skill set was a good match for the ambitious plans of the company.

At the board meeting David Pickering revealed that turnover for the previous year had reached £104 million up 104% on the previous year and a net profit of £1.7 million. When you consider that just two years prior, they had sold their main business to Northern Foods and were literally starting again from scratch, it was phenomenal growth and it highlighted just how important retaining the two families' milk supply was when they had made the sale to Northern Foods. Yes, they had added many more suppliers in the two years but without the hard core of their own milk it would have been that much more difficult to convince dairy farmers that Bodfari could provide them with a good and reliable income.

There was also great personal joy as Angela and Marc provided David and Sue with their first grandchild, Mabli, born on the 4th of April 1996. Just prior to the birth, Marc attended a City Club Dinner with David, at the Grosvenor Hotel, where David was able to introduce him to Geoffrey Mitchell, Senior Partner of Lovelock Mitchell Architects. Marc, a qualified architect, would, shortly thereafter, take up a position working for the firm and some twenty-two years later is himself a Senior Partner in the same company.

At Siglen Farm, son Nick and his wife Claire had finished building their house, giving them some surety in the family business, and of course adding further value to the property, which while still struggling to make a profit, was performing better. All would be fine if the price of pigs remained solid but that seemed to be something over which no one had control.

Son Stuart was also enjoying his time of learning as he spent five weeks on a Princes Trust Business Management Course and then twelve weeks working with a group at Cheshire Fire Brigade. He was accumulating skills that would later prove vital in his chosen profession and he enjoyed his time at these two superb establishments.

New Hall Farm, however, was particularly problematic. Unfortunately, Noel and Kath Morris, the operators of the farm, were in the process of getting divorced and, as is the manner of these matters, there was a significant argument about the value of their stake in the business and who was entitled to what amount of money. On production of the accounts, it became even more apparent that this farm had been losing significant money in recent years and had been propped up by David for quite some time, so attributing any value was a difficult one. David was called in to officiate and duly this property was placed on the market. In some way the divorce forced David's hand. It was a loss-making business that David felt a personal attachment to try and save for the sake of the family involved. Yet the disposal of the property, which he was now being forced to sell, had the desired effect of closing a loss-maker without having to take the responsibility for the decision. Again, the day you close it down is the day you cease having to spend more money propping it up and so it was with New Hall. Another chapter finished.

Chapter 50
Learning a New Skill

As the weather improved, the walking group that David had joined decided a trip back to Scotland was in order. So, Stuart Morris, Peter Ladd, Tage Weiss and David set off for the Ballchulish Hotel at Glencoe near Fort William, where they would make base camp and attempt an attack on the summit of Ben Air. They comfortably made it to the summit and then enjoyed not just the amazing scenery but the unique descent, which was even more thrilling. It was the first and only time they had all taken part in Glissading. The principle is a simple one. You sit down in the snow and ice, on a very steep slope and then, with your feet slightly held off the ground, you let gravity do its thing, as you hurtle down the slope using your snow pick as a rudder and brake in the snow behind you. David described it as exhilarating. The slopes were extreme and the snow and ice perfect.

Back from Scotland the offer of another Chairmanship arrived, this time from the newly established, Conservative National roll out, of CEWTEC. The thinking was that the UK suffered from a lack of skills at the technical level and that everything possible should be done to get people upskilled in the new types of job that were being offered across industry, and for which we appeared to have a real shortage of suitable applicants. CEWTEC would fund specialist training programmes for employers who would be encouraged to take on less skilled applicants knowing that they could have the "on the job" training subsidised by the government. It was a strong programme, delivered right across the UK and its aims were solid and reasonable. David was only too happy to add this to his workload and oversee this Government Quango. This was a government initiative that did make sense and a difference.

There were also changes within David's office as Jane Dewhurst needed to step down as his PA and, in her place, David appointed Anne Rowley-Williams. Anne would now take on the task of learning all the various businesses that David either represented or had invested in, compile the meeting notes, print agendas and minutes, and keep his diary as up to date as possible with the many meeting requests that he received in any given week.

David also assumed the Presidency of the recently formed Chester Business Club, something he and Chester Public Relations stalwart, Bob Clough-Parker, had put together. Their aim was to get Chester businesses working for a common good and to see how others did things. With that in mind a trip to New York and New Orleans was arranged. Business Club committee member and Chester Hotelier legend, the then Grosvenor Hotel GM, Jonathan Slater, had amazing contacts through his travel and trade networks and he put together a terrific itinerary that not only saw them stay in some wonderful hotels but allowed contact with other similarly minded groups in these American cities.

Jonathan, David, and Bob were joined by Ron Smith, Stuart & Dianna Begbie, David Birkett Evans, Eddie & Hazel White and Tim & Margaret Steward. They were treated to some unbelievable hospitality whilst in America and brought back stories of business in the USA that was shared with the wider group on their return, in what was a real eye-opener for the team.

David was asked to speak at the Chester Banker's Dinner this year. He had been outspoken during his fight with the MMB and at the forefront of so many new initiatives, both in farming and politics, so it made perfect sense for his voice to be heard by the Bankers of the city and their guests. What they got was a forthright account of the state of farming across the UK. He also gave a stark warning about the possible dangers of CJD being linked to BSE (Mad Cows Disease) and what might happen if it spread through the beef industry, with information based on a report which had just surfaced within government. He issued a timely reminder for the bankers of their responsibility and how important it was that they keep the country going, through their continued support of the wealth creators. They needed to support the people who, day in and day out, risk everything to create profit, employ people and generate wealth for the UK and that without the investment in new machinery and people, there is no wealth creation. The banking sector had a responsibility to show unwavering support through lending, to the wealth creators of industry, or, he believed, it would grind to a halt, recession then sets in and that hurts everyone. He hoped they were all listening.

Later in the year a couples golfing trip to the wonderful Penina Resort on the Algarve in Portugal produced quite a surprise. As they unloaded the car at the airport to check-in, there was an extra set of golf clubs in the boot. It seemed, without David knowing, that Sue had been secretly having lessons at nearby Old Padeswood Golf Club and she was now ready to join the others in a round of golf. As the saying goes — "if you can't beat'em — join'em".

Whilst most of the year was enjoyable, what wouldn't go away was the problems with Mike Hanson and Cawley Lodge Farm, which was still haemorrhaging money, as was BD

Technology. Worse still, the newly formed Residual Milk Marketing Board, who were charged with collecting even more back unpaid levies, had raised their ugly face, and were making hefty demands on Bodfari Directors for their past debts. They wanted another £1.2 million from David and were determined to get it.

Chapter 51
Royalty, Millionaires and Arseholes

Politically, Chester's MP, Gyles Brandreth, was doing well at Westminster and was quite the favourite with the party leaders. He was appointed Lord Commissioner of the Treasury and would in time be responsible for effectively reducing business Capital Gains tax by increasing the threshold at which payments start from £2 million to £10 million. This was of course most helpful for any business that was taken over and encouraged more entrepreneurs to invest in their start-ups, without fear of losing substantial amounts of their hard-earned profits to HMRC. It was also particularly relevant to any future deals that Bodfari might consider, a point not wasted on the Pickering family.

Gyles invited David, as Chairman of the Chester Conservative Party and an active sporting participant and fundraiser, to lunch with the Duke of Edinburgh to discuss the National Sports Fields, an agenda close to the duke's heart and something David had personally been involved with through his work at Deeside Ramblers Hockey Club. For David, it was a memorable luncheon with an iconic British personality and one of the most important Royals of the twentieth century. The Duke made quite an impression as a man who knew what he wanted and how he was going to get it. He was surrounded by people who were capable of delivering his vision and this was a lesson that David was keen to learn being as he was someone who was often guilty of failing to devolve responsibility and ask for help.

That was not the only brush with Royalty that year as David

and Sue attended the annual Buckingham Palace Garden Party. This really is an extraordinarily, quintessentially British event. Held on three separate days during the summer, where 27,000 cups of tea and 20,000 sandwiches and cakes are served to the assembled masses on the grounds of the palace. One must apply to attend and after a significant vetting process you may get the all-important invitation. David and Sue's credentials stacked up and they were able to experience something rather special in the grounds of the Palace.

In late summer David received another invitation, this time to take part in the annual Millionaires and Arseholes Golf Tournament. This was an annual event organised by Stuart Williams. The Williams family were synonymous with Chester and well known for their TV and Electrical businesses, a sector that boomed from the 1960s for almost forty years. Latterly Stuart was making a significant presence around Chester in the property game; he was also a county golfer, having been a decent rugby player at Chester as well. He had owned bars and clubs across the city and Stuart, like David, knew everyone. His golf tournament involved bringing together an eclectic mix of people and, as the tournament name suggests, a few of them were millionaires and titled people. On the list were The Lord, Francis Stafford, William Corbet Winder, owner of one of the best shoots in the country, Lord Peter Greenall, Bobby McAlpine, Ces Jenkins, Chris Fleet and of course David Pickering to name but a few of the millionaires or would-be millionaires. The principle was that these people would be paired with those of the "lesser" world who just happened to be cracking people with whom to have a beer and also happened to play a decent round of golf, unkindly called, "the arseholes". The teams of two were drawn from a hat, you would then bid money to own a team and in the ensuing competition the winners would take the pot.

Stuart owned the Links Hotel at Morfa Nefyn, so everyone

would arrive the night before the competition at his hotel, have an exceptionally good meal with some outstanding wine, and sort the teams for the following day's tournament, which was played at the picturesque Nefyn Golf Club. Up for grabs this year was a pot of £6,000 and the competition as ever, was stiff. Stuart was able to assess the golf games of those who did not play as regularly as others to make sure there was an evenness to the competition and one's Nefyn handicap was invariably different to the handicap shown on the board at your local golf club. There was no room for sandbagging here and Stuart rarely took the word of a Lord as Gospel, sage reasoning! He had been around too long in the golf game to know whose handicaps needed some attention. It was an excellent two days, with lots of laughter, some great golf but not on this occasion a £6,000 win for David. He did, however, learn a lot from his first tournament and was keen to return if asked.

He was just as successful at Eaton where he and Terry Allen won the better ball pairs championship and with his handicap now just ten, David was clearly playing good golf. In the years to come he would venture into single figures from time to time and then lack of practice and regular play would see him drift back up again.

Staying fit and healthy had always been important to David and so with his regular golf and of course his weekly tennis matches, plus the significant annual bike rides, he was achieving his goal of staying in good shape. When the opportunity presented itself to challenge his fitness further, at the Territorial Army Warcup facility in Cumbria with the Cheshire Regiment, he was up for the fight. A gruelling two days of obstacles courses, water challenges and physical assessments resulted in him getting a glowing report and a deeper understanding of the military and their preparation both physically and mentally.

Chapter 52
Syndication, Commitment and Communication

As 1997 started there was the regular, by now, Skiing trip to Les Gets and meeting up with Marielle and then a little later the Deeside Ramblers would make their way to the Alps; that year to Serre Chevalier, a major ski resort in South eastern France. The resort encompasses a large skiing area, with 250 km of slopes and boasts, amazingly, three hundred days of sunshine a year. If only the lads had got outside the bars a little more often, they might have got a tan!

New Hall Farm had been on the market for a little while now and there was a deal to be done. There was talk of developing an area for housing, but David was keen to sell and move on. He needed to lighten the load. While he had managed to hang on to most of his money during the previous year and business at Bodfari was good, his personal affairs were still precarious. The new threat of the RMMB was very real and his overdraft was well above £1 million now. That coupled with his new, larger, commitment of £4 million at Lloyds, meant he was at the mercy of events outside his control and at any given time real disaster could strike and that is not a good way to live.

The IRA unexpectedly raised 'its ugly head in this year as well. With horse racing very much a part of day-to-day life, David was invited to attend the Aintree Festival, of which the feature race is, The Grand National. Simply the most famous horse race in the world and one with which the family had significant history. On Saturday, just before the tapes came up for the big race, the course received an appropriately coded message that warned of a bomb on the course, which required the immediate evacuation of the public. David fled the course with the other 69,000 attendees and everyone spread to various pubs and hotels around Liverpool, where people tried to re-unite with friends and work out how to get back home. No bomb was detonated but by the time the course was cleared, the race could not be staged and in true British style they simply rearranged the race to take place on the Monday evening. The winner, for the record, was Lord Gyllene, trained by Steve Brookshaw, who had at one time ridden for George Owen, David's brother in-law. It was also the only time in the race's history where it has not been staged on the Saturday and it was yet another Pickering link to this wonderful race.

Shortly after Aintree, David launched Bodfari Stud. He was still in partnership with Bobby McAlpine at Tilstone Stud, but he could see how creating his own stud partnership would allow multiple ownership possible within the company and he had a ready supply of yearlings from Tilstone that could race in the famous Light Blue and Dark Blue diamond colours. He contacted several friends and within no time he had a dozen "syndicate" members of his Stud. He also launched the Bodfari Times, a monthly newsletter, printed as an A4 magazine that featured articles and pictures of their horses. It was an informative piece on relevant racing stories written by 'The Colonel" who was, in reality, Bobby McAlpine and he covered results and upcoming entries for the Stud horses. It was ahead of its time both in the collection of people in the business and his marketing and communication to those people.

The Stud enjoyed a successful first season. They had

nineteen horses under their control, eleven of them two-year-olds. They won six races during the year and most importantly one of those wins was at Chester. Bodfari Distinction won around The Roodee. It couldn't have been a better start. With so many members of the Racing Club being Chester based, a Chester winner was the icing on the cake. Things looked promising for Bodfari Racing.

As had happened previously in his life, just as the sale of New Hall went through at £1.4 million, the final bill arrived from the RMMB. It was £1.2 million, so by the time David cleared the small loan outstanding on the farm and paid the agents fees, the amount left was exactly £1.2 million. As the cheque arrived at his account for the sale, he wrote a corresponding one to the RMMB for the same amount. He never saw a penny of what looked, on paper, a very profitable property deal. In fact, the profit was significantly less when you considered losses on trading over the years, all funded from his personal account. No point dwelling on the losses; it was two less things that could "bite" him and cause serious problems. David's fights with the MMB in all its guises was now finally over and despite the fines and levies, there was no doubt the Pickerings had won.

Chapter 53
Canvassing for God and Country

In Chester, David was now Gyles Brandreth's election agent, which basically meant it was his job to coordinate the re-election campaign. These six-week vote gathering events, which precede a general election, are frenetic. Nationally it was the Grey Man, John Major versus the smooth talking, New Labour candidate, Tony Blair. It was obvious to many that times were changing and that the Blairites and their left of centre policies were making Labour electable, after the failures of Foot and Kinnock and the far-left loonies, who had held the party back for so long. The country wanted a change. Whilst that may have been the national agenda it does not always transfer to the provinces, particularly in long held seats, but as Gyles and his team marched the doorsteps of Chester, it became obvious that they were in a battle against Labour's Christine Russell and with the very real chance that the Liberal Democrats, now being led by Paddy Ashcroft, could also steal vital votes from Conservative voters looking for change; things were tense.

Given his significant involvement with Gyles in the election, David decided not to stand as Councillor in the county election and instead to concentrate on the campaign of his sitting MP. He would also stand down as Governor of both Christleton High School and Lache Park Infants, as he lightened the load for the fight ahead. Gyles and David both knew they were up against it and there was a very real chance that, for the first time since 1906, someone other than a Conservative would hold the Chester seat, and that for the first time ever, that might well be Labour. And so, it was, that on the night of 1st May 1997, David, as Chairman of the Chester Conservative Party, and Gyles Brandreth MP were forced to concede defeat to the Labour Candidate, Christine Russell. Her majority was a whopping 10,553 and a massive 15,000 turn-around from the 1992 election. Whilst the national swing was 8.8%, in Chester, it was a staggering 11.1%. Chester not only sided with Tony Blair, but they were angry that the Conservatives had, nationally, taken them for granted and put Gyles into their midst in what they mistakenly thought was a safe Tory seat. Former Tory voters right across Chester did the unthinkable and voted Labour. It was a distressing night for all concerned and some soul searching was necessary both nationally and locally.

There was added pressure at Chester Cathedral as well. The Song School budget was now up to £1.5 million and with a shortfall of £700,000, against what had been raised to date, David initiated a bid to the Lottery Fund and the Arts Council. These processes are incredibly time-consuming and whilst many are successful, getting money through these avenues and the "hoop jumping" required is extreme. It would be some time before they would know the outcome of either. The only alternative, if they were not successful, was to borrow the money. The good news was that work was finally completed on the floor of the Nave and everyone was delighted; all eyes were now on the Song School project.

In late June, David and Sue took a trip with friends Tom and Christina Bartlam to Royal Ascot. This was becoming a more regular visit as everyone enjoyed the quality of racing, the wonderful hospitality and of course the sheer Britishness of the top hat and tails worn by those in the Royal enclosure. The presence of Her Majesty the Queen, and the sense of occasion that this brings, always makes it a special event. Nowadays horses come from America, Australia, France, Germany, and South America to take part in this festival of racing, held in June every year.

A holiday to Runaway Bay in Jamaica with Sue made the dark nights of winter a little more bearable but the year did not end well as David's mother was in poor health. Everyone was worried about her in the lead up to Christmas.

Doing his usual reckoning between Christmas and New Year David was not only worried about his mother he was also worried about his Lloyds positions. That £4 million liability was an uncomfortable position to have but the figures showed it had been very profitable. He calculated that he was due 8% of £3 million, that being £240,000 for 1995. For 1996 it was 6% of £3 million which was £180,000 and for 1997 he should get 4% of £4 million or £160,000; those returns and the £200,000 in his capital account gave him a figure of £780,000 credit at Lloyds. In addition, he had his significant share portfolio on deposit with them and further reserves, totalling in all, circa £1,150,000. In theory he was in a good place — but just one major problem anywhere in the world and he could be wiped out — again. His various salaries and incomes had amounted to £460,000 for the year and yet he still had nothing to show for it after paying out for all the loss-making businesses and of course enjoying some quality holidays and events. That overdraft will still more than £1 million and growing and the fear factor at Lloyds was higher than he wanted it to be. How was this possible?

Chapter 54
It is All a Question of Timing

David made the decision at the start of 1998, to halve his position of liability at Lloyds from £4 million to £2 million. The gamble of going big when faced with adversity three years earlier had paid off. Whilst he had not exactly enjoyed the latest good run at Lloyds, it had been very profitable but the fear he felt meant he could not operate on a daily basis at £4 million liability. He was simply over trading, and that always ends badly.

It was now time to behave a little more responsibly. The halving of liability at Lloyds freed up both capital and assets and meant he could take the full payment that arrived from Lloyds in January. He could now forward fund his commitments into 1998 with the proceeds from Lloyds which meant decision-making was that much more positive. By not having to scramble for money and with some diligent work on his loss-making businesses things could look a whole lot brighter by year end.

The first decision of 1998 was to appoint his son Nick to run both Siglen and Grange Farm breeding units. David was convinced that the secret to this was getting the costs of fattening the pigs down using more careful controls. He feared that those without a vested interest in the business were less inclined to care about costs and that with his son in place he could reduce costs and improve margins. For Nick it was somewhat of a poisoned chalice. No one had made it successfully work in the last ten years and even David admitted in his yearly appraisal that with the price of pigs what it was now and likely to be for the next six months the chances of this business turning a profit was extremely low. Nick was somewhat envious of his younger brother Stuart, who had just started a house building and renovation business with his partner's father, Eifion Griffiths and they seemed to be doing rather well.

The Deeside Ramblers set off for their winter skiing break shortly after David and Sue had returned from Les Gets; this time the Ramblers visited the gateway to Alpine Skiing, St Anton in Austria. The travel guide suggests that St Anton is equally famous for its apres-ski scene. Hard to see the attraction for these battle-hardened Hockey players! You would have to say the Deeside Ramblers were true to their name, covering the Alps from all angles. One wonders if they collectively covered as much ground on the hockey pitch during the season.

On his return to the UK things were getting lively at Bodfari HQ. The board meeting saw the directors vote in favour of a £5 million investment in a new Casein Processing plant. Casein is a protein found within milk and by isolating this in the production process you can provide an even more transportable, versatile, and durable product. This was cutting edge technology and quality investment and of course no small risk.

In addition to this major initiative the board were forced to release a statement to all shareholders to advise that the non-executive directors of Bodfari Producers, that being, Pete Samuels of Decoy Farm and Andrew Chadwick of Gorstella Farm, would be resigning their positions. The two believed they and the company they represented had a conflict of interest with the parent company. They did not believe they could truly represent the many Dairy shareholders of Bodfari Producers when Meadow Foods, who sold all of their produce for them, dictated the price the farmers received for their milk. Given that both had enjoyed not just excellent milk prices that were above and beyond the average farmer for many years, and that they received a salary for their position at Bodfari, it was a strange decision. However, they made their point and, as regularly happens with these things at corporate level, they were replaced by people who did not see it as a conflict and things continued as they were. This whole episode was really a reflection of the lower milk prices across the UK. The seasons had been brilliant for grass and cattle and as such there was a plentiful supply of milk which had the effect of forcing prices down. This was echoed in the share prices of Northern Foods and Express Dairies which were both lower by 30%. With significant investment in both companies and the shares he owned in them acting as security for David's ever-growing overdraft at the bank, the lower milk price was as much a concern for Bodfari as it was for David personally. Better news was that turnover for Bodfari in the 1997/98 year had hit £129 million, up again and profits were £3 million for the year. A full year dividend of 2.0 pence was paid, which was the largest to date and it did a lot to regain the trust of the milk producing shareholders.

Chapter 55
Big Personalities and Blind Ambition

As the new racing season approached at Chester, David was appointed to the Chester Race Company Remuneration Sub Committee, where he quickly ensured that fellow Directors received a much overdue pay rise. This is always a popular move, particularly if you have ambition to be on the main board and David did!

There was also an article in North West Business which detailed the newly launched Bodfari Stud. It reported just how well they had done in their first year and explained David's vision going forward. He was quoted as saying that he expected the Stud to be at break-even within a year and to have a Group 1 winner within five years. Lofty ambitions indeed. The appointment of Goldford Stud Owner, Richard Aston, as the Bodfari Stud MD, only strengthened that claim. Richard's own stud, at Bickerton, near Cholmondley, was also featured in several racing publications as they were doing sterling work raising juveniles. Richard and his wife Sally were preparing yearlings for sale that were fetching £100,000 at auction and cutting quite a dash as a handsome couple, who were extremely good at their work. David was, again, surrounding himself with professional people; he was most definitely learning how to bring together a strong team.

Bodfari Stud would send out eight winners during 1998 making it a very enjoyable and successful season. Their horses numbered fifteen in total. Trainers included Tarporley based and l Chester Racecourse winner, Alan Bailey, the wily eman Mick Easterby, Paul Felgate, Steve Gollings, ills, and Oliver Sherwood. They had specialist flat trainers, specialist 2yo trainers, Chester specialist trainers and specialist jumps trainers. It was a heady mix of racing knowledge and no small commitment financially. If you consider that to train a horse in 1998 was about £1000 a month, with racing entry fees and transport normally adding roughly 35%, if you were lucky enough not to encounter Vet bills, then the monthly cost for these horses was running at about £20,000. The average prize money on the flat for winning a race was £4000, so you needed five wins a month just to break even. You do not need to be an accountant to realise just how expensive horse racing is and just how difficult it is to make it pay. Many have tried and most have failed, very few have succeeded. Of course, as a horse wins a race, they become more valuable and if you breed and own that horse and then sell it, you may well make a profit to add into the prize money pot, which all helps. Alternatively, if they develop slow horse disease, for which there is no known cure, they may be worth little and whilst they are in training, slow horses eat just as much and take up just as much training time as fast ones and are worth less. That is the gamble.

If 1998 was remarkable, as David aptly described it in his diary notes, then one of those remarkable sets of events would certainly be that he may be one of the few people who have ever had three sets of golf clubs stolen in the one year and most certainly the only living person to have got the insurance money for all three sets; now that is remarkable. The first set was stolen from Eaton Golf Club, the second set from Delamere Golf Club, and the third from the boot of his car in the car park on Pepper St adjacent to the Albion pub. Most remarkably his insurers, NFU, paid up on each occasion. For anyone who has had the misfortune of trying to claim from most insurers, getting paid once is tricky, three times impossible. This anecdote might well be the best advertisement NFU Insurance could have.

In another remarkable series of events in 1998 David was almost run over, twice. Once when leaving the footpath at the Amphitheatre in Chester as a Van careered over to his side of the road and narrowly missed him as he waited to cross. The other was at Doncaster Yearling sales where a car, again, all but side swiped him from the pavement, as the driver appeared to lose control momentarily. Both incidents shook him considerably. After the second incident David decided he needed to recognise his good fortune in being uninjured, not once but twice, in such bizarre fashion, so he sent Jack Berry, the wearer of the Red Shirt, racehorse trainer and chief protagonist of the Injured Jockeys Fund, a cheque for £500 for the charity. It seemed a fair trade.

In late July David investigated the affairs of Widnes Rugby Club. They were a little like Chester FC, perennially in financial difficulty but with a traditional fan base and perhaps dissimilar to Chester had experienced some good years as a dominant force in Rugby League. The attractiveness diminished as he saw the extent of their debts and the lack of assets that sat behind the club so he walked away before making a serious offer.

Just as he thought his days of looking at sporting clubs was over, a read through the Financial Times on the 31st of July revealed that Mark Guterman, the current owner of the recently acquired Chester FC was putting up for sale 94% of Chester FC. In effect relinquishing all control of the club. David already had a plan for Chester FC, from his time as a director, and this seemed the perfect opportunity to put that plan back in to play. He immediately registered and created a company called Chester

City Football Club 1998 Ltd and started negotiations with Guterman. To sit on David's board, he had already secured Mark Astbury, Tony Durkin, Barrie Hipkiss and Bill King, all people with significant experience of Chester football and most importantly the respect of the fan base. These people had worked with David when he had previously tried to help the club and knew of his motives. The Pickering bid was based around shares being issued in the newly formed company that would be bought by supporters of the club and that money being used to support the club, but not to pay Guterman a vast sum of money so that he could walk away, from what was a financial mess. David's plan would ensure this was a fan owned club with a future if he could get Guterman to accept the deal.

With negotiations going back and forward between David and Mark, eventually the Pickering consortium accepted they could not gain control of the club without having to pay Guterman a large sum and with the serious debts Chester had, they had no choice but to suspend their bid. Later that year Mark Guterman did find a buyer and the club continued to lurch from one disaster to another. Rumours circulated Chester that the club had fallen into the hands of known criminals. These rumours were never substantiated, however, with the high-profile appointment and subsequent sacking of Manager and former Liverpool legend Mark Wright, the poor Chester fans never knew from one moment to the next what was happening to their team. It was another sorry saga in the chequered history of Chester FC and a further disappointment for David as he tried and failed, yet again, to put the club back in the hands of the fans.

Chapter 56
To Travel is to Learn

On a brighter note, David's daughter Belinda was about to start her Business and Accounting degree at Edinburgh University, which was cause for some celebration after some previous traumas at school and her suspension after a boy was found in her room! While that move to Edinburgh University gave cause for optimism, the same mood did not prevail in David's report to the Chartered Accountants, where he was the Agricultural Special Interest Group Advisor. It was a damming account of the Agri industry, where he highlighted the various problems and summed it up with;

"Virtually every sector of Agricultural production is in a mess".

He was uniquely qualified to offer that opinion and he highlighted the disparity between production costs and income received, as evidence of this disastrous sector. He went on to explain that the industry not only relied on government subsidies but could not exist without them and that this was simply unsustainable at every level. The report has stood the test of time as we still try to reconcile the Agri-sector whilst attempting to leave Europe and the massive hole that the lack of EU subsidies to the sector will leave when they are no longer available in a post Brexit world. It was a prophetic piece of work and one that should have been acted upon long ago.

The cycling bug had well and truly bitten David. On the 1st

of October he set off for Cuba to ride the 777 miles diagonally across the island in aid of the National Deaf Society. Dissimilar to his previous solo efforts this was a trip organised by the Deaf Society. Those who wanted to ride had to commit to raising £2000 for the Deaf Society; they would then get their flight and accommodation paid for and a bike supplied for the ride. It was great for David and brilliant for the Deaf Society. The society's costs were £1000 per rider and with ninety riders this event made them almost £100,000. For the participant you got an all-expenses trip paid, in return for raising the two thousand pounds; everyone won. The society did about twelve of these in different places each year and were making £1 million just from these cycling events.

On the first morning in Cuba, David went down to breakfast at the hotel and dined with a 70-year-old man from Devon by the name of Jim White. Jim was a farmer. Naturally, they had plenty to talk about. After breakfast, the ninety cyclists set off on their journey and suddenly the peloton came to an abrupt stop. The lead cyclist had spotted a large hole in the road and avoided it, whilst shouting out to those who followed, however, because of riding in such close proximity, the ones further back, were blind to the road ahead and one of the group careered into the pothole, coming off his bike and breaking a collarbone, with other riders careering in to the back of him and creating an almighty pile-up. All were treated quickly by the team and after forty-five minutes, with bike repairs attended to, the remainder set off again. It was only a matter of an hour later they again stopped suddenly. This time there was a cyclist lying on the road. It was the man David had been breakfasting with earlier, Jim White. He had a heart attack while riding and the medics were unable to resuscitate him. He died in Cuba.

After such a bleak start David wondered what else Cuba had in store for them but the remainder of the journey passed without serious incident and it was an enlightening and invigorating ride. He rode across a country where the poor seemed happy with their lot; a country that had somehow lived in the squabbling shadows of the two superpowers since 1960. David's personal problems back in the UK seemed somewhat less important when he returned home. It was a poignant reminder of just how fortunate he was to live in the UK.

An opportunity came up, not long after the return from Cuba, for David and Sue to visit fellow Chester Business Club Director Ron Smith, at his holiday home, in Florida Quays. David worked out that he could then travel on and visit the Keenland Yearling Sales in Kentucky with bloodstock agent David Minton and follow that with a day at the Breeders Cup at Kentucky, the home of Horseracing in America. It seemed like the perfect trip.

Ron Smith's house was suitably impressive, and the Florida Quays made for a special place to relax and enjoy their time away. David Minton did indeed find a yearling filly for Bodfari Stud, even though many of these yearlings were changing hands for sums greater than $500,000, which was a bit out of David's comfort zone. To then see the American Equivalent of Ascot, at Kentucky, was a one-off experience, with the finest dirt bred horses in the world competing for the Breeder's Cup Classic, the highlight of a ten-race card at the home of the "Run for the Roses", Kentucky. They also managed to work their way North East and take in the famed Saratoga Race meeting in upstate New York. Much lauded for its mention in the Carly Simon song, "You're So Vain", where well-heeled New Yorkers go north to play in late summer. This trip had delivered on so many levels.

As the year closed out, for the first time in quite a while,

David's only major concern was that Bodfari & Meadow Foods looked like recording their first backward steps since they had reformed the group. Turnover decreased from £129 million to £115m, with profits of just £1 million, and whilst that was by no means disastrous the downturn was of course attributable to the lower milk price but more worryingly the margin was tiny, at less than 1%.

Chapter 57
Turnover is Not Profit — Tough Decisions

When the figures for the trading year were released in March of '99 what became apparent was that much of their AMF was being sold at the wrong price and in some cases being sold at a loss. Supermarkets were demanding lower priced goods from suppliers and, whilst it was great to have five or six major clients like Nestle and Mars, if they are being squeezed by the Supermarkets then they are going to squeeze producers for even lower input prices. The customer squeeze and the lower milk prices in the marketplace were a very real worry. Even more so was that having paid the £2.5 million installation cost of the new Casein plant, the first products they were selling from this innovative process lost £500,000 in just six months. A combination of learning the production techniques of the new plant and not knowing what the right price was to sell the product had caused the losses but the board were confident this was a learning blip, and they would make it right very quickly.

Given the downturn in Bodfari and his recent run of good fortune at Lloyds, David made the decision, at the start of 1999, to resign as a name at Lloyds. He simply did not want to push his luck any further. This would have a two-fold effect. The first and most important is that it would return almost £1.5 million of assets and capital and secondly it would mean he could release a little of the pressure he was feeling daily, as the spectre of a disaster loomed at any given time. Lloyds had been good to him;

even with those years of, cumulatively, £450,000 in losses, he had made over £1 million in just over twenty-five years and that was from a starting base of just £60,000 in assets back in 1972. Time would show what a wise decision resigning would prove to be.

It was also reporting time for David's personal businesses and that did not make much better reading than previous years, in fact things had gotten much worse. Picks Pigs had now lost almost half a million pounds in the last three years; you just wouldn't have thought it possible to lose so much in such little time but the accounts didn't lie. The problem was that weaners were now costing £28 to produce and were selling for just £15. It was simply unsustainable. So, when son Nick decided he could do this job no longer, David finally came to the decision that enough was enough. With Nick leaving he had no family reason to carry on this loss-making business anymore and so he set about liquidating Picks Pigs.

It was a difficult decision to terminate the Pigs business as this was what had started him at Rough Hill, but losses were totalling close to a million and no one could say he had not tried to make it work. As news of the liquidation surfaced, the local press were scathing both in Chester and Anglesey, as they saw "Fat Cat" businessman, David Pickering, "Mr Chester" and golden boy of the Conservatives, close his business with the loss of jobs, the debts of the business and worse still the farmhands on Anglesey had mercilessly shot all the pigs and bulldozed them into a massive pyre for burning. This did not read well, and David was mortified.

Both Chester and Anglesey are places that are particularly incestuous, where most people know other people's business and jealousy is rife. If you put your head above the parapet then there will be plenty of people happy to take a pot shot at it. This was the ammunition that a number had waited some time for, so they could aim directly at the head of David Pickering. They say you need skin like a rhino to survive in politics and it's probable that David had benefitted from his experience as a Councillor during this difficult time. The criticism was aggressive and scathing and he could do nothing but take it. The only good part about closing a loss-making business is that the moment you do, you stop losing money and that was the case with Picks Pigs. The bleeding, financially, was now over and in time the headlines would only be visible as the wrapping for fish and chips.

Just when David thought there could not be much worse news the phone behind the bar rang at Nefyn Golf Club, where he was again playing in the annual Millionaires and Arseholes Tournament. The caller was his stockbroker who advised him that S Daniels shares had now fallen from 40p to just 20p and that Northern Foods Shares had tumbled by a third from £1.50 to just £1. All these shares, remember, were now acting as security for his overdraft at the bank. He would face some uncomfortable conversations to assure his bankers that all was okay. If things continued in this vein, then next year at Nefyn he might be playing in the arseholes team instead! Despite the untimely interruption and in a real show of mental strength he managed to keep his golf game together and share in the first prize of £12,000. Not a bad day's work but against the back-drop of a share portfolio that had depreciated by almost £280,000 overnight, it was hard to get too excited.

Slightly better news at Chester Racecourse though. New CEO Richard Thomas was welcomed by a board of Directors that now included David Pickering. His working relationship with Bobby McAlpine, the Chairman of Chester Race Co, had awakened Bobby to David's skill set as both a man of figures and marketing and he was keen to have him support Richard Thomas with the ambitious projects to progress the Racecourse in the coming years.

As the hymn says, "When darkest seems the night morning is near" and it seemed very dark when the news that Donald Bateman, Sue's father, had failed to recover from his earlier fall where he broke his leg at Grange Farm and had died. He would be greatly missed. A wonderful father to Sue and a genuine friend to David as a father-in-law. While this loss hung heavy over Grange Farm for some time, morning did start to arrive, and things again started to brighten.

Chapter 58
Let's Party Like it's 1999

Nick's decision to leave Picks Pigs was not just about the parlous state of the pig industry it was also a reflection of his newfound duties as a father. He and Claire had produced another grandchild for David and Sue with the arrival of baby Declan. Belinda was also doing well at Edinburgh where she was out on placement at ICL in Stevenage, so things on the home front were now improving and for Bodfari Stud things took a significant turn for the better as well.

Bodfari Cream won at Doncaster, Bodfari Quarry won at Wolverhampton, Bodfari Signet won at Stratford and Leicester and Bodfari Komaite won at Musselburgh. Better yet, David sold Bodfari Cream (the horse) for £40,000 and he sold two unnamed foals and two yearlings for £100,000. This was more like it. Prize money and the sale of horses was exactly the reason that Bodfari Stud was created. It seemed the pendulum was swinging back his way when he also won £1600 at Muirfield Golf Club playing in the Doncaster Bloodstock Sales Golf tournament and with this win and his previous big win at Nefyn he had to briefly declare himself a professional golfer to accept the prize money. So, in one way or another he was finding ways to make racing pay.

Carrying on with his biking adventures, this year David signed up again with the Deaf Society, to ride from the Sea of Galilee to Jerusalem across Israel, a route that was just over 400 miles. He also managed to convince friend, and RBS Bank manager, Peter Overmeer to join him on this epic journey. It was an eight-day ride averaging 50 miles a day and, whilst this tested Peter, for David it was a much gentler ask than some of his previous efforts, although the temperatures were much higher than his other rides. Dissimilar to Cuba, this ride went without a hitch. Armed guards at every check point of the journey into Bethlehem meant it was not without its tensions, but the riding was enjoyable and the scenery stunning.

Peter remarked that everywhere you looked you were surrounded by biblical history" and for a religious man like David this was incredibly special. In a postscript to the ride, some two weeks later, David was reading the lesson at Hope church and it happened that the story was from Mathew 4:13. In it, Jesus based himself at Capernaum and without thinking David decided to tell the assembled congregation — that this was "where he was riding through, just two weeks ago". He thinks God would have approved of the interjection and it certainly livened up the worshippers as he indulged them with his own pilgrimage across Israel to Bethlehem.

Keeping up his commitment to try and raise 10% of his annual salary every year for Charity David instigated the Millennium Ball for the benefit of the Cathedral Appeal and Hope Church. The celebration of the arrival of a new millennium was to be the biggest party the world had ever seen and for that reason venues were charging fortunes to stage events on New Year's Eve. David secured the Racecourse as a venue for the event and with his small team set about selling it. It proved a lot more difficult than anyone could have imagined. It seemed people just were not willing to pay the hyper-inflated prices for this once in a lifetime event and so, despite eventually selling all the tickets, when they totted up the accounts there was a £20,000 shortfall. Given that he had underwritten the event the bill for the shortfall was sent to David to settle. The two tickets for him and Sue to "see in" the new Millennium had ended up costing him £20,000 plus drinks. He was right again — it was a new year he would never forget! On the plus side, the two charities made £1500 each from the raffles and auctions, so not all bad news. The small profit barely reflected the many long hours put in by David and his team of volunteers. In retrospect he would rather have given each charity £5,000 each and had a great night at Grange farm with some friends for half the price but that was not to be.

Chapter 59
During the Bleak Midwinter

As 2000 got underway and with the, by now, annual trip to Les Gets skiing behind them there was a return to Serre Chevalier for some more skiing with the Deeside Ramblers before he made it back to Grange Farm, where bad news awaited. His mother Margaret had suffered a severe stroke that had left her barely able to move. At best she had some hand response but not much more. It was a real trial for David. His mum had been the one constant in his life. Always there and always cheery. Now he was seeing just how cruel life could be as she struggled for some quality of life at home.

A similar bout of ill-health saw the then Chair of Eaton Golf Club have to resign, and David was asked to stand in as Chairman, adding to his list of responsibilities. His golf handicap was now down to ten and, as Chairman, no doubt he would be expected to play even more golf at Eaton, although that was the least of his worries as the new Eaton Golf Course had some serious challenges ahead.

David and his walking buddies set off to conquer the slopes of Cader Idris in Wales this time and Sue decided she liked the idea of the walking challenge and joined them. On his return to Chester the board meeting for Bodfari would reveal that turnover was back on track returning to £135 million, but for all that extra turnover, profits were stubbornly below the million mark and the dividend remained unchanged at 1.5p per share. Milk prices were remaining low and that hurt margins. John Morris was brought in as the head of production; such was the need for specialist labour and John had a real understanding of this rapidly evolving industry. David also bolstered the financial ranks by bringing in an Assistant Financial Controller as the workload in the accounts department was increasing at a similar rate to revenues.

The Bodfari horses performed poorly in the early part of the flat season but June was a sparkling one with Bodfari Pride winning twice at Goodwood and Chester at 14/1 and 2/1, Bodfari Komatie went in at 4/1 at Catterick and Bodfari Anna won well at 14/1 at Southwell. Shareholders were flushed with success and at decent odds as well. July was even brighter for David, as Angela and Marc announced the birth of their first son Ffen. He was just what everyone needed to bring some joy into the Pickering family. Belinda was also working now for Texaco. She and partner Ed were living in London and enjoying life.

David's work at the Chester Cathedral was ongoing. The project of building the Song School was now expected to reach £1.3 million, down by £200,000 but still well over the initial estimate of £800,000. David figured the only way to fill the gap was with an arts council grant of 300,000, so the back-breaking work of filling in the various forms started and the task of trying to convince nameless bureaucrats that this project was worthy of their support. He was not hopeful. To make matters worse, just as he thought his work was done, having Chaired the successful raise of the £750,000 that the original project was expected to cost, the Dean and the Bishop asked him to stay on and chair the new structure as they fought to find a way to deliver the project. They were determined that work should start in spring 2001. The Cathedral needed David's experience to oversee the building programme. Somewhat reluctantly he agreed to stay on.

It was a bleak time all round on the theology front. At his home Church, Hope, the Reverend Gerald Griffiths finally succumbed to the pressure of his fundraising efforts and he was cut down by a stroke. He had been in pitched battles for years with local MP, Lord Barry Jones, urging him to assist Hope Church in its aims to renovate. David was asked to step in and take control of this project as well; he could hardly say no. Fortunately, word came through quite quickly that the Reverend's prayers and remonstrations with Lord Jones had not been in vain and they had got the money. It was £540,000 on the building works, £10,000 for lighting and a further £40,000 extension. The Reverend Griffiths had won the day. He got all the funds from both the Welsh Ancient Buildings fund and Lord Barry's various government agencies. David delivered the project on time and budget. Work was completed in November. Gerald saw this as a fitting time to announce his retirement. He really had given everything he could to his church and further efforts could have had far worse consequences for his health. He was leaving his Parish in a lot better condition than he found it, and no one could ask more of him.

The Deeside Ramblers deviated from the norm and decided not to go skiing as winter approached and decided they would have a pre-season tour to La Cala Golf Resort near Marbella. Not sure that any Hockey sticks made the journey, but as a team building session the reports were encouraging. Some encouragement also with horses as Dime Bag had thrown a foal called Pawn Broker, bred by Bodfari Stud. Pawn Broker had won and been placed in quality races as a three-year-old, with trainer David Elsworth explaining he would be an even better horse as he got older, with group aspirations next year. It was wonderful recognition for the small stud, and it put them on the map with their mare.

At Bodfari Foods, the New Zealand Dairy Board came visiting and David was on hand to show them around and explain just how the business worked and what the future might look like. They were impressed and discussions ensued about a possible takeover in April of 2002, if things felt right, at an amazing price of £30 million. Whilst it's easy to talk figures when you don't have to write the cheques, the discussion was meaningful, and it gave all the Directors a boost knowing that was the sort of valuation they might expect if and when the time came to sell.

The year rounded out well with Northern Shares recovering to £1.50, which pleased David's Bank Manager. There was a wedding in Grenoble, where Marielle's daughter got married and a quick golfing trip to Cannes with the usual couples which meant it was a busy late autumn. It was a nice way to finish yet another challenging year, but most concerning was the continued poor health of David's mother and to make matters worse her sister was also not well.

Chapter 60
Losses Mount at All Levels

Whilst it was the normal start to 2001, with another skiing trip to Les Gets with the family, quickly followed by a Ramblers skiing trip to Courcheval, all eyes were on Nick and Claire as they were expecting their first child in late January. Their daughter Jucinta arrived, and all appeared well until it became apparent, she could not clear her lungs, which were building up with fluid. Despite the best efforts of the Doctors, they were unable to treat her and she lost her battle with life. It was, of course, the saddest of times. The loss of anyone is sad but a newly born baby is always a tragedy and this hit everyone hard.

As the old wives' tale goes, things happen in threes, and after the tragic loss of Jucinta, in a truly cruel blow, David's mother would die on the thirteenth of March, followed three days later by her sister, David's Auntie, Fon. Just some of the words spoken at his mother's funeral reveal the love and respect the family held for her, as the two sons recalled her putting lunch on the table at twelve thirty every day, where John and David were told to be prompt because the news was on the TV at one p.m. When working in the office she made them lunch every day until her stroke. After her stroke, she had a series of Reiki sessions to relieve the pain and suffering that plagued her right up until her death and in one such session in late December she opened her eyes and said; "*Have a cup of coffee, I have a joint of beef in the oven*" and "*I have put a bet on for you David*". Nobody will know if the horse won but as David said to the congregation when he read out those words during her eulogy, *"we have all been a winner knowing our mum"*.

It was an incredibly tough time yet again and, in some ways, put the financial problems David had experienced into perspective. How he would swap any of the fortunate events of the last years to be able to bring back the people he had lost. His mother had been the one consistent supporter throughout his life, through everything and now she was gone. It did, however, make him really focus and ensure that he did everything possible to keep making things right and keep doing the little extra things that make a difference in life.

For the farming industry the news was also devastating. In mid-February, the first cases of foot-and-mouth re-appeared in Essex, which was, of course, incredibly concerning for everyone involved within the farming industry. The country shut down in ways that could not have been imagined. No stock could move around the country and tourists were forbidden to visit rural areas as the government fought to control the spread. In total 3.7 million animals would be slaughtered, and the industry was once again on its knees.

The death of Sir Donald Wilson of Oldfield Farm, Pulford, one of the original farmers to supply Pickering Dairies, was yet another sad piece of news in what was proving to be a truly awful year. The Pickering's and Wilson's families had been doing business together for fifty years and Sir Donald had been there with Den back when they were forging new partnerships and taking on the MMB. He was prickly with David, as David was always the one who had to chase the money, but he and John got on extremely well.

If the Chairman of the Northwest Food Alliance was less

than optimistic about the future of farming and food producers generally, perhaps we get a glimpse as to why, with the events of the year to date. Nevertheless, David's quote in his speech to the assembled group hinted at a lot more than just personal losses as he explained;

"Farming productivity is rising but at the cost to the environment and the image of the farmer and his products as a primary producer, we will need to think long and hard about our relationships with our buyers and the land going forward.

The public perception of farming has deteriorated (the public view is)

- *set aside — farmers being paid to grow weeds.*
- *feeding and cleansing the land by crop rotation and animal fertiliser has been replaced by pesticides and growth promoters.*
- *blame for disease-spreading habits that brought us salmonella, BSE and Foot and Mouth*

Farmers feel they operate in a hostile environment ...our position is precarious when wheat accounts for less than 1% of the cost of a loaf of bread"

The housewife wants cheapness, freshness and value.

Household expenditure on food is now only 10% of income and it was 30% in 1970, just 30 years ago.

The price of food should be less important than the security of what we eat — food is our first medicine. Imported foods may be cheaper — that is because they do not have to conform to costly health and animal welfare standards".

David was looking into a complicated future of supply chains, supermarkets and their extreme buying power, that included wider aspects, much more than just how much cereal or how many animals could be produced. He recognised in 2000 that the farmer had an important role to play in the future of not just the industry, but the planet and farmers were going to need to find a way to make it pay in the new trading world that was surely coming. The continued downward pressure on producer prices would inevitably result in problems and how right he was, with horse meat scandals, supply line traceability disasters and many, many farmers going to the wall.

In his own business they were experiencing real problems with pricing policy and maintaining their wafer-thin margins. There was definite demand for the new Casein protein product but it seemed no one knew how much to sell it for to make a profit or how strong their selling position was in the marketplace. Turnover for 2000 was back up to £147 million but the profit was just £2.1 million — it should have been higher, and something was wrong. To be making a gross profit of just 1.4% was perilous. Better of course than losing money but milk prices were recovering and they should have done better.

The margins at Bodfari were small, but they were doing better than Express Dairies, in whom David had a significant investment. Their share price had fallen from 80p to just 15p and his pet project S Daniels had fallen from an already lowly 25p to just 10p. It really was a wretched time. The opening of the new Business Link (they took over from CEWTEC) building in Ellesmere Port was some cause for celebration as David lunched with Prince Andrew, who in 2001, was without controversy at the time.

Chapter 61
Say It Like It Is

It seemed that in some way or another everyone that David cared about was leaving, as Belinda and Ed looked to explore India in a six-month escape and the Dean of Chester, The Right Reverend Stephen Smalley, with whom David had worked for so long and was as close an ally as he could have at the Cathedral, was to retire. Interestingly, in his leaving remarks he mentioned David by saying.

"This catalogue of one donor's generosity is impressive, if not yet complete".

The out-going Dean was not about to let David off the hook with his fundraising, even after he retired. The Dean also reflected on their first meeting in Abbey Square, where a tracksuited David had just returned, by bike, from Rome, after an audience at the Vatican, whilst raising money for the Cathedral. The Dean was impressed with David's,

"calm ability to record in an apparently tiny but ultimately expansive notebook the major events in the crowded canvas of his active life".

The Dean summed David up quite well.

Slipping under the radar was that David had been appointed a Director of Primary Capital back in 1999. They had been looking for someone with board experience who could advise them on investments in the food sector and, in that regard, David fit the bill perfectly. It was in May of this year that the Primary

Capital team held a top-level away day conference at the world-famous Cliveden Hotel. Famous, as it was the venue of choice for Ms Keeler and Ms Rice-Davies during the Profumo Scandal of the late '60s. An incredibly impressive building set in huge grounds overlooking the Thames and the wonderful Berkshire countryside near Maidenhead. In keeping with the history of the place David created his own scandal by telling the board some home truths. They really did not like it and he was duly sacked as a director. He never really had been one to just bite his tongue and just take the money; how much easier life might have been if he had!

Back in Chester, as Chairman of Eaton Golf Club things were not going well either. When the Duke of Westminster decided it was no longer safe to have a golf course on his estate, no matter how well-heeled the members were, he told the members that they needed to play their golf somewhere else now. The Duke found them another parcel of land they could use near Waverton, not far from Chester but far away from the duke's house and he told them they needed to build a new course. Now building new golf courses and clubhouses is expensive stuff and somebody had to fund it. The committee decided that all members should pay £1300 for a share in the business and then of course a further fee each year as their annual membership. The problem was that not enough people were happy to pay that amount of money for a new course on a notoriously wet piece of land. It would be years before it was a good course and even amid a golfing boom, numbers of new members were slow to come on board. This was a significant financial problem for the new Eaton Golf Course and real problems were not far away if something could not be done about recruiting more members.

They needed new members quickly and David suggested to

the committee that they should decrease the share price to £300 to get more members signed up. It was a close-run thing but Bill Jones stood up at the meeting and suggested that the sub-committee were well advised and the rest of the committee would do well to back them on this proposal. The motion narrowly passed, and the following week sixty new members signed on. The course was now financially secure again as the steady flow of new members kept coming. It was a seminal moment for what is now one of Chester's best courses.

David's next major move at Eaton was to appoint Kerry Jones to run the club on a day-to-day basis. She had overseen the Rhosneigr Sailing Club, perhaps not the traditional background of a golf club secretary but she was most definitely the right person for the job as she is still in charge in 2020. The course and its day-to-day operations have never been better. David did manage to find some time to play golf during his tenure as Chairman and in fact with Paul Thomas, he won the Seniors Greensome, which got his name on to the newly erected honour boards.

A highlight of the year was undoubtedly a dinner held in the name of Mick Easterby at the Mount Hotel in York in September where the Bodfari Stud members attended. Mick is a larger-than-life Yorkshire character in every way, who definitely refers to a spade by its true name. He is also a canny Racehorse trainer to boot who oversaw several Bodfari horses and was probably the Stud's most successful trainer at the time. David created an environment over dinner, of speeches, some roasting Mick, and some roasting others around the table. There was Pimm's served in huge brandy balloons, the most amazing beef all carved by Mick, at the table, while he entertained with racing stories throughout the night. It was a fitting tribute to Mick, as Bodfari

Komaite and Manzoni, both horses he trained, had won at Chester in the year. Bodfari Komaite had managed to win twice at the Roodee, whilst Manzoni had another win at Musselburgh and Redcar to add to his Chester victory, which kept the shareholders happy and eager to enjoy the company over dinner. The total winners for the year was seven, which equalled their success of 2000. With a few seconds and thirds keeping the prize money ticking over it wasn't a bad year for the stud.

Tilstone Lodge Stud had another outstanding result in the first weekend in November as Guys and Dolls, a horse they bred, by Efisio, out of their mare Dime Bag, scorched clear in a Group Three race in France, again showing the merit of Dime Bag and her progeny. It was the only high point in a month that will forever be remembered as the month that changed the world as the Twin Towers in New York succumbed to the most vicious terrorist attack ever seen. One of those seminal moments where we can all recall where we were when it happened, and we saw those stark images of planes crashing into these iconic buildings.

As David totted up his year he could only reflect on the personal loss. It seemed to hang over everything. Yes, investments were in a poor way with lower-than-expected prices, but he was still here and those investments could always recover. The events of 9/11 also made him realise that he was not as hard done by as he thought. Had he remained in Lloyds of London he could now be staring at life shattering losses as the insurance claims came in from the damage caused by Al Qaeda. If nothing else that was something for which to be grateful.

Chapter 62
Honouring Your Commitments

With all the problems of the previous year David had lost track of his own personal finances which were now showing at an all-time debt high. His personal overdraft was an eye-watering £3.6 million. His bank manager had continued to support him and of course David had signed over all the assets as security for the bank that were previously held for his positions at Lloyds. Despite the asset backing, the overdraft was a concerning figure for both him and his Bank. At a modest 8% per annum, you must make £288,000 just to pay the interest each year on an overdraft that size. Now that is a big figure to have to earn after tax in anyone's language and it clearly was not sustainable.

There was a brighter start to 2002, as on the 18th of the month Nick and Claire were able to celebrate the birth of their daughter, Kumara. Thankfully there were no complications, and everyone was delighted for them. With that worry out of the way the grandparents were able to go on their annual skiing trip to Les Gets and link up with Marielle and later in February to take a couples golfing holiday to Penina. This wonderful resort course on the Algarve is steeped in history and is a highlight of golf in Portugal.

At the annual board meeting for Bodfari, David announced that he was standing down as Chairman and that David Newton should be his successor. This was supported by the board as Newton had been groomed, since his first appointment as

Director, to take on the role. They also revealed figures for the 2001–02 trading period that had topped £176 million, an increase of 20% over the previous year's turnover. This was obviously a particularly good performance and the new protein production was obviously proving popular, but at what price? In effect they had bought the turnover, as losses on the year totalled £1.39 million. The sales team explained that they needed to get people on to the new product and it had to be financially viable for the big companies to take the risk. They were confident they could push prices up as people realised the quality and adaptability of this new product. It was a challenge for the new Chairman but one he was ready for and one he had dealt with at Hillsdown Holdings during his time in charge as their CEO. It was also time for change at Executive level. Simon Chantler had been sharing the CEO role with Norman Oldmeadow but, with the enlarged group requiring even more management, it was decided Simon should be sole CEO and Norman Deputy CEO. They would then strengthen Management below Norman as well. The group, which included Bodfari and Meadow Foods, would also now be known, simply, as Meadow Foods.

Further announcement was made of the purchase of Holme on Spalding Foods, in Yorkshire. This business manufactured Chocolate Crumb and sweetened Condensed Milk and was seen as a linear production acquisition that would not only make a profit but increase Meadow Foods' position in the marketplace, as a key supplier to the confectionary trade. The principle being that if you want to supply conglomerates and do so profitably, you need to grow big enough to be able to sit at the price negotiating table knowing that the loss of just one customer is not going to have a material effect on your business. On paper, this was a sound acquisition.

Good news in Chester came in the shape of an approval for the new radio licence covering the Chester area, for the consortium headed by Ron Smith, of which David was a director. This was quite a feather in the cap for the local group as new radio licences do not come up very often. The new station's working title was Chester FM, or as it is now known, Dee 106.3. David put some money in to the business and helped set it up, bringing in many of his contacts to help launch the station. Ironically, it was only a matter of a year later that he was, again, sacked from the board. The reason? For speaking his mind and being just a little too forthright — would he never learn? He was, however, able to sell his shares and at least get his money back, so no damage done financially. Dee 106.3 still exists to this day and its unlikely that there is a radio station that operates anywhere in the UK, that is run on as small a budget as this one. Only the dedication of the presenters and the determination of its CEO Chris Hurst keeps this station afloat. It is unlikely David's investment in the station would ever have yielded a substantial return, so he was not too unhappy about no longer being involved.

Another shot in the arm was the announcement that the Song School at the Cathedral was to get the go-ahead. David and his team had secured the final funding for the £1.5 million project and work would start during the year. It had been a long slog to raise the money but now it was done David could simply oversee the building works, something he had done on many and varied projects, and then he could gracefully retire from the scene, safe in the knowledge that another project had been completed on time and in budget. After the terrible problems of 2001, this year was starting better all round. It was also a nice time for the new Dean to be installed, the Right Reverend Dr Gordon McPhate. He was taking over from Dean Smalley and was inheriting a significantly better Cathedral than the one his predecessor had been handed.

Chapter 63
Taking Over and Takeovers

In the late spring Bodfari Creek won a bumper at Haydock. Bumpers are races for jumps horses who are starting out in their trade. They don't jump anything at this early stage of their career but they get experience of the racecourse whilst learning how to race. They are so named because these inexperienced horses can, quite literally, bump into each other on the track while they learn how to race. A win at this level normally means a decent racing future is assured as these races are hotly contested by the bright new crop of horses about to embark on a jumping career and Haydock is a Grade 1 track where the best horses come to find their feet. This was one of the few successes during the year and, in July, David announced that the Bodfari Stud would be wound down. The reasons were two-fold. The first being that the business this stud reflected in name was now called Meadow Foods and as such there was little publicity value to keeping the racing name going. The second and most important was that, despite the successes at Group level of Pawn Broker, there seemed to be little appetite from members to keep funding the operation.

Bodfari Stud had been in operation for six years, had sent out forty-five winners and provided lots of enjoyable times for its participants. They had experienced great race days out at tracks across the UK and of course many winners at Chester, with the Bodfari name being seen right across the UK. David had organised golf days, dinners with trainers and provided regular updates, via the Bodfari Times. Much of what David put in place for this racing group was the forerunner to the racing Syndicates of today on which the small trainers rely so heavily. He signed off by telling members he would find single horses from time to time and invite people to be part owners with him if they wanted further involvement in racing. One thing we know of the Pickering's is that this racing bug is a tough one to shake and he would no doubt return but for now it was over.

2002 was also the year that David celebrated his sixtieth birthday, as did the Queen, with her Jubilee. The previous two decades had just flown by and that was what prompted his decision to announce his retirement from the Chairmanship of Meadow Foods. He fancied slowing down a bit, the problem was he did not really know how!

His new PA, Alison Dutton, had started and whilst she would no longer have to prepare documents for Bodfari meetings or newsletters for the stud, there was still a mountain of projects to attend to daily and a diary that never appeared to have a gap in it.

This was also the year that David finally stopped losing money in S Daniels. A Hong Kong company offered 14p a share to buy them and the offer was accepted. It is ironic that David had been nursing losses on paper of £500,000 on these shares, which was of course terrible, but you never actually have a loss until you sell, and the irony is that as soon as you sell you get money back so this proved to be a timely cash injection and a significant capital gains loss to set against any gains in the current financial year. Sometimes that is the way you must look at losses or they just eat away at you. It had certainly been an expensive way to get a seat on the board of a listed company and the saying, be careful what you wish for, never so apt.

Trips during the year included a visit to meet Ed's family in Ireland. Ed and Belinda were back from India, so David and Sue took the opportunity, when it became apparent that more permanent arrangements were imminent in their daughter's life, to meet the respective in-laws. Ned and Una, Ed's parents, lived in Mallow, Munster, a beautiful part of southern Ireland. Everyone got on famously. The Pickerings added to their time away with a fabulous holiday to Belek in Turkey. With so many golf courses on this resort and such good value, it was an ideal place for a family holiday and both David and Sue loved it. A victory on the green baize, with Snooker partner and good friend Ken Probert, meant there was some added bragging rights in the City Club as well to round out the year.

So, by the end of 2002 there was a mild recovery in every way. David had celebrated his sixtieth year by winding down some of his commitments. His work at the Cathedral was all but done and Hope Church was now in a good place. Bodfari Stud would cease to be a drain on his resources, and he had sold most of the horses during the liquidation of the syndicate. His family was recovering from some terrible personal losses and he had managed to reduce his overdraft from £3.6 million to £2.2 million with the final sale proceeds from S Daniels. The overdraft was still a hefty commitment but at least it was going the right way.

After holidaying in the new year at Les Gets and an escape to the delightful island of Madeira with Sue to play golf, David was enjoying the lightening of his workload. No pigs to worry about any more. The reins of Meadow Foods were in the safe hands of David Newton and Simon Chantler and almost all the fundraising projects at the Cathedral and his own Church, Hope, at an end. He accepted the position as Sexton at Hope Church. This combined his job as Warden with the duties normally associated with the Verger, a sort of PA to the Reverend in charge and something he thought would not be terribly demanding. In fact, he was delighted to report to the Parish that his planting of Lavender in the Church grounds was really growing rather well. That is the sort of pressure most people can deal with and gives a good level of satisfaction.

Just as it appeared things were quietening down, John Ross, the Chairman of the World Famous, Chester Mystery Plays, died and it was Jo Sykes, the Managing Director of the Plays, who accepted David's offer of help. She put it to the board for David to step in as interim Chair. The group were awfully close to delivering one of their five yearly set of plays and they needed help. Jo knowing that she could not possibly handle all the other logistical aspects, as well as producing the play, was keen to get David on board.

The mystery plays date back to 1568 and, after being banned by the Church of England for their praise of the Pope at the time of the reformation, they were restarted back in 1951 in Chester, to help celebrate the Festival of Britain and have been staged every five years since. The dates altered slightly over the years, but July of 2003 was to be this year's date and production was in full swing. It was a steep learning curve for David, who quickly brought in assistance on the financial side, with friend and RBS Bank Manager, Peter Overmeer. As Neil Large from the Health Authority said earlier, David had developed a deft skill for involving others in his various projects (perhaps a skill he learnt from his meeting with the Duke of Edinburgh) and Peter was a willing servant for the Mystery Plays. The confirmation of a royal visit from their Royal Highnesses the Earl and Countess of Wessex only added to the pressure.

Whilst David and Peter took control of finances and

sponsorship and with the news of the Royal visit, a bit of arm twisting by David convinced The Lord Bishop of Chester, the Right Reverend Peter Forster, to agree to stage a garden party, with the Royals as guests of honour. Tickets to attend went on sale and went quickly, which then of course bolstered much needed funds for the Plays. The 2003 plays were deemed a total success, both in content with very strong reviews and financially, as they made a small profit. It turned out to be simply perfect all round. At the conclusion of the 2003 plays, after an evaluation process had taken place, David agreed to stand down as Chairman and allow Jo to take back control for the 2008 round of plays. It was the wish of previous Chair John Ross that Jo succeed him and now David was able to make that happen. He had stepped in to help and was equally happy to step back out again. Sue Pickering, however, had enjoyed the experience so much that she agreed to stay on to help with production for 2008 and to take a part in the plays, which meant there was a lovely continuity of involvement and the Pickerings have remained a friend of the Mystery Plays to this date.

Chapter 64
Turning Down an Offer

On the board at Chester Race Company things were moving nicely. CEO Richard Thomas had suggested a couple of years earlier that Chester Race Co should utilise their car park a little better and create a hotel. They would easily fill it on race days and with other key events staged at the course and the city needing more affordable hotel accommodation the investment seemed right. The board agreed and the building went ahead. The Hotel opened to universal approval. It was a sign of both the CEO's and the Board's ambition to grow shareholder value in the Company. The shares are like gold dust to get hold of, most only being handed down from generation to generation. They now trade hands at not far off £100,000 a share, if any become available. The Pickering Family had owned their shares for quite some time and during the reign of Richard Thomas and the period that David was on the board, Chaired by Bobby McAlpine, they had seen value go from around £20,000 to a figure five times that value. It was shaping as a most profitable period for Chester Race Company and its shareholders.

At Conservative Party, Chester HQ, the members elected Paul Offer as their Prospective Parliamentary Candidate (PPC). Paul was from the Midlands and was a successful Business Consultant with a likeable manner. David Pickering's job was to integrate Paul into Chester Society and see if they could make both the party and Paul electable in the year 2005, when the next

General Election was due. After the shambles of the 1997 election, followed by the loss of the 2001 election by PPC David Jones, there was much ground to make up.

David Jones, the 2001 loser, had gone to Chester Law College, so at least he had some link to Chester but being a Welsh Speaker and born in London he really was not the ideal connection. Again, one wonders if anyone in London knew anything about the Chester seat and if someone in London had seen the proximity of Chester to Wales and assumed Mr Jones, would be ideal because of his Welsh connection. How wrong they were. On the plus side at least this time Conservative HQ found someone with a vague connection to the city. Mr Jones did manage to reduce Christine Russell's majority a little, but he would eventually find his seat for the Conservatives in 2005 representing Clwydd. Unsurprisingly he was a perfect fit as a candidate for that seat!

That meant it was Paul Offer who was next in the firing line to try and regain this former Conservative stronghold and, as nice a man as he appeared to be, they had still failed to appoint a Chester person to win a Chester seat as Paul was based in the Midlands. Would Paul Offer fare any better than the previous two incumbents? David was determined to give him the best start and went about introducing him to the great and good of Chester and working hard to ensure people in Chester knew who he was. Something that had painfully failed with David Jones, given that the average person in the street had no idea who he was or what he stood for. It was not long before most people in Chester knew who Paul Offer was!

Just as David was able to hand over control of the Mystery Plays, so too, his tenure of Eaton Golf Club was ending. A chairman's reign is three years at Eaton, and he had served his time. The Golf Club was now in great shape both financially and physically. He had overseen the major drainage work that had been necessary to alleviate the flooding areas and it had well and truly proved effective. Eaton Golf Club was now a thriving successful and very enjoyable place to play golf. It would only get better with time, as golf courses normally are considered mature after twenty years. As David left his position of authority at Eaton, Sue took up the mantle at the course, where she was also now a playing member. She agreed to be the English Golf Union appointed Competition Secretary for the club.

David Newton delivered his first trading report mid-way through the year and he revealed that turnover had gone down in Meadow Foods, from £176 million to £161 million, but even more disappointingly they still had not solved the margins issue and they reported a loss of almost a million pounds, making it £2.42 million loss in two years and no dividend payment. No one was panicking yet and in percentage terms the loss was significantly less this year, but they had to continue increasing margins on their sales for this business to work properly and to recoup the nearly £5 million of capital investment in the Casein Protein Plant. Meadow Foods was the UK's first Reverse Osmosis (RO) operation, where they held a distinct first adopter advantage and whilst that was significant, if all the work of the last two years was to be worthwhile then they needed to start generating profit. That was the task for 2003/4.

On the family front things were developing nicely. Ed and Belinda were Married at Soughton Hall, a wonderful place in Flintshire, set in its own grounds, halfway between Rough Hill Farm and Mold. David was able to treat Ed's parents to a special day racing at Chester while they were visiting, which also happened to coincide with the first year of the other special Irish relationship at Chester Racecourse, that being the World's Number one trainer, Aiden O'Brien, bringing over his Derby and Oaks hopefuls for the very first time. The all-powerful Coolmore boys were in town and they would have outstanding success over the coming years bringing their superstars to Chester to learn their trade around the tight, twisting track of the Roodee. O'Brien's theory was, that if the horses were balanced well enough to handle Chester, they would handle the undulating slopes of Epsom and so it proved with Derby and Oaks winners coming out of their respective trials at Chester. In 2003 it was the Sir Michael Stoute trained Kris Kin who won the Dee Stakes and went on to win the Derby; latterly O'Brien winners at Chester who have scored in the big one at Epsom include Wings of Eagles and Ruler of the World. The fillies have also flourished with the Cheshire Oaks prep race, including the world's number one mare Enable, trained by John Gosden, and owned by Prince Abdullah, who won in 2017 before winning the Oaks at Epsom and the Prix De l Arc De Triomphe in Paris. Over the years Chester racegoers have seen the absolute best line-up at this amazing course and that year Ed's parents saw the Derby winner at Chester.

Whilst Nick and Claire were happy to be able to move to Denmark Cottage in Oswestry, emotions were mixed with Marc and Angela. They had another child, Mia, born in August which should have been cause for great celebration, but Marc was diagnosed with the debilitating disease ME, similar to the symptoms that John's wife, Jo, had endured years earlier. Marc would learn to live with it and work out how to keep it under control, but it was a struggle for the two of them, with demands from work and young children, sapping vital energy. David's son Stuart had also achieved planning permission to build a house on Grange Farm. Using the outbuildings left after the pig business was closed made good sense. It seemed good use of the land and it was nice for Sue and David to have him living nearby. He also had plenty of storage space for the machinery and tools for his Groundworks business, which was doing well.

Chapter 65
All Change, For the Better?

At the Cathedral, work on the Song School was well underway, which was keeping David busy; his aim was to be open in spring 2004. He had also got involved, as Chairman, in the City Club Investment Fund, which was called Centaur. Here a group of City Club members would propose a share, discuss its relative merits and then the group would invest and see how they did. It was meant to be a bit of fun and interest for those who had time on their hands. It was also keenly contested as each member put forward their own ideas and why they should invest in that specific listed company and then of course the waiting time whilst they see which share does well and which does poorly in the coming months and years ahead.

As the year came to a close, the final piece of good news was that the sale of the Dene Hotel had gone through, which again looked on paper to have made a profit of about £120,000 but with losses across the years was probably more break-even, if you were smart with a pencil! This too would help to lower the overdraft which by the end of 2003 now stood at just £1.4 million. When you consider it had topped out at £3.6 million, this was a huge reduction in three years. As good as this was the interest, annually, on £1.4 million was still £112,000, or over £2,000 per week!

In 2004 the decision was made not to continue the skiing holidays after Sue had damaged a knee on one of those wretched button lifts the previous year, but a golfing trip to Majorca with the Proberts was the early season trip away. The Proberts had a particularly nice Villa at Puerta Andratx. David and Sue would follow that later in the year with another visit to the Hotel Xanadu at Belek in Turkey. This was proving to be irresistible with its fabulous facilities, that included fifteen different golf courses, two floodlit tennis courts, and reliable warm weather.

A re-assessment of his banking facilities saw the need for a new valuation on assets. Most were now in strong recovery. David was pleased that Northern Foods were now back to £1.70 and his own house Grange Farm was valued at £750,000. More good news followed with Meadow Foods reporting 2003/04 figures up at a record £215 million and pleasingly profit had returned at £1.56 million. Still thin margins but going in the right direction. The only negative was that David Newton was retiring from the business.

The appointment of the new Meadow Foods Chairman, Paul Deakin, followed shortly after. Paul's CV was an excellent one and in a lot of ways mirrored David's past. He started as a Chartered Accountant at Price Waterhouse, went into Investment banking with Rothschilds and then worked with Bank of Scotland on the United Milk project at Wiltshire. His pedigree was indeed a good one and he was inheriting a company that was again trading profitably and with growing revenues. It seemed the excitement was back again at Meadow Foods.

Having relinquished his Chairmanship at the Cathedral with the completion of the Song School, David could afford a mini golfing break. This time the trip to Nefyn wasn't financially as successful as previously in that David didn't win the big purse on offer, but neither did he get the terrible telephone calls about plummeting share prices, which made for a far more relaxing time. With an overnight stay at the Holyhead Golf Course on the way back the three-day golfing trip was great fun.

On his return to the office the invitation to head up and Chair the Regional Skills Council, an organisation put together by the North West Development Agency and Steve Broomhead, was one he could not turn down. It was an opportunity to work with Canon Fran Hulbert again, who described the creation of the new entity and David's role.

"From 2004 the NWDA held the lead role for all nine Agencies with three Government Departments. This began with the piloting of a bold and simplified model of business support and skills, expressed in the form of a regional skills strategy, overseen by a Framework for Regional Employment and Skills Action, which matured into a single business led Regional Skills Partnership. Throughout the development process David played a central role, becoming Chair of the RSP in 2000.

David exercised his personal skill and business influence and provided highly respected leadership both at regional and national level, leading his counterpart chairmen in ministerial meetings, and playing a key part in the Northern Way developments. He drew on his direct personal experience of creating a highly successful company, activating private sector support and influencing public sector provision, always underpinned by a quiet commitment to skills and employment. With his style of unassuming humour and incisive questioning, he always demonstrated a rare blend of private sector acumen and clarity alongside sustained and patient support for the complex and unwieldy public sector skills agencies. Within the more local Chester community he is highly regarded for his ability to draw together the interests of business and commercial networks with the academic and civic communities to the benefit of the city and the regional economy — "the quiet ambassador".

The improvement of work/life skills was something David had nurtured from the early days at CEWTEC, through Business Link, and now the newly funded organisation was just what was needed to bridge the gap between employee skills and employer requirements. With just the one new role in 2004 and no extra burdens, it meant that this was an enjoyable year. The management team of Simon Chantler and Paul Deakin were doing sterling work at Meadow Foods and in David's world there was a relative calm. At now, sixty-two years of age one could imagine this was how life was meant to be. But could it last?

Chapter 66
A Quiet Reflection

As 2005 got underway David felt his personal finances were in reasonably good shape, and with all the work he had undertaken in the last ten years, it was time to both reflect on what he had achieved, what he had failed at and then to spend some quality time with Sue and enjoy some of the fruits of the labours.

The summary table he compiled included all the many Chairs he had held and the businesses, charities, and quangos he had influenced. There was of course the terrific success of Pickering's Dairies, Bodfari and Meadow Foods, without which life could have been so different. The turmoil of Lloyds, the Pigs and the numerous loss-making businesses weighed heavily on his mind and he did not dare add up just how much money he had actually lost through these failed ventures in the previous decade. He concluded that his risk management between 1991 and 2000 was haphazard and careless and that it should not happen again. It was chaotic and driven by both ego and greed. He wasn't happy admitting to these failings, but they needed addressing. There had been quite a bit of luck involved in getting out of trouble and David had longed subscribed to the saying, "that the luck you have, is the luck you make" but as he said earlier, one should not need to get in to trouble just to prove how good you are at getting out of it. He simply must do better and his personal notes, whilst admitting all the failures also related that he had made a lot of money to be able to lose it, as well.

Admonishments done and new aims written, he was at least proud of the charity fundraising he had done and the committee work that had helped the Cathedral, Hope Church and Eaton Golf Club and he felt John and he had really made something special out of Rough Hill Farm. No doubt his father would have been pleased. He would have also been delighted that his son had bred a Cheltenham Festival winner. In March, the horse, Inglis Drever, part of the Tilstone Lodge operation that he and Bobby McAlpine ran, won the World Hurdle, and signalled his arrival as the pre-eminent staying hurdler of his generation. He would win again in 2007 and 2008 and in total record earnings of over £796,000. Traditionally the breeders received 5% but records do not show how the nearly £40,000 was divided up between the two partners although David recalls Bobby McAlpine did send him a case of Champagne!

In the build-up to the 2005 General Election David decided that the Conservative Party needed a boost before the hard work of door knocking. Something to rally the troops and it was decided that a cocktail party at Chester's number one restaurant, Paparazzi, would be the ideal start to the campaign that would hopefully see Paul Offer elected as Chester's MP. David had managed to convince party darling Boris Johnson to be the guest of honour and whilst most only knew him from his appearances as the bumbling guest on *Have I Got News for You* it was obvious that greater things were expected of him. The event went well, Boris was charming, he sold and signed lots of books and had the crowd eating out of his hand with just a few, well-rehearsed, one-liners. Paul and David worked the crowd, the Chester Conservative Party were very bubbly, and they all genuinely thought that they would retake the Chester seat from Labour at the upcoming election.

Regretfully, for Paul Offer, he did not quite make it, losing by less than 1000 votes. A tremendous performance, pulling back a 7000 majority in such a short space of time. You would imagine that the local Conservative Party would be overjoyed. Not so, what happened next was something rarely spoken of but it would be hard to be proud of the party and their behaviour during this time. As Chairman it was David who had to adjudicate, in what was a terrible set of circumstances, dominated by nastiness and ambition. Not on David's part. He has always described himself as Kingmaker and not King; in this case he was forced to be King Slayer.

Shortly after the 2005 election Paul Offer was reported to senior officers, by party members, for having had his car parked overnight, outside a lady Conservative councillor's house. The inference was that the two were involved in an extra marital affair and that this constituted conduct unbecoming of a PPC for Chester. Of course, the story was "leaked" to the press and despite the fact it carried little weight in terms of established fact it made great headlines with the Labour dominated press and it required the local party to act.

Paul refuted the charge, but David suggested that, as he had not moved to the city from the Midlands and there were those questioning his commitment, he should take his counsel and that it might be best if he resigned his position and returned to his own family home. To Paul's credit — he did. Paul Offer was left with little alternative because those clawing their way to the top of the party had big plans and they seemed hell-bent on creating a "ruckus" over this story and removing him. It was obvious to most that at the next election the Conservatives would be victorious in Chester and those in committee had their candidate ready for the coup they had created. With another four years until the next election the party were in no hurry to appoint their "chosen one" but getting rid of Paul Offer was the number one objective and they had achieved their goal.

With the election over and the problems in the short term dealt with, now was a time for doing something special for David and Sue and first on the list was a visit to South Africa. They flew firstly to Cape Town and enjoyed the wonderful city that sits at the foot of Table Mountain and overlooks the two great seas of the world as they join. They saw whales at Hermanus and drove along the beautiful garden route, through to George, before heading inland to the Sabi Sabi Game Reserve in the South western section of the Grand Kruger National Park. These luxury lodges are a wonderful way to experience a truly remarkable view of nature, taking in the quiet, spectacular sunsets. It was an ideal place to relax and feel incredibly special, experiencing the sights and sounds of the animals of Africa. There is a deafening silence created by the noise of the animals when you sleep under the star filled sky in Africa, broken only by the roar and smell of a Lion, as it tends to its kill. It is a unique experience where the excitement you feel and hear makes sleep almost impossible on your first night.

News at Meadow Foods continued to make things even better as turnover for the year was reported at £208 million, slightly down from the previous year but profit was £1.42 million, and everyone was happy. The new investments were paying off and the new Management team working well.

About the only disaster during the year was on a personal note and that was the booking of a golfing holiday for the group of couples who regularly went away, this time to Hammamet, in Tunisia. It was a cheap deal and perhaps that should have been the warning because no one enjoyed the accommodation, the food, or the golf course. However, you must kiss a few toads from time to time and this one had a line put through it very quickly: a definite toad. Golf trips back in the UK to Hawkstone Park, the marvellous Royal St David's at Harlech, one of the great British Links courses and a must visit for any keen golfer, as well as another trip back to Nefyn made up for the disappointment of Tunisia in a year that got a diary note that said — enjoyable. A good way to finish 2005.

Chapter 67
Never Too Old to Learn

After a mid-winter break in early 2006 to the Hotel Abama on the Island of Tenerife and a bit of golf for Sue and David it was time again to take stock of his current positions. Financially things had improved immeasurably. David was pleased not to be under the extreme pressures of the previous years. His financial liability to the businesses he had formerly owned was considerably less and that was also helping to relieve the pressure but he still had a host of other commitments and now at sixty-four years of age he was looking for an easier life.

David's directorships included Chester Race Company, which was one he enjoyed, so keeping that was top priority. He was inspired by the work ethic, vision and determination of the CEO Richard Thomas and was certain things would continue to grow at the Roodee. He wanted to be around to see that growth. He was Director of the Chester and County Unionist Building, which was the Headquarters of the Conservative Party in Chester and he really wanted to move things on with some development of the building but this was a stubborn group, frightened of change and change was proving difficult to bring about. His other directorship was with Total People, a company set up to provide "proper jobs" for people who had re-trained and this was a cause he believed in and sat well with his Chair roles, one of which was as the Chair of the North West Regional Skills Partnership. This was the body created by the North West Development Agency, headed up by Steve Broomhead and the two worked actively trying to deliver a more skilled workforce in the North West.

Sitting side by side with the Skills Partnership was his Chairmanship of Business Link, who were another important cog in this quest to get the country up skilled. There cannot have been many people in the UK who were committing more hours to the very urgent need to upskill the workforce of UK PLC.

David was also coerced by the Vice Chancellor of the University of Chester, Tim Wheeler, to sit on the University Council, a task he was happy to take on. The two had met back in 1998 at one of Dean Stephen Smalley's business breakfasts and had got on extremely well; they would become lifelong friends. Tim had shown a real appetite to move the University on, from what was once a small college, to become a major force as a University in the North West. David was impressed with Tim's ambition and his appetite to succeed. He could see Tim's vision and he was keen to help, so he agreed to join the University Council, where he would, initially, take up the role as Chair of the Audit and Risk committee. Now there is a task that if Mr Wheeler had read this book prior to the appointment, he might have thought twice about, given David's aggressive attitude to risk and his aversion to auditing. Of course, on the face of it he seemed ideal and he was always far more prudent with other's assets than his own.

The two made a good partnership and were together during the expansion explosion of the University from 2,500 students to over 16,000, in a decade. The University assets increased over ten-fold and their annual income, approaching £200 million. An amazing Chester success story. It was over dinner, as talk turned to horses and breeding that Tim was keen to point out that his own wife Marilyn was indeed from good stock. We are not sure

Marilyn enjoyed the parallel argument that her husband was making, which of course brought a silence to the table from everyone. The table bid him continue and he duly explained that Marilyn's Great-Grandmother had been in service to the Marquess of Anglesey and that during her time working for the Marquess she had fallen pregnant. Whether out of duty or kindness, his ilk not normally known for the latter, the Marquess granted Marilyn's Great-Grandmother a pension and a house in which to live. Under today's laws, with deaths in the family, it is possible, over time, Marilyn's grandparents could have claimed the title. Not many assets slipped through the Wheeler fingers over the years. They would, however, win many more battles and in honour of the story David would name one of his horses after Marilyn, so something positive came from Tim's story at least.

Another of David's Chairmanships, a little closer to his normal skill set, was as Chair of the North West Food Alliance. This was an organisation that was funded by DEFRA and whose task it was to get the Agricultural sector back on its feet after the devastation caused by Foot-and-Mouth. The aim was to try and create a stronger "farm to fork" alliance, regionalise food and drink and create a greater awareness of the farmer and his/her role in supplying primary produce to the UK food chain. His CEO was a lady by the name of Pat Foreman. They did not always see eye to eye, but their shared goals meant they went about trying to deliver good value for the DEFRA pound. They worked closely with the various tourism bodies across the North West and they reported back to both DEFRA and the NWDA, who were becoming a strong presence in local politics in every sub region.

As he looked to lighten the load of work, one of the Chairs that David resigned from was that of the Chester Conservative

Party. The ugly wranglings during the time of Paul Offer had taken their toll and loyalties within the party were split. However, the local party were not keen to see David leave, and he was appointed President in the hope he could keep the fractured friendships intact. This was more a figurehead than an admin role and one he was comfortable with. One of the many skills you acquire over time is that of statesmanship and David moved comfortably between groups offering advice and conciliatory messages and broking deals. He had spent too long fighting for the party to just leave, so the position suited him and the party. He would get to act as a referee in any disputes and attend on the party's behalf any events that required representation. It seemed an appropriate compromise.

David then took up a similar role at the Chester Business Club. It was now a thriving and important part of Chester life and under the steady hand of Bob Clough Parker, with whom he helped set up the club in 1987, they were in a good place. Bob described his many years of working with David, firstly as PR Consultant and latterly with the Business Club.

"David could appear Aloof and distant to some" but he believed it was his underlying shyness that gave that appearance, he went on to say, "*beneath it all beats the heart of a generous, loyal and worthy man".* Fine words and certainly befitting of their time together.

In late January brother John had what David described as his "indulgence party". John had, through his wife Jo, inherited a run down, former Manor House, on the Dulas Estate in Anglesey. This three story "mansion" was being used by the local poultry as a fabulous roosting area and was as ramshackle as could be imagined when John took it on as a project. After a difficult time dealing with planners and a particularly expensive three years, it had been restored to its former glory and John proudly showed it off to many of his shooting pals and family. John felt he owed it to his father-in-law to set the house right and he had done a wonderful job of restoration. It was most certainly his "indulgence" and one of which he was enormously proud.

As the AGM board meeting for Meadow Foods approached David flagged up his intention to come out of both, being a director and a shareholder. He advised the board in advance and whilst they accepted his resignation as director, there were no takers for the nearly 20% of shares he controlled on behalf of both himself and various family members. It was a strange board meeting all round. They reported turnover of over £200 million which was strong, but they had lost £1.62 million in the year. The loss was not surprising to David.

The company, on Norman Oldmeadow's recommendation, had agreed to buy Quantock Cheese in 2005. It was an interesting business. The principle was sound. They bought short-dated cheese stocks and distressed label cheeses, repackaged and then resold to market traders. The margin was often good, if you had good stock control and a good relationship with your customers, to move stock quickly. It became apparent they had neither and in the space of just one year Quantock had lost £1 million. This was unsustainable. After the realisation of the deficit, it was unanimously decided to cut their losses and "bin" the business. It had been an expensive mistake. David reiterated that he wanted to sell and preferably by the 28th of May 2007, when he would be sixty-five. It seemed an appropriate time to get out completely.

After a trip with the Proberts to their villa on Mallorca, David returned to find he had been nominated to become a Deputy Lieutenant for the Shrievalty of Cheshire. The DL, as it is known, is an assistant to the Lord Lieutenant, currently David

Briggs. The Lord Lieutenant is the Queen's representative in the county and in former times it was his responsibility, with the help of his DL,' to raise the militia on behalf of the Crown; thankfully these days we have little need to raise a militia, so he now uses his DL to do the Queen's work across the county. It is more of an honour than a chore and it was recognition of the sterling work David had done on the many committees and charities that he had represented.

July saw the Open Golf Championship, staged at Royal Liverpool, Hoylake, and David with others from Eaton Golf Club, were in attendance over the four days. It was wonderful weather and they saw, arguably, the best golfer the world has ever seen weave his magic around the links of Hoylake. Tiger Woods dominated the tournament, a colossus striding the fairways, just as he had since the turn of the century and anyone who witnessed him up close knew they had seen greatness.

Closer to home David was showing off his own skills on the course yet another hole-in-one came his way on the seventeenth at Eaton and this time he was in the company of lifelong friend, Edward Walton, who graciously agreed, given it was also his birthday, to buy everyone in the clubhouse a drink to celebrate, even though this is normally the responsibility of the player who achieved this rare feat. David dodged another bullet!

He was in rare form that summer as success came his way in the Mixed Invitation at Delamere Golf Club, where he partnered Fay Dilliway-Parry. They combined well to lift the trophy with a stunning fifty-one stableford points, pipping a couple who had got in much earlier in the day and had already planned their acceptance speech, with what looked like and would have been on almost any other day, a winning score of fifty points.

Chapter 68
Festivals and Fun

In 2006 David was invited to attend, on behalf of Chester Racecourse, a meeting conducted by the Chester City Council. Mike Dix, who oversaw the culture portfolio, was keen to get a joined-up agenda across the city to ensure there was sufficient funding for the burgeoning number of Festivals that were now taking place in and around Chester. As one of the major players and venues for events and festivals the council were hopeful of having representation from Chester Race Company. I was also invited to attend as I was responsible for the largest event to be staged, outside of racing in Chester, the Taste Cheshire Food and Drink festival, held annually at Chester Racecourse. It was here that I started on a journey with David that would touch many different facets of corporate Chester and teach me the workings of politics and people.

As the owner of various restaurants in Chester from the mid-1990s until 2010, I was aware of David Pickering because he was simply everywhere in the fabric of Chester. Our paths had already crossed indirectly in business as I had applied for a Food and Drink Grant to help stage the North West Food Lovers Festival at Tatton Park and the North West Food Alliance assisted with some funding. The application passed before David's committee on the way to approval. As the owner of a couple of Chester's best restaurants and bars, it was impossible not to know who David was. He was a director of Chester Race Company, a member of the Chester City Club, member of Eaton Golf course and that was when Eaton golf course was on the Duke's estate, the Chairman and latterly, President of The Chester Conservative Party and committee member of many other Chester Institutions, I am sure. In fact, in just about every way it was possible, David Pickering was somehow involved in the city of Chester. His friends owned jewellers and estate agencies, they were senior partners of Accountancy and legal firms, they ran banks and building societies. They met on the golf course, or at the Chester City Club to play snooker and billiards, in the members stand at Chester Races and in the best restaurants and pubs of Chester and Cheshire. As the UK and Chester blossomed, from the '80s onwards so too did this generation of Chester citizen. They were Maggie Thatcher's workers, and they were finally being handsomely rewarded for their work. The stock market just kept going up and with it their pensions, investments, and salaries. They owned British Telecom, British Gas and any other British share issue that was going, they made money and they liked it. This was the generation who shaped Chester into what it is today and now I was getting to work up close with one of the lead actors.

My first meetings with David were on the golf course, at Morfa Nefyn in the Millionaires and "Arseholes" tournament, referred to earlier. In fact, we were partnered on one occasion. We did not win but we were placed. Suffice to say David was in the Millionaires team — I was not! After that event David then came to me, as the owner of Paparazzi Restaurant and asked if I would help the newly appointed Conservative Prospective Parliamentary Candidate (PPC) Paul Offer, get to know people in and around Chester and perhaps help with some of the marketing, for a man who was a new face to the city. Chester can be notoriously "cliquey" and getting off on the wrong foot has finished the career of many a person.

David knew that I had a strong following at my restaurants and that I had staged the Chester Food and Drink Festival at Chester Racecourse on numerous occasions and done a lot of different projects. I had a good understanding of the local media, more than a little success marketing and he was right to ask. My network, whilst not as powerful as his own, was significant in number and meant it was easy for me to get Paul amongst those who regularly ate and drank in my places. These people were opinion shapers in and around the city. I was happy to oblige. I made the restaurant available to Paul for meetings and lunches and picked up the tab to help.

I liked Paul Offer and I liked his ambition, however, his story of Chester has already been replayed in this book and so back to our initial "festival" meeting in the Holiday Inn Express at Chester Racecourse. The intention of this meeting was to create a body, called Chester Festivals. A body that would bring all the festival and event agenda, for the newly formed county, under one umbrella. This would mean that all events that wanted local government assistance would pass through Chester Festivals to ensure that there was one major calendar and that major events did not compete with one another. The bonus was that the public money would be allocated by an independent board and would favour festivals with ambition, economic impact potential and those that attempted to raise the bar in terms of quality and provision. These were solid aims; it was a competent proposal.

The council at that time were funding a Music Festival, A Literature festival, and numerous other small events. They were handing over small amounts of money to all sorts of strange happenings, without a clear understanding of what their strategy was or some accountability for the public spend. Event organisers would approach councillors and pressure would be applied to officers to allocate budget to whatever whim was currently popular. It was not efficient, and this proposal was a significantly better way to function.

Once the assembled group understood the Council remit, the figures involved and the structure, the intention was for a newly formed Chester Festivals to take control and deliver on a Service level Agreement, the aims and ambitions of the stakeholders and council. It was David who was elected to Chair that process and I was elected interim Chief Executive.

Out of those initial meeting did not just come Chester Festivals but Andrew Bentley (now the General Manager of Storyhouse) arrived from Liverpool and David charged him with working out how we could bring a Theatre back to Chester and what it might look like. Andrew took control of the "arts agenda" born out of this renaissance and went on to deliver the Theatre in the Park and worked with the Council to deliver Storyhouse. Storyhouse is a wonderful, if not well overdue, success. All the planning for it came out of this original committee chaired by David and by working with Mike Dix at Cheshire West and Chester Council (CWAC) and council leader Mike Jones, who gave full backing and support to this entity. It was a very productive era that started in late 2006 and David was again at the helm. Despite his ambition to unburden himself from other roles during 2005–6 David now had yet another Chairmanship, although he did explain to the board that this was, in his eyes, an interim position and that as soon as a suitable replacement was found he would step down.

As 2007 got underway David attended a Farmer's conference in Oxford. This was part of a group who had been meeting for many years and every time David attended one of these events, he felt he had increased his knowledge around the sector. It was, in his eyes, important if you were in a position of influence, to be up to date with what stakeholders were saying and experiencing and this was the ideal format to get up to date with agriculture and its many problems.

It was also the year that good friend Neil Large was appointed Captain of Eaton Golf Club, which would mean a lot of golfing days away for David with the Captain and even more so with his wife Sue, who was appointed Lady Captain, at Eaton. A proud moment for one who took up the game later in life.

At the end of year reporting board meeting for Meadow Foods, David made his retirement as a director official. He had advised them earlier of his intention and he was also keen to know if anyone had taken up his offer to buy his shares. The company reported turnover, again above £200 million and they had righted the ship from the losses of the previous year with a break-even performance. Not brilliant but decent and a good indication that next year would be back to strong profits. Perhaps no one purchasing David's shares was a good thing.

Chapter 69
A Monk's Pilgrimage

On the 28th of May 2007 David turned Sixty-five and with it came two further resignations. He handed over the reins of the North West Food Alliance. His conversations at the Farming conference convinced him that the recovery work of the Alliance was now complete. He also ceded the Chairmanship at Business Link. This entity was less important now the Skills Partnership had taken over and he could see that without further funding it would be difficult for Business Link to continue in its role.

David and Sue then took a little time out to enjoy a trip sightseeing in Barcelona visiting the awe-inspiring Gaudi Cathedral, La Sagrada Familia and taking in the Las Ramblas before David set off on yet another bizarre challenge.

It was connected to the Cathedral and involved Fundraising, hardly a new combination for David. This time it involved the celebration of The St Werburgh Festival, something hitherto that had passed each year without notice. As Interim CEO of Chester Festivals I had agreed to help make this small festival a more important event in the Chester calendar and David decided to bring about a significant focus by re-creating the St Werburgh Pilgrimage.

St Werburgh is the Patron saint of Chester. She was the daughter of Wulfere, King of Mercia, born in 650 AD and was revered for rejecting the advances of a Viking Warrior called Werebode by running away from him and becoming a nun.

During her life she created, as the Abbess of Ely, nunneries at Trentham, Repton, Weedon and Hanbury. After her death she was very quickly beatified.

To become a Saint, you first must be dead; this happened in 669 AD, in Trentham, so that is the first tick. Then you must have achieved a minimum of three miracles. It was not long after her death that the stories of her miracles began to circulate. The most famous and the one for which she is regularly pictured is her healing of "the goose". Quite a thing in the Dark Ages apparently, goose healing that is. Subsequent miracles were then verified as people made pilgrimages to her resting place in Hanbury in the hope of assistance, which, legend has it, regularly occurred. In 875, the Danes invaded Britain and the people of Hanbury feared that those who worshipped the Norse Gods would vandalise St Werburgh's remains, something the Vikings were in the habit of doing, so they relocated the remains to Chester in 907 by trekking across country from Stoke to Chester, with her remains. St Werburgh then carried on her good work from her resting place in Chester.

One such miracle, quite spectacular, if legend can be believed, involved King Gruffyd of Wales. Known as the last King of Wales, he besieged Chester. St Werbergh's shrine was lifted to the battlements and as the King looked upon it, he was struck blind, whereupon the siege was abandoned as the army fled in fear — you don't mess with divine intervention. St Werbugh had saved the day, again.

History lesson over, we return to David, who put together another small group from his walking pals, who were going to re-enact the pilgrimage by walking, dressed as monks, from Hanbury to Chester and arrive on the final day of the St Werburgh festival, a fitting tribute. It was a festival that had already included a two a.m. performance in the Cathedral grounds over two nights of Shakespeare's, *A Midsummers Night*, put on by Chester Festivals, made all the more stunning for those who attended as the sun began to rise at the conclusion of the play.

On Sunday the 17th of June, David, who was wearing the habit of the monks, was bearded for the journey and had adopted the name of Cedric the Conversus (a conversus is a trainee Monk), set off from St Werburghs in Hanbury. His fellow pilgrims, for the first sector, were Peter Overmeer, Duncan Evans, Roy Willis and Richard Hoffman and their logistics manager was Jim Storrar. After celebrating a special St Werburgh mass in Hanbury they started on the paths and canals towards Chester. Their trek took them through Newborough and Abbots Bromley before joining the Staffordshire Way and the Trent and Mersey canal. The first overnight stop was planned for St Bede's school, Bishton Hall, Colwich.

The eccentrically described Headmaster of St Bede's, Hugh Northcote, and his wife were terribly excited to welcome the modern-day monks. They shared beer with the headmaster before joining Sir Charles Wolseley for a stiff whisky and then dinner. The evening meal was served in the school dining room under the gaze of the nearby rich and famous. The menu was a tribute to the event, having recreated Vegetable Soup with nettles, stuffed lamb, and crumble with custard. After a long walk the rewards of bed, following dinner, weren't quite as they had hoped, as they slept on the gym floor in their sleeping bags, but this pilgrimage was meant to be a test, not a luxury.

On the second day after breakfast and prayers and a blessing from Canon Chris Humphries, the pilgrims discovered that map reading whilst in heavy rain, wearing a brown smock and not much else, was not easy and the serving six covered an extra two miles on their way to Stafford. Once back on the right track, progress was slowed again as previous weeks of heavy rain had flooded the areas surrounding the rivers Trent and Sow, making for long diversions. On one occasion, trapped between the flooded plains and a row of houses, the six monks were forced to climb a barbed wire fence into a back garden, where a kindly homeowner seemed unperturbed by the arrival of the monks and duly escorted them through her house out onto the road. One can only imagine what the neighbours thought as the miserly monks filed out from the front door. Later that day in the Navigation Arms the welcome sight of a pint of Abbotts Ale was both appropriate and needed.

Day three became problematic early. In a cavernous, gloomy rock-cutting, the towpath was ankle-deep in mud trodden by cattle and in many places the old path was nettle ridden and overgrown, making the sandal covered journey very tough. But beat on they did and when they arrived at the Bridge Inn for a shower and food, they were met by the Vicar of Audlem, Helen Chantry, along with Chief Executive of Chester Cathedral, Annette Moor and the local press who had come to see and support the pilgrimage.

The following day's journey was a hard slog of sixteen miles, from Audlem to Beeston Locks. As they passed Nantwich, afternoon tea was provided at NWF HQ and a greeting from CEO, Graham Scott, a former ally of David's, from his days on the board there. Along the towpath they actively collected donations from the people who were by now coming out in numbers to see them, thanks to the attendant press attention. One or two got more than they bargained for as David led the group in stretching exercises on the canal tow path. They inadvertently revealed a little more than just their character, as the habits rode up their legs; a passing Canal Boat Helmswoman was particularly impressed with the muscled monk's morning activities!

Eleven Monks prepared to make the final journey to Chester from the Dysart Arms in Bunbury. At 8.55 a.m. lay preacher Eric Wallington gave the party a blessing at the lock gates and placed his hand-written prayers in the casket they had been carrying, for delivery to the Cathedral. By the time they reached the Cheshire Cat they had many others walking with them, including school children. They had been told of this story during class as part of a local history lesson and were allowed out to join the pilgrimage. Everyone in Chester came out to see them. They held back the Viking Hordes en route, were challenged by Chester's Romans at the Eastgate and then finally the train of people worked their way up St Werburgh Street to the Town Hall.

The greeting was both buoyant and welcomed, with many dressed in the same monks' habits. There was music, dancing and of course the delivery of the casket to the Sherriff of Chester, Andrew Storrar, followed by a welcome from the Dean. The official party then walked down to the West Doors and entered the Cathedral where the casket was delivered for safe keeping to the Chapel of St Werburgh. It was a spectacular end to an incredibly special event, designed and conceived by David. It raised money, yes, but most importantly it connected the city with its heritage and told a story that many did not know, and others had forgotten. I was lucky enough to be involved in helping put just a little of this together and I had nothing but admiration for David and his pilgrims. It has never been repeated in Chester — more is the pity.

David followed this with a short break to Portugal with Sue, to play golf and recharge the batteries. Ireland was also high on the list for a visit, as Belinda, David's daughter, who was pregnant, was moving with her husband Ed to Cork to start a new life and new jobs for both.

As October arrived it was the Ruby Wedding anniversary of David and Sue. They decided to invite thirty of their friends away and everyone went to Polruan in Cornwall for a weekend of dinners and good fun. It was a fabulous part of the world where they had been a few times previously with Edward and Jilly Walton. On this occasion it was only Jilly, as she and Edward had separated in the July.

Chapter 70
Managing a City

It was during 2007, whilst working on Chester Festivals, that David and I became aware of a glaring omission in the stakeholder provision for the city of Chester. The council, who had previously managed the role of Chester City Management, decided they could no longer justify funding this position from within their Management and that previous outputs of this entity did not give a good return on investment. There was a definite need for a leadership role to be taken for the stakeholders of Chester.

Anecdotally, footfall on the high street had been declining at double digits for the previous three years and the number of vacant shops was climbing by the day. Chester needed to make a stand against the growing tide of out-of-town shopping centres, online shopping and decaying public provision. With this as a backdrop, David and I approached the Council and asked if they would be prepared for David to become Chairman of a new entity, called Chester City Management (CCM) and for me to become the Chester City Manager. Our goal would be to take a small amount of public funding (£30,000 annually) and recruit the private sector to contribute financially to a series of campaigns. We would unite the stakeholders and present the city to both locals and visitors in a better light by challenging the Council to do more in the public realm. We wanted, directly, to increase footfall and entice operators back on to Chester's High

Street. The council agreed and we went about creating a new board of Chester City Management. Despite his best intentions to avoid major roles, David was yet again Chairman of another influential body in Chester.

As 2008 started, it was the ambitious plan that I presented at Chester City Management that had captured David's attention. Getting the stakeholders to believe that there was a way forward was going to be difficult; they all had their own agenda, were incredibly cynical of anything in which the Council were involved but they did agree that if we did not work together, it was never going to get better.

David told me on day one, that as my chairman, we needed to be seen to be always working together and that what we said was crucial and that there was never to be so much as a cigarette paper difference between our public views, if this was to work. A special word for both Julie Webb, the General Manager of the Grosvenor Shopping Centre and the General Manager of Marks & Spencer. They were both forthcoming with important information around footfall as the city had no counters at this time. They helped with national trends and allocated budget to CCM, without which we simply could not have staged any events. They helped us get the ball rolling and for that reason Chester owes them a debt of gratitude.

It was agreed that our first campaign was to be something that showed everyone Chester was back. It required the recruitment of major retailers and small retailers, cabinet member councillors and resident's association leaders as well as the local media, all to sit and discuss how the group could make a difference. David chaired the meetings, and it was obvious that there was a genuine will around the table to make good things happen, none more so than Eric Langton, the then Editor of the

Chronicle Series. Eric is no longer with us but during his time he paved the way for a better Chester. Had Eric not got behind CCM then it's voice would have been so much less heard. Prior to David and I sharing our vision of CCM with Eric, the local government were not enjoying a good relationship with the press. We believed if the city was going to succeed then we needed the press on our side and, with regular briefings to journalists and the support of Eric, the tune changed significantly for the better. Eric helped spread all the good news stories and for that we will always be grateful.

The CCM first venture was the Smile Campaign. The campaign was prompted by the closure of the Hoole Bridge, an arterial link to the city and a connection between the trendy and burgeoning suburb of Hoole. Both groups of stakeholders were concerned and so was the relaunched Chester City Management. CCM set about telling a story of positivity, a story that everyone could buy into, a campaign of everyone working together. The vision CCM had was one of inclusivity and a shared ambition to make the city great again. The campaign featured over 140 different retailers all offering a discount or a value-added item, during a festival of shopping and it caused quite a stir.

CCM followed the Smile Campaign with a strong Fashion Festival with fashion parades in the precinct, on the back of trucks, in the main streets, in pubs and hotels. People could see vibrancy back in the city and they liked it. The CCM premise was that Chester was a place people liked to visit but they needed an extra reason to come. CCM started, with Chester Festivals, to formulate a city-wide plan to give people what they wanted. The aim was to create an experiential shopping experience, before that term became vogue. An experience you simply couldn't get online or in one of the many soulless shopping centres. A Chester experience that was special.

CCM also undertook the first customer survey of the people in the streets of Chester, something that had not ever been done. Both David and I found it incredible that people who were meant to be promoting our city had no idea who their customer was or why they were in Chester. By way of example, locals were screaming in the paper that car park charges in the city were killing the footfall and to a certain extent they were right, but to the day visitor, from outside Chester, on a ranking of the ten most important things in deciding to visit Chester, the visitor ranked car parking ninth in importance, whereas the local person ranked it number one. Understanding these things helped CCM frame policy.

Making decision based on fact and not theory made for a powerful forum and in 2008 the work was well underway. It was made a little more difficult because Chester City and Cheshire County Council were in the process of being dissolved and morphing into Cheshire West and Chester Council (CWAC) and Cheshire East Council, both with roughly 350,000 residents and the demarcation lines were fuzzy.

Chapter 71
The Birth of *Free After 3*

The CCM Chester City survey work discovered that between ten a.m. and three p.m., 72% of people on the high street described themselves as day visitors, 22% said they worked in the city and so had a reason to be there other than by choice and only 6% were locals shopping. David's challenge to me was to find a way to get Chester people using Chester again.

David wanted to know why local residents didn't use Chester. The overwhelming reason was that the out-of-town free parking at rival centres like Cheshire Oaks and Sealand Road made Chester unattractive to locals, who had to pay to park. They said it was simply too expensive to park when they had a choice of free parking at out-of-town locations.

The footfall counters of Marks and Spencer's, Tesco's, The Grosvenor Shopping Centre, WH Smith and others showed that at three p.m. the footfall just died. Perfectly logical, day visitors who formed 72% of the high street, were keen to pick the kids up from school, miss the busy traffic of later and get home to prepare the evening meal. Hence the mass exodus at around three p.m.

David instructed us to survey the council car parks and count the number of cars who came in after three p.m. and this showed the council that the average revenue in their three car parks after three p.m. was just £100 per day and that the loss of £35–40,000 a year against the possible return to Chester by locals shopping was an investment worth making. They agreed and Free after 3 was born. This proved to be one of the most successful campaigns ever. In the first six weeks the footfall figures had risen by over 28% and this figure grew to over 40% within six months. On the back of this success and many other initiatives, Chester City Management was a shining beacon of collaboration and one that David had contributed to in the most fundamental way. His way was to guide, coax and support, getting all the partners to understand the importance of working together, taking a few chances and it was working. In fact, so successful was CCM that it was mentioned by the Chester MP in Parliament as a shining beacon of success. This at a time when the Government was desperate to reinvigorate the High Street. Mary Portas had been commissioned by the UK government to try and rejuvenate the UK High Street and many of her recommendations, Chester had already started and was leading the country in High Street recovery. Cities all over the UK started to replicate the Chester *Free After 3* campaign, again with great success. Not a bad start to year one but David had even bigger plans and by bigger, I mean, much bigger.

Chapter 72
Chester the Giant City

For David it was a chance meeting in 2008 with Dave Roberts, the head of Chester's Giant Family, and a lady called Kristine Szulik, that saw the creation of something truly sensational. It was a project called, Chester — The Giant City. A phrase that intuitively appealed; a perfect sense of irony. Chester is wonderfully proportioned and incredibly attractive to the eye, but the one thing Chester is not, is giant! Yet deep in Chester's history is a story of the Middle Ages when Chester was the Giant Making capital of England.

Why did you need a Giant? —To ward off evil spirits of course. Of the giant makers in Chester, there were none better. What is a Giant? It is a super-structure resembling a human about fourteen foot high, into which, an actual human, climbs and then carries that effigy on their back. The principle being that at the Summer and Winter Solstice your village would display their giants to the spirits and of course no spirit in their right mind would attack a village with fourteen-foot people in it. Not when there were easier options elsewhere — job sorted. This was another unique and quirky selling point that truly captured the imagination of David Pickering.

Chester was striving for its identity and he was convinced that by proclaiming to be Chester the Giant City it would certainly become just that. It was a bold plan and one that again he backed with significant sums of his own money. He also enticed many others to help. Who knew before this project that there was a High Sheriff's fund, or that the Lord Lieutenant was the Queen's representative in the shrievalty of Cheshire? David as Deputy Lieutenant did, and he was on first name terms with all of them. When he asked them to help, they did not know if this was something special or if he had taken leave of his senses, but they did help.

It was not just a marketing plan though. David's plan was also a social enterprise where underprivileged and disadvantaged people could learn a trade, where artistic talent could be fostered decorating the Giants and, in mid-2008, David chose Kristine Szulik, to manage this project for him. A project into which he would invest over a £100,000 of his own money.

Giant making aside, David and Sue took a break to the enchanting island of Mauritius and played a bit of golf, enjoyed the sun and a great value holiday. Ed and Belinda had now settled in Cork and named the house they built— Roughlyn, which was a fitting tribute to where it all started and the families Kings Stand winner back in 1966 and, just for good measure, David again won the billiards at the City Club.

David was hit hard financially by the next big event of 2008. There was a free fall of stock markets across the globe in September. This was triggered by the extraordinary level of defaults on sub-prime housing loans in the US which resulted in the collapse of more than just the one bank. It was a staggering blow to confidence in financial markets and showcased the greed of modern banks, who had been playing roulette with investor's' money using complicated financial instruments — and they had come unstuck, in a big way, requiring State Aid to avoid bankruptcy. The UK stock market fell from 6500 down to 3700, almost 50%, and it took with it much of David's available capital.

Whilst on paper he had lost a lot, he fortunately did not need to sell any shares and he felt confident they would recover in time. It was a period of great uncertainty in financial markets but now was definitely the time to be doing something positive, if as David predicted, things recovered quickly.

Chapter 73
A New Era of Hope on Track

The re-organisation by the newly elected David Cameron Tory Party meant much of the regional funding was stopped and the Labour Party devolved; Development Agencies were replaced with sub regional Local Economic Partnerships. David resigned his Chair of the Regional Skills Partnership as he could see this would have little budget or role going forward and with it, he thought the time had come to cut free from the Chester Business Club. He was not in business anymore and his voice less important. He was also terribly busy with Chester City Management and Chester Giants, where he believed he could now make a significant difference to the local landscape and he was right.

Busy as David was with his newest involvements, he had been out of Horse racing for some time and somehow, as we have seen, that bug never left him for long. He had an idea to get back involved in horse ownership, prompted by the start of two new training establishments in Cheshire. Rob Lloyd Racing at Spurtsow and Michael Owen, the former Liverpool Footballer, had created', Manor Farm Stables, at Malpas, these both caught David's attention. He took me with him to see both sets of stables and after an unfortunate meeting with the then trainer at Michael Owen's place, well before Tom Dascombe took over, he opted for having a horse with Rob Lloyd.

Rob invited David to his training establishment, set in the

shadows of Peckforton Castle, to meet his trainer, Pat Morris; it was an offer too good to refuse. Rob was enigmatic and David took to him quickly; he had huge plans to develop his site into a major training establishment and in the last six years Rob had enjoyed a meteoric rise to significant wealth.

Things did not go right, almost from the start. You see Rob Lloyd was a corporate gambler and his companies very highly leveraged. The listed company he owned, Eatonfield, went from 165p to just 5p almost overnight after the crash and the banks wanted their money back. The timing of the 2008 crash could not have come at a worse time for him. He was put under incredible pressure by his banks and it became impossible for him to deliver on his ambition for this training centre. He simply did not have the money to finish the project. He was, himself, fighting to survive.

It was also tough on Lloyd's trainer, Pat Morris. He, his young wife, Sharon, and two children both under five years of age, packed their bags on the Curragh, in Ireland, and took the gamble that they would be the ones to deliver Rob Lloyd's dreams. A dream they bought into and gave everything to try and deliver, but with half the gallops built and less than half the facilities promised it was never going to work. It did not work out for the Morris family, as Rob was forced to leave the site and surrender most of his business assets. Pat was able to stay and train on site for a short period of time, with the permission of the administrators, but without the quality horses he was promised or the facilities, he was just another trainer with the worst problem of all — slow horses.

By the time it became apparent that Rob would not be resurfacing out of this financial quicksand there was a fire sale of Rob's previous assets, principally his horses — enter David

Pickering, sniffing out a bargain and able to buy several horses at less than half their original purchase value. This appeared to be the perfect way back into Horseracing. Surely if someone thought they were worth double what you were going to pay, it must be a safe investment. Problem was, the original purchase price had already been inflated by those eager to take some of Rob's millions off him and so David inherited a group of horses that, whilst being okay, just were not great. In essence he got what he paid for and no more, but he was back in the racing business.

With a small group of horses, David launched The Chester Racing Club with his pals, and I was given the job of assisting with the placing and liaising with the trainer, whilst reporting back to David and the Racing Club on the horse's development. Whilst negotiating his string with Pat Morris, David had also put two mares in foal and we visited the foals at Goldford Stud, owned by Bangor Racecourse Chairman and former Bodfari Racing CEO, Richard Aston. They were simply marvellous. A Chestnut coloured colt who David named Roughlyn, by the sire Haafd, who looked every inch an athlete out of a mare that David and Bobby McAlpine, the chairman of Chester Race Company, jointly owned, called Dime Bag. As you may recall, they had some success with this mare as she had bred a horse called Pawn Broker. He had won a listed race and been placed in Group Races on the flat, so hopes were high. They had also bred an exceptionally good Cheltenham Festival winner called Inglis Drever, the horse that earned just over £750,000, so they had seen success before with this mare. The other was a tall, rangy colt, by Rail Link, out of a mare called Singasongasixpence. David named this one Another Journey. He had high hopes for both.

It had been another good year for Meadow Foods, who reported turnover in excess of £220 million and profits exceeding

£5 million. Secretly David was pleased no one had accepted his offer to buy his shares in 2007. The shares were undoubtedly worth a lot more now and with Simon Chantler doing such a good job of running the business, he could only see the company being worth more in the future. A company in which he was not having to do any work anymore and that had a gifted individual in Simon running your key investment. Once again, fate had played a hand and things were looking up.

In the winter of 2009, David's reflection on the year that had just passed, left him with the following words to mull over: Live, Love, Learn, leave a legacy — they would all feature in his aims for the new year. Of his own character he looked for improvement in honesty, openness, confidence, calm and consistency. He was very ready to focus on becoming a better person and working towards creating a solid family environment.

The year got off to a good start at Meadow Foods. They purchased Nene Valley Foods in Peterborough for £4 million. This now gave the company a production and distribution base in four areas, equally split across the UK. Dissimilar to Quantock Cheese, Nene Valley was making money. It was another good deal by Simon Chantler; not only was turnover again rising, this time through acquisition, but more profits would flow in the following year once they had absorbed this new business into their accounts.

Things were not going quite as well at Chester Race Company. David had been receiving quite a deal of publicity in his new role as Chairman of Chester City Management and interim Chair of Chester Festivals. CEO Richard Thomas and I were working on a plan to put a new Theatre, Conference centre and large underground car park on the Little Roodee car park and had a number of meetings with the Leader of the council Mike Jones and his Portfolio Head of Culture, Richard Short. They liked the idea and of course I had briefed David about it. Part of the City Management communication plan was that we had regular briefings with the press and David, aware of this scheme, offered it up to the press as a beacon of hope. This seriously annoyed Richard Thomas and from that moment on the relationship deteriorated. So bad was it, that at the lunch break during the Board meeting of Chester Race Company, a meeting that always preceded the AGM, Chairman Nigel Churton asked if he could have a word with David. This he agreed and Nigel expressed that he felt it was time for David to step aside and resign as a director. David asked if he was being sacked and Nigel sheepishly replied that surely it would not come to that. Reading the writing on the wall David went back into the meeting after lunch and offered his resignation. Of all the appointments that he had over his lifetime, the loss of this one hurt the most. He had enjoyed his time and thought he had done a good job but a combination of what appeared to be his personal ambitions, and the dislike of anyone creating a higher profile through their position at the racecourse, had alienated him from the Chief Executive and Nigel was simply pulling the trigger.

They tried a similar tactic with Sir Charles Lowther but this one failed when Sir Charles decided he did not want to go quietly, and he rallied the other board members to support him. The board did support Sir Charles and then demanded the resignation of Nigel Churton, which he duly offered. It was only a minor setback for Thomas, as he soon had in place another Chairman with whom he could work but David was not amongst his directors. David's only positive to take was that it was probably better for his liver not to be involved any more as there was an awful lot of drinking and lunches required on race days and, with the acquisition of Bangor Racecourse, there was double the commitment!

Chapter 74
Months of Misery, Moments of Magic

It was interesting to note that in David's diary he put, for the first time, that on April 1st he saw a Swallow and on April 30th he heard a Cuckoo. There is no other year where he records anything like this. Perhaps, now he was simply taking the time that he had never had previously to look around; he cannot remember but it is there in his notes, never repeated.

There was plenty of golf during 2009, but none more entertaining than when David was playing with John Iles as part of a four ball. John teed off on the sixteenth hole and hit an all too frequent poor drive. The ball was careering at speed towards Gordon Hamilton, who was crossing the small bridge, chasing his errant shot from the thirteenth tee. The polite thing to do in golf, when someone is about to be hit by a golf ball, is to shout — fore! John, David, and partners in unison, seeing the impending collision of the ball with Gordon, screamed fore. This had the unsettling effect of panicking Gordon and he overbalanced backwards, attempting to avoid the ball. As he overbalanced, the bridge guard rail caught the back of his thighs and he ended up somersaulting backwards into the water below, miraculously, landing on his feet. The mood on the sixteenth tee went from fear, to astonishment, to helpless laughter as the very wet Gordon Hamilton made his way out of the pond to find his ball.

It was not all bad news on the racing front either, which

makes a change. Neil Large was by now a fully paid-up member of Chester Racing Club and he and David went to Dalham Hall Stud in Newmarket, the UK home of Godolphin, the brainchild of Sheik Mohammed, ruling leader of Dubai. Dalham Hall was the home of his Darley Stud breeding operation, their amazing mares and of course a training and schooling set-up, second to none. To say they were impressed would be an understatement. On their return things improved further because, shortly thereafter, The Chester Racing Club juvenile, Schoolboy Champ, scooted away to win his maiden at Haydock and the future looked bright. It was the first Chester Racing Club success and, as David said previously, it was "months of misery and moments of magic", this was one such moment. When your two-year-old wins a maiden, the sky is the limit as far as you, the owner, is concerned — just how good could he be? Time would tell.

In mid-summer brother John suffered a mild heart attack and there was concern. John enjoyed life to the full and whilst he was a lover of good wine and rich food he was not in the same shape, physically, as David, who had always kept his weight in check and remained active. Summer also meant another Garden Party at Buckingham Palace and here David saw former fellow Race Company Director, Sir Charles Lowther, who was there in a more official capacity as Aide-De-Camp. The party was again fabulous but on leaving there was a torrential downpour and David, Sue and their fellow guests were soaked through.

As the leaves fell to signal autumn was upon us, Ed and Belinda, again, needed to up sticks in Cork and this time move to Gibraltar where Ed had secured more work with Lovelock Mitchell, the same firm that David's other son-in-law Marc worked for, on a big reclamation project. Whilst that move was difficult for the young family, they had a rare piece of luck:

Belinda won £10,000 on a scratch card in Gibraltar. What a great start to married life on this rather strange British territory. It seemed luck was also heading the way of David as well; a chap by the name of Noel Coakley had approached Simon Chantler, with a £23 million bid to buy Meadow Foods. That would value the family stake, that David represented, at about £4 million. The euphoria did not last long as Simon worked out quite quickly this chap simply didn't have the money, but the exercise was done in terms of a valuation and, even if he had the money, Simon was not sure that was enough to buy Meadow. Now that was a nice way to finish the year, with the realisation Meadow was now probably worth more than £25 million.

David and his walking pals decided this was the year they would start the Offa's Dyke trek. This 176-mile footpath, which legend says was created by King Offa of Mercia, to delineate Mercia (England) from Powys (Wales) is a regular haunt of walkers and, as it is literally on their doorstep, they decided the time was right to attack a portion of this famous trail. The group, led by Stuart, the navigator, as he was the one in charge of directions, started their border walk. The aim was to cover about half the journey this year and complete it in the following year. They enjoyed excellent weather and the scenery was nothing short of stunning.

Chapter 75
Bigger, Stronger and Better than Ever

David, on his return from walking Offa's Dyke, was busy back in Chester. Before he left, he had challenged me to create something special for 2010, something that would be a legacy, so I did. I put together the most challenging programme of events for Chester City Management and Chester Festivals, ever. David then set about helping find the money to make it happen by getting Mike Jones from the Council and Rita Waters from Chester Renaissance, all contributing. The event was called Chestival.

Chestival was the Festival of Chester and it was the biggest event Chester had ever seen. It ran from the 11th of June to 14th July. It featured a three-day Roman themed long weekend with over 250 Roman Soldiers living in Grosvenor Park, and fighting in the amphitheatre. It staged the very first Giant Weekend, with over 50 Giants on the streets of Chester, all adding to the Mid-Summer Watch Parade. There was the World Town Crier Championships, an outdoor cinema in the amphitheatre on a giant screen, the annual Music Festival took place in this period and we also staged a top UK Show jumping event on the Roodee. It was a staggering array of events on the streets of Chester. Chester City Management was the glue that brought it all together and it was our biggest and most successful project to date. The streets of Chester were alive and buzzing over the Summer of 2010. Tracy Lynn, who took on the role as Director of Chester Festivals on a full-time basis was integral in this success. She and her team helped to deliver this simply amazing programme of events. Most of all it showed what could be done if we got everyone working together. This was something David had wanted to see for many years, his city all working together. This was living proof that when it happened, it worked.

Good things were also happening at the enlarged Meadow Foods as well. Not only was turnover up, as you would expect with the acquisition of a new business, but most importantly profit had now exceeded £4 million, for the first time ever. Encouragingly for David, they had forecast profits of £10 million for the year 2010/11. On a lowly, four times profit multiple, that made the business worth at least £40 million and David was looking after shares, of both his own and other family members, totalling almost 17%. That worked out to something in the region of £6.5 million, which was a significant improvement on the figure he might have taken two years ago when he first put the family shares up for sale.

The year finished on an even bigger high as Chester City Management put together the biggest and best Christmas that Chester had ever seen and none of it would have happened without David's support. David's challenge to me was, again, to think big and in 2010 we put a sixty-metre giant Ferris wheel on the Castle Court Car park in Chester. We had an Olympic sized ice rink, children's rides, fireworks events and fifty Victorian styled Christmas traders in attendance.

To do it, we had to commit to raising £150,000 and to get the ball rolling David put in £25,000 of his own money. Raising the rest was not easy but we got there. It was incredible and it was a massive success. It really got people believing that we could do great things in Chester. People still talk about "that" Christmas now and as much as the current offering is a good one, it does not have the scale or excitement that was created back in 2010. The big wheel was a shining example of Chester's newfound ambition. You could see it from almost every point on the A55 motorway. Even from Grange Farm in Higher Kinnerton, the lights were visible at night but without David putting his own capital at risk, we would never have been able to do it. That really is putting your money where your mouth is, where so few others have.

Chapter 76
The Year of Golf, Giants, Gee-Gee's, and Animals

Not many know that the origin of the phrase going to the gee-gees, when referring to horses, is a Chester invented term. Back in the early 16th century Chester's Mayor was a chap by the name of Henry Gee and history says he was the first person to stage organised horse races in the UK. Those horse races were staged on the Roodee, home of Chester Racecourse, with the first one being in 1539. His surname became synonymous with Horse Racing and hence it was called, going to the "gee-gees". Prior to his staging these events on the natural amphitheatre of Chester, horses would race over much longer distances from one village to another. The horses would go from one Church, with its steeple, to another and hence the phrase steeple chasing, which is still used today for those horses who jump fences during the National Hunt programme. So, horses are indeed deeply ingrained in Chester and English life and, as you will have read, very much a part of the Pickerings and their story.

In 2011, the Chester Racing club, and more particularly David Pickering, had five mares, all in foal, and another eight racehorses all in training with Pat Morris, at the, what was soon to be, former Rob Lloyd Racing Centre. For it was not long into the year that Eatonfield officially went bust and administrators were appointed to deal with the assets. Pat Morris, with whom David and I got on very well, informed us he would no longer be able to train the horses, as he had accepted an offer to be a pre-racing trainer for Dr Marwan Koukash, one of the country's biggest independent horse owners. It was great for Pat, not so good for Chester Racing Club. Pat recommended that we take the horses in training to local trainer Lisa Williamson and that his mares go to Richard Kent's Mickley Stud, in Shropshire.

David was unable though, to get too involved in the racing process, he was appointed Captain of Eaton Golf Club for the year and that involved, having to play a serious amount of golf. During the year, his handicap flip-flopped between ten and eleven and he played all over the UK. It is the tradition of Captains to invite other captains to come and play at their course and David did not wish to offend anyone by not accepting their invitation. There was also a fabulous opportunity to play at the Ryder Cup venue in South Wales, Celtic Manor, where he would play with other Cheshire Captains. This did not work out quite as was planned because, despite the fact it was a very good spring and summer for golf, on the day they played at Celtic Manor, the heavens opened and, after just four holes had been played, they had to abandon the course, which was underwater in numerous places. They returned later in the year and completed the round, but this was a disappointing day.

David's year as captain was full of strange and unusual events, none more so than when playing in a Captain and Pro Challenge, a competition where two members try to beat the Captain and Club Professional. David and Bill Tye, the professional, were up against friends Neil Large and John Iles. John, whilst walking backwards looking for a ball, fell straight into a pond. It seems Gordon Hamilton had wreaked revenge after John had forced him into the very same pond in the previous year. And whilst that was humorous and without consequence the same could not be said for Steve Aylott who experienced the ultimate in bad luck.

In a bizarre set of circumstances, Steve, who was looking for a ball, returned to find his electric trolley and bag were missing from where he had left them. His playing partners and he searched high and low and simply could not find it anywhere. They even enlisted the help of the captain (David) and his playing partners, who were on another hole playing at the time. Annoyingly for Steve, who really did not see the funny side, he had found his ball but without his clubs he could not continue and was forced to concede the match. It was days later the trolley was found in long grass at the foot of a large hill. It had clearly set off when no one was watching and buried itself in the long grass. Technology — hey!

In a similar vein of misfortune, David was playing in a four-club competition at Runcorn Golf Club and as he hit his drive it collided with a Seagull in mid-flight, the ball deviated out of bounds and David ended up carding a rather miserable eight on that hole. Things, though, were a lot worse for the Seagull as David needed to dispatch the critically injured bird. One of the rare occasions where a birdie at golf was not welcome.

Despite the odd mishap, it was a successful golfing year with victories in the winter tournament, Texas Scramble, Mixed AmAm & Seniors 9 Hole as well as lots of fun at lots of other golf clubs. By way of a thank you for all the support he received as Captain and to commemorate ten years of golf at the new Eaton Course, David and Sue hosted a drinks party at Grange Farm, which was a lovely event to close out the year of his Captaincy.

David did, surprisingly, have time though to take up an engagement as Trustee at Chester Zoo. This entailed overseeing the application for £30 million of funding to create the latest addition to Chester's award-winning Zoo — The Islands Project. After a trip to Hanover Zoo to see how they were positioning themselves, he returned to the good news, that the funding was given the go-ahead and the project could proceed. More good news for Chester and yet again David was on the board where big things were happening.

It was a similar story at the University of Chester where the announcement was made that their bid for money to build the NoW Food centre had been successful. This multi-million-pound development is a shining light of food and drink development and part of the massive building work that the University of Chester, under Tim Wheeler, achieved. Simultaneously, David was very much involved in the purchase and development of the Thornton Science and Research centre at Stanlow, which also happened during this time. It was an amazing rate of growth that Tim Wheeler, as Vice Chancellor, created.

David and Charlie Woodcock, who was from the University, met regularly to work out how to get European Funding for the University, so that it could continue to grow and provide quality tertiary education right across Cheshire. Charlie was exceptionally successful in finding pots of money and turning that money in to positive Cheshire Gross Value Added (GVA) and both Thornton and the NoW Food Centre were clear examples of their combined success.

Somehow David and his fellow walkers found time to complete the other half of the Offa's Dyke Walk, which was part funded by David having £100 on Ballabriggs in the Grand National at 14/1 — it won and was a nice return and yet another Grand National success. It was, however, small change by comparison with the monthly training and keep bills for his horses, who really weren't performing very well. There were a couple of winners but nowhere near enough to cover the costs. Same old — same old!

After another sterling year of events in Chester, where the Giants had their own two-day festival as part of Year 2 of Chestival, with over one hundred Giants out on the streets of the city; David, and the Giant team, with the help of John Iles, secured £60,000 of funding from the People's Lottery Fund to create sixty Giant Queens for 2012 to celebrate the Queen's Golden Jubilee. The grant team were impressed by the Catherine and William Giants that had been made to celebrate their wedding and during the year these two Royal Giants were seen all over Chester: at the Food and Drink festival, the Summer Ball, outside the racecourse and in the city centre. They were a spectacular example of what this social enterprise could create and now they had the money to make an even stronger statement in 2012.

Chapter 77
Knowing the Value and Not Just the Price

In essence it had been a strong year, with all but David's horses performing well. His pulse quickened a little more when he found out that First Milk were in talks with Meadow Foods for a buy-out at £50 million. At that price, his shares were most certainly on the table, but he would leave that to Simon, who so far had been faultless in his negotiations. Whilst that was good news what followed to finish the year was devastating.

Earlier in the year brother John had a bad fall whilst skiing and was heavily concussed, requiring him to come home from Grenoble. To add to his problems, when he returned home both he and his wife Jo were bundled up from their beds and tied together by armed robbers who broke into the house and robbed them of valuable assets. Whilst those two events were terrible and left an awful scare, worse news was to follow as John was diagnosed with leukaemia. Whether it was damage caused by the fall or the shock of the attack, or a combination of both, that triggered the Leukaemia, we will never know but it can be no coincidence that after a series of misfortunes and shocks, John was faced with a life-threatening disease. No amount of good trading news could sweeten that bitter pill for him and his family.

In 2012, the first concern was John's health and how he would respond to treatment and his illness. John was determined that life would go on as normal and asked that everyone respect those wishes. David decided that a trip to Sri Lanka would be an exceptional place to experience and a place that he and Sue could see the simplicity of life at its best. His key words and focus for this year were ordinariness, simplicity, health, happiness, and family and this was the right place to reflect and take on board what those words really meant.

The Chester Racing Club horses had not performed well during this season. They simply weren't very good. David did, however, try to bring some publicity to his beloved city and for his friends with the naming of the horses. He named his two-year-olds, Deva Victrix, The Chester Giant, Chester's Little Gem, Roodee Queen, Gilly's Giant, after Neil Large's wife and Professor Tim, after Tim Wheeler, Marilyn's Marquessa, after the title on Anglesey that Marilyn never got, Eaton Oak and Roodee Lady. Sadly, in most cases, the horses really didn't live up to their illustrious names.

The wins totalled only three for the year in 2011 and the prospects did not look great for 2012. David decided there would be a cull and he would get rid of all but four racehorses and four mares. He had twelve horses in training in the previous year and that was not sustainable. One bright spot was that Roughlyn was looking like a useful prospect and with that name everyone was hopeful they could get a win out of him.

For David, the Queens on the streets of Chester were a high point for Queen Elizabeth's Golden Jubilee. With sixty queens all on display and the attendant publicity, which was exceptionally good, this project was a considerable drain on David's resources. He had invested almost £100,000 of his own money into the project and it seemed there was little hope that this business would ever be sustainable. Which was a shame because the aims were good but in its current format it was just an expensive charity that did not give enough value for money. One hope was that the Giant theme would really be adopted by the city and that is where David dispatched me to meet one of Chester's most colourful characters and the owner of 'The Crocky Trail', Ed Whalley.

Ed had a love-hate relationship with the authorities and needed a mediator. Ed was not great with authority, having once, allegedly, tried to run down a planning officer who didn't agree with Ed's interpretation of the rules! He was always pushing things to the limit at The Crocky Trail with his health and safety issues and that didn't endear him to the authorities either. Ed strongly believed that children should be allowed to play outside, take risks and develop their character through confrontations and that is never popular with today's 'snowflake' administrators.

My meeting was arranged because Ed had a 100ft Giant sculpture made of wrought iron and he wanted to put it up somewhere. Both David and he thought it a fitting tribute for Chester. It would then truly be, The Giant City, with its 100 ft Giant sculpture: perfect! Together they identified the land that was bordered by the M56 and the M53 as the ideal gateway to have Chester's own Angel of the North — a proper welcome to Chester the Giant City. His instructions to me were simple — meet Ed, find out how much it will cost to put it up, he will give the sculpture for free and get the council to approve it, then we find the money for the erection of the giant. Simple.

A 100ft sculpture bordered by two motorways, needing planning approval and transport from its site in Waverton, to its hopeful resting place. No problem! Well, yes there was, but with the help of local planning specialist, Justin Paul, and his group of contacts we very nearly did it.

It took months of meetings with highway specialists, with nature experts and logistics managers and all agreed it could be done. We ran campaigns in the local paper and in the main the public loved it. Interestingly when I met with the Council Arts people, they hated it. Not the idea of the logistics, they hated the Sculpture and were quite animated. How dare Ed Whalley thrust this art upon us, what right has he got to do this — he is not a sculptor, were the comments I faced. However, they could not get away from the fact that the people liked the Giant and it was, quite a statement about the city, of that there was no doubt. The only grounds on which the planners could turn it down were planning rules and we had them all covered. The question of taste? Beauty is in the eye of the beholder. Had the funding come through for the various costs to erect the Giant it is fair to say we might now have an amazing sculpture that signalled your arrival at Chester and I think that, while it divided opinion, like all good sculpture should, Chester is a poorer place for not being able to see this fabulous structure. It sits rusting in a field in Waverton, a forlorn figure that never achieved its greatness, perhaps a metaphor for the Giant project itself.

During David's tenure as Chairman, Chester City Management had key partner meetings with Transport providers, UK Highways, bus operators, train companies and Liverpool Airport. They all sat around the table talking in a way that had never happened before, to properly coordinate and communicate to the public, things like city roadworks, major events, joined up marketing. Anyone who resides in Chester will understand these meetings also never happen now, as the building works, bus lanes, empty shops and city profile have become shambolic.

We were lucky to be the favoured vehicle of Council Leader Mike Jones. Without his support things would have been different but it was David's connection through the Conservative Party that greased these channels. Mike Jones encouraged us to constantly challenge the council and the North West Development Agency. With Chester Race Company we put on a Show jumping event and with NWDA assistance got it to become an Olympic Ranking event within just three years. One of only two in the country. We had caught the attention of the regional body as we sought to bring together a bigger focus on Chester. When David challenged the NWDA as to why Chester and Cheshire, proportionately, received so little funding, they hit back by saying, that "you never bring us anything worthwhile that we can fund". In the short time before they closed, David changed their attitude, created dialogue, and accessed money for the good of Chester and Cheshire.

The newly formed Marketing Cheshire, headed by the canny Scot Chris Brown and ably assisted by Barrie Kelly, were convinced by CCM to make Chester the attack brand for the county and marketing campaigns started to appear to tempt people North on the direct train links from London. This was a big feather in the Marketing Cheshire cap and something everyone involved should be proud of. Two hours, or thereabouts, from London Euston on a direct train was just fabulous. Eight trains a day made commuting that much more possible and Virgin Rail were happy to talk about partnerships. It was less than a year until Virgin were bringing 1600 people a day to Chester and the visitors liked what they saw. The streets were cleaner, there were many less vacant shops and with an increased programme of events, the place started to feel buzzy and busy again. All of this happened on David's watch as Chair of Chester City Management.

During the year, I approached David and told him I thought the funding route for Chester City Management was all wrong. I was spending 70% of my time trying to raise money to deliver

30% of the activity that the city needed to keep the strong footfall figures in place. I suggested to him that City Management needed to become a Business Incentive District — a BID. The Council had tried this some years earlier but at that time it was a Council led project and with the council in such dire trouble the stakeholders did not trust them, and the stakeholders voted it down.

From 2008 to 2012 we had put the city back in good shape and people trusted Chester City Management. David agreed with the proposal for a BID and after approaching Mike Jones, Head of the Council, who also agreed, we set the wheels in motion to get Chester to become a BID. The BID would allow CCM to become a professional body with an annual assured income of £500,000. The vote was successful and we both left the new BID in charge of the city with a fabulous annual marketing budget, where they would be able to market the city professionally and ensure the stakeholders got an excellent return on their membership.

Regretfully, even with that funding in place, the current BID delivers significantly less than the CCM of 2008–2012 and David's vision of a Chester BID that would market the city with ambition, style and scope has never eventuated. Chester is now once again full of empty shops, footfall declining and in dire need of a real boost.

Chapter 78
The Long and Winding Road of Fate

In late Summer, brother John arrived, during one of David's grandchildren's parties at Grange Farm and David was convinced he wanted to tell him about his treatment. When John asked if they could have a quiet word, that was not the subject. John wanted to discuss Meadow Foods buying out David's block of shares. John offered him £2 million for all the shares David represented. That valued the company at less than £10 million. Given that talks had already been taking place with First Milk and figures in the £50 million bracket discussed, David told John the offer was derisory. He sent John off to go and think about what a proper figure might be and was more than a little annoyed at both the intrusion and the ridiculous offer.

Some of David's winter nights were taken up with a new Bridge Club he had started, called the Pinewood Players. It included Edward Walton, John Heath and Tage Weiss and was a lot of fun but it still was not filling all the extra time he had in a day. To keep his mind more active he decided he would try to help some smaller businesses and do some Angel investing at the University of Chester Riverside Innovation Centre. An ideal place to try and make a difference. It is a sort of breeding ground to nurture start-up projects, as part of the University of Chester programme. He asked me to go and look at a few of these that he had invested in, only small amounts at the time, up to about £10–20,000 per business. My task was to see if I could help with some marketing ideas and some practical route to market advice. I was happy to do so.

The investments included a company who was going to transform how Children learn through online tutorial models, called Learnerverse. A good product but one that could have been so much better, held back, again, by the Management. Like so many I have seen before, the lack of understanding in how to turn a good idea in to one that makes money is the biggest stumbling block most face. This was no different. A senior management who wanted to do things their way and would not sanction any outside support or ideas that challenged what they believed. I feared for David's investment on this one, which was a shame as it was an excellent idea and in the COVID-19 world of 2020 should have been a massive winner.

A brilliant Bike company, called Bikmo, saw investment from David. They catalogued every part of a bike and made all the spares available to the world, online, for comparison, purchase and of course payment of commission from the seller, back to Bikmo. These guys were seeing the rise of the bike in society and were keen to cash in on a marketplace that had not as yet been disrupted. They did not really need my help. They knew what they were doing and how to do it. Smart people running it and David was very keen to see them progress. He would support them much more going forward.

And finally, a sort of T-Shirt maker/fashion brand. In an ultra-competitive marketplace, they did not seem to have a unique identity that people could buy into, or at least that was my thoughts. They had a market to sell to — being university students and if they could create a "cool" brand that was aspirational then it had a chance, but they seemed to spend a lot of time talking about logos and not enough working out what it was they were trying to sell. David also had a small investment in a Soup making business that was based at the Now Food Centre, but this was short lived.

The year ended on a real high, as Simon Chantler appeared on the doorstep of Grange farm wanting to talk Meadow Foods business. He offered David a figure of £7 million for the shares he controlled on behalf of himself and other family members and David said he would talk to all involved and get back to him. This valued Meadow Foods at £40 million and was far more logical. It was after a discussion with Sue, where she said to David, what would Simon do if the roles were reversed and David knew what the answer was straight away. He had seen Simon do it many times before. David would accept the offer if it were increased by 10% to £7.7 million. He went back to Simon, who agreed the deal and that payments would be made in two tranches of 50%: one now and the other in September 2013. It made for a special Christmas in the Pickering family of Grange Farm. David and Sue and the various family trusts set up for Children and Grandchildren were now in an extremely healthy state.

David was now out completely from Meadow Foods and the family had done amazingly well but it was the end of an era. David and John had continued the Pickering tradition of working the land and assets at Rough Hill and now the business that dominated the site was no longer one that he had an interest in. He had been general dogsbody, pig farmer, Director and Chairman. The business had gone from £500,000 turnover annually, when he and John took control, to over £250 million in just over thirty years, and now the business David helped to build was in the hands of others. With John's health deteriorating and the Leukaemia becoming more aggressive to the point where it seemed that treatment would make little difference, neither brother was now having any involvement in the day-to-day running of Meadow Foods.

To add to the nostalgia in the year, David's special home bred horse, Roughlyn, who was simply the most gorgeous looking horse, made his way to the course. It is fair to say that his first couple of runs were not great. He was being trained by Kevin Ryan and really was not shining at all. Kevin was convinced there was a race in him but, when it all went horribly wrong at Beverley, Roughlyn was pulled back from Ryan's yard and joined the rest of the string nearer to home at Lisa Williamson's stables. It took seven more runs for him to break his maiden but on the 5th of December 2012, amateur stalwart jockey Serena Brotherton gave him a peach of a ride and he duly picked up the winner's cheque. He was in training in total from January 2012 until December 2016 — he won once from twenty-five starts and made a total of £4,459 in prize money. The joy of winning is a strong drug and Roughlyn did at least do that but as you can see with circa £50,000 of training fees for about £6500 of earnings, it was not a great return.

Chapter 79
Time is the Real Enemy

As 2013 started there was a weight of expectation around David's horses. Chester Racing Club had at least nine horses that would come to the track in 2013 and they were all with Lisa Williamson, local Chester trainer. Lisa is one of the lesser-known trainers and, whilst she does not have access to some of the fancy equipment and treatments that some of the big names in the sport at Newmarket have, she is fine conditioner of a horse. If it can win, it will win with Lisa. That said, her ability to place the horse in a race that it is capable of winning is sometimes tempered by logistics, owner politics and day-to-day knowledge of the horses in the race. Let me explain.

As a trainer, it is all well and good getting the horse fit and keeping them well, but the trick is then to find a race where your horse is just a bit faster than the others and that is the hard part. It is tough to keep up with every horserace every day and have a view on form of all the other horses that might be in a race, when you are looking after forty horses at home, who demand full time attention. In horseracing placing horses in the right race is as important as training them and often overlooked by owners. It is also fair to say that Lisa's horses in training mostly operate in the "bargain basement" of horse racing and that is where it is mighty competitive. They are not there by choice; they simply are not superstars. The problem is that it costs as much to train an average horse as it does an incredibly good one.

At the lower echelons of horseracing, there is so little margin for error in sprint and middle-distance races and most times for owners of these types of horses it is about what might have been. Could the jockey have switched quicker, did the horse miss the break, what if we went a little further next time or perhaps drop back a furlong or two? Perhaps the ground was too soft, too hard, too undulating, too tight, too anything that might have stopped it from winning and after all those conversations the owners normally decide to give it another try and so another month's training fees, as the owner hopes next time it all falls right. That is the conundrum David faced every time one of his horses ran.

Not by choice, David's horses, one by one that year, ended up being in the bargain basement and, despite all sorts of reports by me about their health, potential, size, and temperament, most just simply weren't very good and were either sold or given away. It was not so much the cost of a horse, remember David got most of these relatively cheaply, but a horse in training at Lisa's bargain training fees, with travel costs and vet bills, is still costing you £1500 a month. What a lot of young horses need, is time to mature and time in this game, with costs mounting every day, is something in short supply.

By way of example, one of Lisa's previous owners, had a horse with David Pipe, for which he paid £60,000. David Pipe could not get it to win and in frustration the owner sent the horse to Lisa. It ran a few times for her but did not show a lot and the owner decided to give it away. Lisa gave it to a nearby point-to-point trainer who put it in a field for a year. The horse matured and grew and then won nine consecutive Point-to-Point Races, climaxing in a £20,000 race at Stratford. Now winning points is different to winning under rules but it was a good example of how time and patience can often deliver results. The question is:

how long do you wait for a horse to mature and when do you know it is time to stop spending money? Fine margins all round and an expensive game when you get it wrong. Fortunately, with foals coming through each year from his mares at Mickley Stud, David was able to move on the horses who could not make it on the track and think about the next young yearling who might be a star. A triumph of optimism over reality.

Every year all over the country hundreds of owners dream that the unraced two-year-old they are watching in training will compete at Royal Ascot and have that special status reserved for Champions. It does not happen for many but when it does… and that is what keeps you coming back. This for David was not a stellar year. Not one winner from nine different horses in 2013. David made yet another pledge to cull the crop and look at placing young horses from Mickley Stud with other trainers. One such trainer, recommended by Mickley owner, Richard Kent, was Jo Hughes, based at Lambourne and training with the assistance of her partner Paul Blockley.

Racing has a way of accumulating interesting people. Back in the days of the Bodfari Racing syndicate, David and his syndicate members were captivated by the larger-than-life Mick Easterby — a Yorkshire racing legend. Well Paul Blockley may not go down as a legend but colourful and entertaining, with a unique understanding of horse racing — definitely. Richard Kent told David of a horse that Paul had in training with his wife Jo (Paul was banned from training for misdemeanours too complicated to explain) and David was tempted. It proved to be a great move. He paid little money for the horse and duly named it Picks Pinta — named after the fact that his dad delivered milk and that is what a pint delivered by David's father was known as. He won two times and finished second four times in his twelve runs for Hughes/Blockley before he was moved on for a profit. Most of David's newly bred foals ended up at Jo and Paul's and, whilst they had a little success in France racing and delivered six winners, they never really did much after that. A lot of cost and more than a little disappointment. David then decided enough was enough — for now at least!

An escape to New Zealand came about in this year. Good friend Peter Overmeer and his partner Sue Petranca were planning on going to Nelson for Peter's son Chris's wedding and asked if David and Sue Pickering might like to join them. Sue did not fancy the trip, but suggested David go, which he did. In fact, of the party that made its way south, it is fair to say David enjoyed it most. They visited Nelson, Auckland, Christchurch, and Queenstown. All in all, it was seventeen days and eleven flights, with every one of the flights taking off and landing at the prescribed time, a rarity in today's world. For David it was sunshine, good food, little alcohol, fresh air, exercise, and stunning scenery. David described it as a great holiday with ten games of golf across the nearly three weeks. For Peter and Sue, it didn't work as well. Their "practice honeymoon" did not go to plan and Sue returned home early ending the relationship between them.

In June, David organised the annual Wye reunion to come to Chester. He sorted the accommodation and meeting rooms at Rosset Hall for the various guests and this year wives were invited to attend. Trevor Trigg, who attended most every event summed up his feelings about this group when he wrote in an email to me:

"What a great achievement that a core of us still reunite annually. The reunions, and those of us involved with them, have continually broadened my knowledge and interest through a wide

range of subjects and topics that we have been shown over the years.

However, I do not think that this would have been able to continue, if it wasn't for David as Chairman, as I call him, and his typically highly efficient ways of recording all the facts about us all. This coupled with his diplomatic way of organising is, in my opinion, the main reason why we all continue to benefit from our friendly reunions."

In September, David was appointed, by Cheshire West and Chester Council, as "The Champion of the Walls." This involved overseeing the significant rebuilding of the collapsed Chester walls and the animation of a few of the areas around the walls so that visitors could understand the important events that took place in Chester. David was honoured to be entrusted with this project and whilst it was a short period of time it was nonetheless an important one. Chester's walls are synonymous with Chester and as a visitor attraction they are second to none in the Northwest. Chester was at last recognising that the preservation of this asset was vital, and they wanted the right person to make it happen. As usual with a project overseen by David, the work was completed on time and in budget. How much more careful he is with other people's money than his own.

Chapter 80
Is There a Doctor in the House?

Ampleforth Abbey in Yorkshire was the next escape for a long weekend retreat and the chance to live like a monk for three days was how David rewarded himself. Chester Cathedral organised this for him and he found it more than a challenge. It was twelve church services in three days and total silence after seven p.m. until seven a.m. the next day. David described it as interesting, demanding and enlightening. The absence of the word enjoyable in his description may be a clue as to how others of us might find the event and it is possible this will not be included in the Visit Yorkshire top ten holidays. However, it was yet another of life's experiences that David could tick off the list.

Much better would follow when The University of Chester recognised David's involvement with them for almost two decades during the time of their greatest ever growth, with an Honorary Doctorate. David Pickering, Doctor of Business Administration was how Tim Wheeler presented David to the gathered crowd. Rarely can there have been a more apt Doctorate or one more deserved. It is one of David's proudest achievements.

Equally enjoyable was a "fact finding" mission to South Africa with Simon Ely. Simon had several business interests, including the wine industry in South Africa and asked if David wanted to accompany him on a tour. The opportunity seemed too good to miss, so together they set off and had a most enjoyable week away. It really had been a sparkling year with the engagement of son Stuart to Paula and the marriage of Sue's nephew Robert to Alissa, the icing on the cake.

Whilst the second tranche of the proceeds of Meadow Foods share sale duly arrived in September the joy of this final settlement was tempered by the extremely poor health of brother John. On the 5th of December John would lose his battle with Cancer and David would stand alone as the last of Den's sons.

John was liked by everyone who knew him. He was a simple man who had an appetite and enthusiasm for life. Never happier than when with his wife Jo on their Anglesey estate at Dullas, with his dogs and his friends. He had been High Sheriff of Cheshire in 1995 but never craved the limelight of public life. He and his brother had done an amazing job of creating something special at Rough Hill and there is no doubt he got a well-earned pat on the back from his father when they were re-united. He is survived by his wife Jo, their two children, Alec and Chrissie, and their three grandchildren. In a fitting piece of Pickering negotiation, while none of the family members have a direct interest in Meadow Foods any more, Alec Pickering remains the landlord of Rough Hill and Meadow Foods are still his ever-expanding tenant. Alec, keeps alive the three hundred years and counting, of Pickerings at Rough Hill Farm. They have gone from tenant farmer to Landlord, the transformation is complete.

By 2014, David's business commitments were significantly less, and he had more time on his hands; not always a good thing, as he tends to find ways to fill his time and not all of them, over the years, have been productive or cost effective, as we have seen. However, when the request from Tim Wheeler, Vice Chancellor at the University of Chester, came, to ask if David would chair the newly acquired, Thornton Science Property, he simply couldn't turn it down. It was an ambitious project: to convert the old Shell Oil research centre at Stanlow, into an incubator hub for the Sciences and it appealed to David. In his eyes, technology and its practitioners should have a home to be creative and to solve problems, to make the world a better place and this was a good project. He was looking forward to making this project work.

In the previous year David had visited both New Zealand and South Africa and he had done so without Sue. There were good reasons why she could not accompany him but looking back during his time of reflection at the Abbey, he recognised it had been a particularly selfish year and he marvelled at the "rock" that was his wife. She was always there, never questioning beyond caution and always making sure her family had the support they needed. As David had more time around Grange Farm, he simply marvelled at just how many different tasks she undertook on behalf of her family and friends and he felt guilty that by constantly pursuing his own goals he had been oblivious to the sacrifices made by Sue. He was determined to make that right in 2014.

David and Sue therefore spent some quality time together on a trip to Antigua, where they stayed at Nelson's Harbour. The relevance of the location was not wasted on David. Nelson's Dockyard was the first in the Caribbean, built for the maintenance and repair of Nelson's fleet. Nelson's ships had copper plated hulls, which meant they were free from the barnacles that slowed up the Spanish and French Fleets and provided the English ships with a vital edge in the success at the battle of Trafalgar. The copper on the ships was mostly mined on Anglesey and processed on the North Wales coast. History aside it was a great holiday at Sugar Ridge Hotel where the two spent time walking the 365 beaches (they have one for every day of the year on Antigua — fact), with just a little golf as well.

The first family event of the year was daughter Belinda's, husband Ed's, fortieth birthday party. A family trip to Cork was full of fun and laughter. Closely followed was the arrival of Jessie, the new Grange Farm retriever, who brought a need for constant walks and attention. All of which fitted with David's new ethos for both he and Sue to remain healthy and active into old age. Granddaughter Mabli was about to start University at York — where had the time gone?

At Eaton Golf Club, David delivered on his promise during his Captaincy, for a roof to be erected over the golf driving range area. An improvement the members were most keen to have in place. He thought this was a project he could get his teeth into. Club Professional, Bill Tye described his work;

"*In his year of Captaincy David questioned all the key staff on how to move the club forward. I raised the subject of covered bays on the driving range, something I had been saying for a few years was needed. David and then Chairman Neil Large MBE, decided that this would be their project for the year, and rather than seek to use club funds, would find the money from like-minded members. The project was soon funded, planned, built and opened all because of David Pickering.*"

There were also some home improvements as well with the Orangery being added to Grange Farm. It was David's intention to spend more time at home and the space and light that this south facing room created was a welcome addition. This was all about preparing to wind down further and bring about a less frenetic lifestyle of investment and constant spending. Whilst the pay out from Meadow was indeed a good one, at the current rate of spending David would have neither time to enjoy it or enough money to survive old age.

If 2014 was remarkable for anything it was David's understanding and recognition of his family, and the role he needed to play in their lives going forward. His walking days, with Stuart, Tage, Bink, Collin, Ken, John, Peter, and Alan were all but over. They had walked over mountains in Scotland, walked as monks in Staffordshire, Cheshire, and North Wales, sailed most of the Irish Sea and the West Coast of Britain and the last of their journeys was what David called the Pilgrim Grandfathers Trek (they were all now grandparents), retracing parts of the North Wales Pilgrims Way, from Basingwerk Abbey to Bardsey Island. His body was now telling him enough, time to stop after this one last journey.

As enjoyable as their time together had been, the walkers simply could not keep pushing themselves, as age was taking its toll. Fellow walker, Stuart's miracle, in heeling his knee with the waters of St Winifrides Well on Anglesey was definitely a one off. No amount of medicine, spiritual or physical could repair the body sufficiently for these feats of endurance to continue. It had been thirty-seven years of fun with rarely ever a cross word. Yet another group of truly delightful people who stood the test of time with their friendship. David's life was the richer for the time they spent together. In his own words, David said "*Life is about experiences and not just about things*" and through this group they had all experienced far more than most and perhaps not as much as some.

By December, the islands project at the Zoo, from a finance and planning perspective was just about sorted, so he could hand that responsibility back. It was a proud moment when they broke earth for this major extension to add to what many believe is the finest Zoo in the UK. That fact that David's requirement at meetings was now complete meant he was virtually free of commitment bar the Champions of the Wall and The Thornton Science Project, which was stalled due to a planning problem. As he considered his time between Christmas and New Year the obvious thought for a man who had filled every corner of every day and night, was "What do I do now?"

Chapter 81
Explore, Invest and Grow

David took a little time to think about what comes next, as he and Sue went back to Cape Town in January, where things did not start well. Sue had her handbag stolen out of her arms as they walked back from the restaurant to their hotel. Normally that would not create too many problems as there was less than £70 in cash in the handbag, but it also contained the car keys. Fortunately, a lady working at their hotel, who was disgusted that they had been robbed, put into action her group of friends and within hours the handbag was found. Without the money but still containing the car keys. Disaster was averted but golf was cancelled for the following day, as it took Sue a day or two to re-gather her confidence. In short time, she did, and they made their way to Stellenbosch and the wineries as well as quite a few rounds of golf in the glorious sunshine and setting of this fabulous part of the world.

While away, David realised all the horses needed to go, they cost too much. So too his commitment to the Chester Giants. The Giants had cost him over £100,000. Unfortunately, the people charged with running this Community Interest company did not understand that it needed to be self-sustaining and that neither the public purse nor the Bank of David could go on funding this forever. The money dried up and the company was disbanded. It deserved better. It was a unique piece of thinking, it brought colour, life and vibrance to the city and it was all part of the regeneration of Chester, post financial crisis. It brought huge crowds when it was featured and provided a small group of people with employment and a belief they could do better in life.

With the right people leading the day-to-day management the Giants might still be there as a lasting and fit legacy but, not for the first time, that was something David didn't put in place. Trusting the people, as he always did, to do the right thing and make it work, was the problem yet again. Now it is just a memory and one that hopefully will not be forgotten. The Giants and the Rhinos — another of Chester's magical street art projects during David's time with Chester City Management, were both unique and exciting.

Fittingly, if you go to Grange Farm the garden has four giant Queens heads in various locations and three Rhinos; at least in Higher Kinnerton, the Giant spirit lives on.

The Wye Group, returned to Hereford in 2015 for their annual reunion and David and Sue joined Jilly Walton at her holiday cottage in Polruan, as they did most years. Golf at the fabulous Aphrodite Hills in Cyprus, was yet another escape, as David realised he had certainly worn himself out over the last five years. For the first time he appreciated that he was getting older and it was becoming harder to do the same amount of work. The latter he did not mind as he often reminded people when they complained of age that they should "never regret growing old it is a privilege denied to many". There was, however, no doubt in his mind that things were a lot harder than they used to be and that he needed to heed the words of Sue and just take it a "little easier".

His strategy in 2015 was a simple one. Secure the family finances to ensure that none of them would have any money worries in the future and then create a "David" investment fund, or as lifetime friend Peter Overmeer described it "his gambling fund/piss-pot". David named it Pickering Enterprises. Peter's description of David and his previous investment strategy fits with the stories we have related in this book, when he wrote.

"Traditionally, for many people, gambling is synonymous with horse-racing but it can take other forms not least in the world of business and this applies in some of David's wider activities. Although he describes himself as an entrepreneur, he has never run his own business as such but has been happy to back others who have taken that initiative. Quite why I have never asked him. For David variety is the spice of life. Allied to that, he was never the best at the nitty gritty of the admin side of business, for him it was the bigger picture, the wider canvas rather than the detailed brush strokes. To him that was boring. Quite why he picked the businesses he did to invest in I have no idea. There is no pattern to them in terms of sectors or industries. Instinct, whim, who knows, maybe just the gambler in him and I say this with reason. On a couple of occasions after his 'investment' had gone pear-shaped he asked me to go in and produce a report on why it had happened to enable him to claim relief on the investment. This proved well-nigh impossible and left me wondering why he invested in the first place. I think on occasions it was a case of flattery to deceive."

David invested in seven companies using his gambling fund as Peter referred to it, or as it is now, Pickering Enterprises, with various amounts of money, from just £20,000 up to over £100,000. They make up as diverse a portfolio as you could imagine. We touched on some earlier when he was helping some smaller businesses at the Riverside Innovation centre and one of those, **Bikmo,** was proving to be successful, so he invested further in this business to help them along the way. They had by now moved on to Bike Insurance, with the irony being that they had become a preferred supplier of Hiscox, the same Hiscox, started by Robert Hiscox, who had advised David during the Lloyds of London Insurance Crisis, that now was the time to "go big or go home", a dividend that paid off handsomely back then and now their two companies were working together. Other investments included **YoYo** — not a small children's toy on a string but a company who designed a unique platform for trucks that could see the entire hold area unloaded and re-loaded in just minutes. This means less downtime for trucks while they waited to be loaded. Ingenious and practical.

Next was **Air Quality Research (AQR)**, a company who specialise in applied charged particle technology, in short, they make things like waste water, safer and drinkable and must have a huge future in Third World countries. **New Lighting Technology** — a firm who produce lighting products for outdoor advertisers that are clearer, last longer and use less electricity. **Pythia (**Ground Gas Solutions) a better way to monitor ground gases and the emissions they produce. **Renewable Hydrogen Technologies**, this is cutting edge adaptation of the newest energy source that will very soon be powering cars, trucks and already powers space rockets and is high on Government investment strategies. Finally, **Storeelectric Ltd**, a company who find innovative ways to store the energy we create through renewable sources. The total basket of investment came to just over £1 million in 2015. They were all start-ups in one form or another and out of the basket of seven David was hopeful that at least two of these would find an exit route to market in the future.

David appointed another long-time friend, Mike Huntriss, to look after his interests in each of these companies and Mike agreed to report back to him on a fortnightly/monthly basis to update on progress and just how they could help the companies move forward. This would be David's reason to get up every morning, read the Investors Chronicle, Financial Times, and other daily papers, keeping an interest, and helping these brilliant ideas come to fruition. Would they work, time would tell and as David quoted to me often in our interviews, *"Never be afraid to fail, be afraid not to try"* They were all working hard, and he was helping them along the way.

Chapter 82
Repaying the Debt

David had made a decision, in the New Year of 2016, that this would be the Year of the Family. He recognised that he had been absent for too long and now was the time to put things right. Not necessarily absent in body, although he had taken many trips, bike rides and walking breaks, away from Grange Farm but absent in mind as well. He was, at times, so tied up in the many different financial ventures and board responsibilities that he often didn't hear the stories being told by Sue or his children, as he mind wandered to matters outside the home. This year he would "de-clutter" and stop trying to push so many "boulders uphill". These were the words he used in his diary notes and now more than ever he was determined to make a change. If he did not, he was in danger of life passing him by without recognising what was truly important.

He also felt the need to be a little less bold. As Peter Overmeer described earlier, his investment style was frenetic and almost compulsive, and he needed to find a way to rein this in. David felt he had backed many, many, people over the years with his investments and very few of them had ever delivered on their promises and potential. Not that they didn't intend to, they just were not capable. It didn't make them bad people. He recognised the fault was his, in not understanding what they were capable of. This had resulted in substantial losses, as we have seen but ultimately whose fault was that. David believed that most people mean well, and he was keen to give a person a break when they needed one. In nearly all David's financial failures perhaps it was his inability to recognise that having a good idea simply wasn't enough, the real trick was how to make a good idea make money.

The appointment of Mike Huntriss to manage his angel investments was a good one. It kept David once removed from the emotional, direct appeals of these companies for more money and he was delighted with the way Mike treated David's money as his own, with care and attention to detail; perhaps even more so than he, himself. It seemed that, in the case of business, more money was rarely the answer and Mike was getting to the bottom of it better than David had done in the past.

Part of "Year of the Family", involved David and Sue taking a cruise on the Royal Clipper around the Windward Islands. The Royal Clipper is a five masted sailing ship that carries just 200 passengers and has the most marvellous feel for the "Grand old age" of sail. Modelled on the fastest sailing boat ever made, it is an incredibly special sailing experience. It tours the small Caribbean Islands, that include Martinique, St Lucia, Grenada, and St Vincent. They are the less busy and prettiest of the cluster and, in the case of both Martinique and St Lucia, very much French influenced. The cruise was a great success, with good food, great company and when they docked in Barbados, it was the refreshing break they both needed and a good start to the year.

On the return home the same could not be said for Peter Overmeer, who David noted looked tired, on edge and in poor health. It seems he had been tempted back to Jolliffe's to take on their office management and had overseen the move of the business to St John St in Chester. The workload and pressure were really showing on his face. Peter admitted that this move was too much and, when it was done, he too was in need of a period of convalescence, a little golf and some fun.

In March David and Sue were joined in Verbier for some Skiing by Belinda and Ed and their two children, Noah and Evie. The year of the family was proving to be something very enjoyable. With David having resigned his role at the University of Chester the load was easing further and family time increasing. To celebrate and reminisce just a little, David and Vice Chancellor Tim Wheeler had their last lunch together with David having an official position at the University. It seemed strange to David. He and Tim had lunched at Senate House, in the University restaurant, at least once a month for the last twenty years. They had discussed the next move, the state of play and the problems that needed sorting and yet here they were having the last of those luncheons. Yes, they would remain close friends and undoubtedly, they would lunch together again but the conversations would be different from herein and the collective need to problem solve no longer required. For David it was a poignant moment. The end of an important chapter, tinged with a little sadness. Yes, he would have some extra time available but bit by bit, him being needed by others to help solve problems, was disappearing. He tried hard to fight those feelings by telling himself his family needed him now and it was time to give them what they had sorely missed. This was something he needed to learn.

Chapter 83
Being Told Where to Go

Whilst the workload was decreasing, occasionally Mike Huntress would highlight that David needed to get involved in one of the seven Angel Investments Mike was managing for him. One such case was in April when Mike suggested they both attend a board meeting in London to discuss Storeelectric. David's investment was greater than £100,000 and this Hydrogen, electric storage "disruptor" had agreed a lucrative funding scenario with fellow investors. David was the Chairman of Storeelectric and the company's Accountants, a top London firm, had agreed at a previous board meeting, that they would put in £1 million of "FREE" fee work. They would then raise £10 million of investment and take a 10% commission on that raise, which would in effect pay for the fee work. It was a good deal for a company who needed that sort of capital so that it could install its own products and prove to a sceptical industry that this new technology worked. They were in the right space at the right time and they needed to show various UK Government departments just how important this product could be. Mike had advised David that the main agenda item of the meeting should be to find out exactly how much Paul Davies and his team of accountants had raised so far, as the company's need for money was growing by the day and the funding was vital, if they were to achieve their lofty ambitions.

Coinciding with this meeting, which was held in the plush

London offices of the accountants, the Sunday papers of that week had highlighted how the big four accountancy firms were finding larger and larger loopholes for their wealthier clients, so they could pay less and less tax. Many of the firms were more than a little nervous of too much press coverage and sensitive about the work they did. And so, with this as a backdrop to the meeting, when David asked Paul how much the company had raised for Storeelectric, the answer came back as zero. Nothing raised at all. At this stage David was seething, given that the company had made commitments based around the raise and would now not be able to meet those deadlines; this would set them back significantly. He told Paul Davies, the lead from the accountants, that he and his company had spent far too long helping the wealthy avoid tax and not enough helping the people that needed them most and that accordingly they could "fuck off", something he had never done before in fifty years of chairing meetings. It was not a pique of anger, as it looked, he felt he needed to convey a sense of shock and urgency and get some sort of reaction — he succeeded. Paul Davies reacted similarly and told David he too could "fuck off" and the meeting came to a grinding halt as David offered up his resignation and confirmed that, without assurances of financial backing, he would invest no further. To Paul's credit, when the dust settled, he agreed to take over from David as Chairman. He found ways, both with his own money and that of others who he would entice to invest, to keep the company afloat. It was a pivotal moment in the company's history and, if they make it, the actions of that day will have gone a long way to creating their success.

On a less frenetic note, the Queen enjoyed her ninetieth birthday in late April and with a house surrounded by Queen Elizabeth statues David and Sue felt particularly patriotic on what was an historic day for the country. Our longest ever reigning monarch is immensely popular at Grange Farm and her continued good health was echoed by her loyal servants in Kinnerton, who were looking after themselves. David was weighing in at 11st 7lbs and other than some arthritis conditions that were relieved with regular physio he was in "good fettle".

In May, David made a pledge to the Cathedral that he would invest £40,000 into the redevelopment of the Refectory. This café style eatery has never flourished. In a city where morning and afternoon tea locations are much sought after by 72% of the visitors who are there for a day out, this should be a busy place. His theory was if you could make it an appealing place to eat and drink then visitor numbers to the Cathedral itself would logically improve as well. David said he would help to increase his £40,000 to £100,000 by getting others to assist in this aim. His premise for wanting to help was a simple one. What wealth he had acquired was from the food industry and this was an area he understood. He also recognised that whilst he still felt an outsider at the Cathedral, never really having been adopted by them, he had been inspired by this amazing building and mentored by Stephen Smalley when he was Dean and that perhaps he was still in their debt.

Sad to think that someone, who had done so much over the years, in terms of fundraising, overseeing development works and driving redevelopment, still felt an outsider but admirable that he could put those feelings aside and still marvel at the building and all it stood for, whilst financially contributing, yet again.

It was also comforting to know that the subdivision of the family money into the NFU and Barclays Wealth was paying dividends as they were doing rather well. Not spectacular but steady and without concern. It meant there was no longer risk of failure and that he and his family would be comfortable for some time. This was a big change for the man who had time and again risked everything in the past. People often talk about big gamblers and retell stories of thousands of pounds bet on a horse, or on a hand of poker but many big gamblers rarely see a racetrack or casino and in David's case, whilst he was no stranger to a bookmaker, his bets on sports and lady luck were modest by comparison with his bets on businesses and himself.

As he looked at the returns on these so-called safe investments, handled by the NFU and Barclays, he recalled the huge losses on Covent Garden Soups, the massive losses on Lloyds of London and then the incredible gains, when he risked all on the encouragement of Robert Hiscox. The gamble of taking on the Milk Marketing Board, defying them and winning, despite having to pay them over £1 million personally. Bodfari had years of profits and dividends on the back of that gamble. Yes, it was a different world today and whilst he still had his Angel investments to get the heart racing and the adrenalin pumping, things were a lot less stressful and for that he was thankful.

Chapter 84
When is enough?

Many years ago, David had set himself a personal target of £5 million and again he was glad it never really got to more than that. He believed that too much more might have seen a side of himself of which he may not have been proud. He had seen how he behaved in an almost reckless way when he had more money than he needed, and it had taken him time to mature and realise how to deal with the responsibility of money. In one's younger years, if you are good at making money, then you worry less about losing it and the money itself has less value. As you get older you start to realise that you will not, forever, be able to make things happen to right the ship and pay the bills and now was that important time. A security blanket of investments was in place and it felt good and right.

It was a hot summer, by English standards, one that included lots of golf, with a nice tournament, which David won at Eaton to celebrate Simon Ely's seventieth. There was also a lad's trip, that David and John Iles organised, to Clonokilty in County Cork. This was followed by a trip with the Diliway-Parrys to Troon, to the Open Golf. David and Sue had made their way around the Isle of Iona, birthplace of St Patrick and the centre of Gaelic Monasticism. It is a key spiritual, historical location and they made the visit before they went to Troon to meet up. While they were together a lot during the year they were separated politically in the big event of the year as Sue had voted for the UK to leave

Europe and David was a "Remainer". The historic vote in June went the way of the Brexiteers. David's comment on losing was his usual phlegmatic self. "We lost the vote — now bloody well get on with it". If only we had.

The good weather made for good walking and the temptation to finish the North Wales trek along the Llyn Peninsula was strong. He had said that the Pilgrims Trek would be his last, but this was 'definitely, maybe', one last walk. He reflected that it was also probably the best. The scenery was stunning, as you go from cliff edge looking across the Irish Sea down to fabulous sandy beaches. Raging seas to inlets protected by the elements, any amount of birdlife and a calm rarely found in the UK. The walkers completed their sojourn, happy that the time had come to end the walks and delighted that it had finished on such a high. On completion of the walk David was feeling light-headed and a little wobbly on his feet and for a man that had enjoyed relatively good health all his life this was another concern. Fortunately, the remedy was relatively simple. In the heat and with all the walking he had let his salt levels get too low. Added to the aching limbs, this was another reason for the long walks to stop.

The Year of the family was not without incident and in July, son Nick announced that he and Claire were divorcing and, whilst that is not a rarity in today's world, it is not without sadness when a family breaks up. This one was no different. Perhaps these family concerns and the lack of projects to focus on, accounts for Alan Dilliway-Parry commenting to David that he seemed restless and pre-occupied.

David's role as President of Chester Walls also finished in the July. They had done a lot of work both in repairing the walls and in getting Chester people to understand the importance of this unique asset but, like all Government funded projects, eventually the money runs out and the project ends. This one was little different, and it was yet another project that now didn't need him and his unique skill set, any more.

The year rounded out nicely, with the regular, eight couples making a trip to Montecastillo, Golf resort in Jerez De La Frontera, Cadiz. The abiding memory was of perfect weather and a series of highly patterned, "shite shirts" that Tim and Pammy Lowe had sourced for the group to wear whilst away, to identify themselves. More akin to something your average, fat, American tourist might wear than middle class retired English people, they certainly stood out from the pack and had everyone laughing from the time they arrived at the resort. This venue was simply perfect.

In the same quarter that America elected Donald Trump as their President the Queen of England awarded Neil Large an MBE. David was delighted for Neil, who had dedicated years and years of his life in service to the NHS and whilst still the Chair of various NHS groups in the North West it was a fitting tribute to a man who had given so much to public service.

The life of a retired man is meant to revolve around having a lie in, games of golf, reading books and afternoon naps and, while David certainly enjoyed plenty of golf during 2017, not all of it was good. His handicap went out from thirteen to fifteen, brought about by an increase of aches and pains in the body and because of those pains, not wanting to play as often. Winter golf was much less appealing as arthritis was making its presence felt and the prospects of playing in the wet and cold far less appealing. The appointment of good friend John Iles as Captain at Eaton meant he would play more often in the summer, but he was fast becoming a fair-weather golfer.

David and Sue welcomed some winter sun when they went

to visit Marielle in Grenoble. It was also the ten-year anniversary of the St Werburgh Pilgrimage and the twenty-five-year anniversary of the Rome to Chester bike ride. In some ways David was a little disappointed these passed without being marked but that was the way of the world — as he would say, in what is a recurring theme of David's life story — "just get on with it".

David recognised his role, both within the family and to his various companies, was that he needed to keep providing financial stability and with that in mind he decided to sell two of the houses he had bought a few years earlier. One was at Vale Royal and sold for £165,000 and the other at Romney, which sold for £285,000. Even though everyone said property was the place to be, investing in houses was boring and the profits modest indeed. However, putting £400,000 back into the pot was a good way to help that financial stability. David added another £65,000 when he sold his remaining share in Chester Race Company. He viewed that future growth for the Racecourse was going to be difficult and he was not using the benefits of being a shareholder anywhere near as much as he used to. It seemed a fair price.

David's seventy-fifth birthday was on the 28th of May and the celebrations included about 120 people all gathering at Grange Farm, where a marquee was erected and the guests turned up wearing the theme, which was sporting apparel. The contemplation of seventy-five years lived was mixed. David had certainly done more than most and maybe not as much as some, but he was in good health, barring the aches and pains, and he had managed to provide pretty well for his family, so it wasn't without cheer.

There was less cheer in June when Prime Minister Theresa May, besieged by back bench "Brexiteers" and abandoned by every lead Brexit negotiator she appointed; none of whom could get the job done, called a General Election. For what reason we know not. It was a disaster, with a good and workable majority given up for one that had to be supported by the Ulster Unionists to get any business done at all — let alone Brexit. The writing was on the wall for the UK's Dancing Queen, with the public savaging her in the vote. The seat of Chester was also a disaster. Whereas Stephen Mosley had lost the seat in 2015 by a mere ninety odd votes to Chris Matheson, the newly imported PPC, Will Gallagher, had lost it by a stunning 10,000 votes. It was an extraordinary backlash against the Conservatives, locally.

With nature as the theme for July and August, David, with the help of Alan Dilliway-Parry, taught himself to catch moles. Alan had caught sixty the previous year on his lawns and David, noticing the damage being done to the grass at Grange Farm, needed some assistance to rid him of these pesky vermin. He learnt quickly and dealt with the problem, as necessary. On the other side of the conservation coin, David and Sue visited the island of Tobago for a holiday and were able to see the baby turtles released on to the beaches to make their way into the sea. David recalled that, despite the attention of large sea birds, nearly all the turtles made it to the water, in what was a moving, memorable, and extremely uplifting scene.

The only bit of bad news during the year was that Granddaughter Mia had broken her leg when falling from a trampoline at a Children's entertainment park, that and Sue suffering from Vertigo, something she had never experienced before. It may of course have been brought on by the realisation that in October she and David would celebrate their Golden wedding anniversary! Fifty years since that time, driving around the duke's estate in David's MG, as the sun set and in the lengthening shadows of Eaton Hall, David had asked Sue to marry him. They had been through a lot together and now in an Indian Summer in October, with the Marquee re-erected, friends and family gathered to celebrate this special occasion. How fitting it was that Grange farm was the setting. They had a lot to be thankful for and this had been a good home over the years.

After the party David and Sue decided to take a little break and stay at the stunning Chateau Rhianfa, near Beaumaris, on Anglesey. It has the most wonderful views of the straits of Menai and David was struck by the early, snow-covered tops of Snowdonia. He didn't think there were many places in the UK where you could be so close to the sea and the coast of North Wales and gaze upon the mountains. Anglesey was indeed a special place and one that had been an important part of all the Pickerings and Owens, over many, many years. He decided then that he would start to chronicle the family history of Anglesey and start pulling together all the stories that touched his family through the years. He had a title for it — Odysseys of Anglesey.

Having been in reflective mood David finished off the year with a retreat to Foxhills, near Frodsham, which is the Chester Anglican Diocese retreat. This former Manor House is set in seventy acres of mature woodland and lawns and is a place of prayer, study and mission and serves its practitioners well. David returned feeling positive about his life, thankful for the various gifts he had been given and hopeful he could continue to have an impact in the years ahead.

David had lost the urge for winter golf, with its muddy fairways, cold mornings, and damp air so the chance to escape in the winter for warmer climes was particularly attractive. He and Sue had enjoyed their time so much on the Royal Clipper, when they sailed the Caribbean, that they signed up for a trip on the

Star Clipper. It was a similar, if slightly smaller sailing ship, that toured the islands of Thailand. Those amazing, beautiful rocks, covered in trees that reach out of the ocean and make one think of *The Man with the Golden Gun,* make for a wonderful setting. In early 2018, they set off for two weeks on this fabulous four masted frigate. At 360ft and with just 170 people on board it has generous staterooms that make one feel special and that was to be the theme for the year. A bit of pampering for Sue and again, more time with the family.

His speculative investing was now well and truly contained within Pickering Enterprises, which was set up for the benefit of the children and grandchildren, with the hope that at least one of the seven companies would "take off" in the coming years. Angel investing is always difficult. Everyone has a good idea and they all sound particularly plausible when you are being "pitched to" by someone passionate about their product. A good idea, however, is less than half the battle, the remainder being organisational skills and a "bloody mindedness" to simply keep going when you are up against it. How many would show this necessary attribute?

Mike Huntress, his Portfolio Manager, was doing a good job with the management teams of the companies within Pickering Enterprises and was regularly reporting and updating to David. This meant when they needed more money, as all start-up businesses always do, David was one step removed from the process and he was then able to discuss things with Mike to ensure some of the emotion was removed from the appeals. It is a process David could have done with quite some years ago and certainly he recognises now how much money could have been saved. He also accepts that whilst his further funding to the many investments that had failed in the past, rarely ever solved the real problems, they did help the people running the business for a little while longer and there was some comfort in that.

The summer saw David back on the golf course at Eaton in what was a good weather year, warm and dry for long periods, making for quick fairways and even quicker greens on a golf course that was maturing into something quite special. He felt proud that he had contributed to that success during the early years.

At the end of summer, the eight couples again made their way out to the Baselo Montecastillo Golf Resort in Jerez, a venue that was becoming most popular with the group. High quality accommodation, a great golf course designed by Jack Nicklaus and at a very reasonable price. In David's words, this was one of Spain's hidden gems. Affordable luxury, not in any of the normal, populated resorts. A place with some style and grace, where manners and respect still mattered.

After returning from Spain, Sue and David made their annual pilgrimage to Polruan to join Jilly Walton and others for a week in Cornwall. This was now a tradition of over twenty years' standing and again much anticipated by everyone who attended. Life-long friends enjoying each other's company in Cornwall. As it should be.

It is fair to say 2018 passed without incident and as David totted up the pluses and minuses of the year in that Christmas-New Year break, he was pleased. His only committee position of note was that of the Development Council at the Cathedral and of course his ongoing work as Church Warden at Hope. For someone who had once been on as many as twelve different boards and committees, this workload was minimal. He was much rested, with finances in good shape, achieving his goal of spending more time with family and stress levels at an all-time low. The perfect remedy for an enjoyable life. Is this truly retirement he asked himself. The answer was a definite 'probably'.

Not long into the following year Stuart and Jo announced they would be moving to Murcia in Spain. Stuart's Garden Maintenance business was great in the summer months here in the UK but in the winter, it was both slow and demanding, with poor weather, difficult working conditions and not a lot of fun. Jo's father had contacts out in Murcia and they believed someone with Stuart's unique skill set would do well offering his services to the large ex-pat population based around the various golf resorts that populated this area, the most famous of which, was La-Manga. They decided to make the move and go to the sunny south east of the Iberian Peninsula.

Sue and David helped them with the move and after packing them off they decided a trip to Tenerife was in order and a spot of golf at Golf Del Sur. This didn't prove to be a great success. The resort is extremely near the airport, on the wrong side of the island and not the sort of style they had enjoyed on Mainland Spain — they would not be recommending this one when they returned home. Adequate but not great was the report.

Chapter 85
Money Does not Stop the Pain.

Back when David first started his work at the University of Chester, he had challenged VC Tim Wheeler to improve the sport offered at the University. Tim accepted the challenge and appointed Gordon Reay as Director of Sport. David offered Gordon his support during the formative years and Gordon did an excellent job of providing a better sporting portfolio. When Gordon approached David to become the President of the University Rowing Club David gratefully accepted the position. His previous rowing experience included him and his work colleague taking a lunch break in the articled clerk days and hiring a rowing boat on the Dee to get to the other side, so they could eat their lunch — surely the perfect Rowing Club President! He had been to Henley regatta a couple of times, which made him marginally more qualified. His first task was to get a blazer made that represented the Rowing Club and both he and the VC were fitted out very shortly thereafter. The remainder of his exploits with the Rowing Club will have to wait for another time as 2020 has not allowed a lot of rowing to take place.

At Hope Church, they had been challenged by the Church of Wales, as part of their 2019 programme, called "Leading Your Community in Growth", to take a leading role in North Wales. David agreed they should join this programme and try to use the £50,000 they had saved, from the original roof development, to bring about a better connection between the Church and the

Community, with a series of initiatives. The challenge to the Hope Church Elders was to work out how best to use their funds in the community and get people to realise the church was not just for weddings and funerals. They needed to be perceived as leaders and supporters in the community. This was a noble ambition and something Churches across the world are grappling with.

One of David's lesser investments, a mere £2000, was in a business called "The Goat Tree". David became aware of this business through the annual University Enterprise Awards, where he and others from Chester Businesses judged the best University Business School ideas, in a sort of Dragons Den way, with the winners going forward to be judged on a national basis. One of the winners this year was The Goat Tree.

Set up by Jess Kelly and Ayoup Jarrai, they created a Coop in Morocco, called The Goat Tree, who would farm Argan oil from the berries of the tree. Argan Oil has great health and beauty properties and the Moroccan berry farming woman, known as Berber's, had a direct family link to the winning team, making this a very personal business. David was so impressed, despite the fact that they received money as a bursary for their win, he matched it with £2000 of his own. Later in the year, when one of the team's fathers was struck with cancer and could not travel, David accompanied the two young entrepreneurs, to Norway to act as chaperone, for the European finals. They didn't win, but it was no small achievement to get to the European finals.

It was also a big year for the University as well. At the Educate North Awards in 2019, the University of Chester achieved six wins, including a Lifetime Achievement Award for VC Professor Tim Wheeler. As one of the UK's longest serving Vice Chancellors, he received recognition for his dedication to education. He retired at the end of 2019, at the age of 69, having spent more than two decades in the role overseeing the most progressive years of the University's history. He was appointed the inaugural Vice-Chancellor in 2005 — his successor is Professor Eunice Simmons who took over in January 2020. David described Tim, as "*interfering, listens to all student complaints, control freak, dictator, agile, quick to respond to change*". None of which seem anything but good qualities and certainly they served the University well. After a long working relationship, David and Tim have developed a strong friendship.

With less evenings taken up with countless board meetings, David's bridge group were flourishing. Once a month, four people, David, Tage Weiss, Alan Park and Richard Edwards would take it in turns to host a night, where a meal would be provided during the evening and of course a drink or two. It was during this year that with Alan as his partner he and David achieved the rarity that is "all the tricks" more commonly known as a "Grand Slam". Supposedly, it is the card players' equivalent of a hole in one in golfing terms, at least with this one you do not have to buy the entire clubhouse a drink.

By mid-summer son Nick was complaining of regular stomach problems and, with ex nurse and mother Sue on the case, concern was growing as the symptoms would not abate. Nick undertook a series of tests and the news was not good. He had developed cancer of the stomach. David and Sue urged him to move into the cottage that adjoins their house so they could help look after him while he underwent treatment, which he did. Despite the best available medical treatment and the assistance of quality specialists, the condition was worsening. David and Sue felt their son was literally disappearing before their eyes.

Later in the year he became so frail that he fell from his bed and did not have the energy to recover. He managed to shout to "Alexa" his in-house hub, to call Mum, and when it dialled, he was able to call for help from next door to get back into his bed. He lasted through Christmas, as a fraction of his former self and in early February of 2020 he lost his battle for life. He left behind his three children, Declan, Kamara and Charla. It was of course a sad loss and one that was hard to take, with the order of things around the wrong way as the child dies before the parents.

Not long into an already difficult year, everyone across the Globe would be dealing with the effects of COVID-19. A particularly contagious Corona Virus that was killing the elderly and infirmed in vast numbers. The UK went into lockdown on March 20th, 2020 in an attempt to try and stop the spread of the disease. Nursing homes were hit hard with fatalities running at about 15% of occupants. Those with respiratory illnesses were hooked up to ventilators to aid their breathing, with a mortality rate of about 60% in the early days for these sufferers. Those with diabetes or severe weight issues were also cruelly hit. It was the most extraordinary time as fear gripped the nation and people were confined to their houses except for an hour exercise a day and no contact with any other person outside your own home.

The mixture of both Nick's death and the daily reported fatalities from COVID-19 prompted David to start recording his life. As usual, he wanted to have some control over the way the events were reported and 2020 was showing him, yet again, the value of life and ensuring you do "get around" to doing the things you always said you would.

And so here we are. The story of David Pickering told. All that remains is my own thoughts on who David Pickering is. As I said in the prologue, you may well have your own ideas by now. If they compare favourably with mine, as shown in the epilogue that follows, then, perhaps, I have done a reasonable job of retelling, what I believe is quite a story. It is not finished yet, but this book is, save a small piece I have kept back, about the seven companies in Pickering Enterprises, what they do and where they are in their work cycle. Maybe you might feel compelled to join David and find a way to get involved financially with one of them. If the history shown in this book is anything to go by, one of them is going to make it big, the question is — which one? That is the gamble. Remember, as David says, "the luck you make is the luck you have". Be lucky.

THE END

Epilogue

It is December 2020. We have all just endured a year that can only be described as an absurd part of world history. The year the world stopped and, as predicted by a few some time ago, it has not been a World War but a virus that stopped us. A simple, sticky, little, nasty organism.

David Pickering is now seventy-eight years of age and as I meet him, after our latest lockdown, socially distanced of course, he looks as fit as I have seen him for some time, never carrying an extra pound and for someone in his eighth decade, he could easily be mistaken for someone ten to fifteen years younger. I have finally completed writing up his story. By that I mean all the words are down in chronological order and I will now pretend that I know what I am doing by attempting to turn these words into something like a book. I will try hard to do that because this is a truly remarkable story about one man's life and if you have got this far then you probably agree.

I made a deal with David that if I wrote the book, he would provide access to all his diary notes and I would write it as I see it. Both of us have adhered to that deal during this process. I think it shows. Now the big question that I said I would try to answer in the prologue.

Who is David Pickering?

I have read the words of his friends who have written glowing tributes in personal emails to me, many of which I have quoted: people like Peter Overmeer have been candid about his faults and generous in his praise. Neil Large MBE, has mentioned

David's social skills and his ability to get people to do things as part of a project, bringing people together. The Right Reverend, Stephen Smalley, former Dean of Chester, was fulsome in his praise for David's incredible work to move the Cathedral on, with his tireless fundraising and various appeals. We have all now read of the work he did at Eaton Golf Club, as highlighted by club professional Bill Tye, as well as the endless meetings of so many committees, organisations, and groups but really — who is he? The answer, in my opinion, is not an easy one to understand, nor does my observation help all that much but I have come to a conclusion.

David is a contradiction in every way; that is who he is.

Firstly, David is a private person; he has kept his personal affairs, until now, to himself, yet he has spent so much time in public service, either as a Councillor, or a President or a Chairman, of so many different organisations. Surely a contradiction.

He has always been the leader in name and yet rarely did he lead the charge. He happily allows others to come up with ideas and run with those ideas to move something forward. Never precious about ownership only interested in the outcome. Yet another contradiction.

He is uncomfortable having a £50 bet on a horse, yet he is one of the biggest gamblers I know — and I know a few. Look at what he did time and again when he risked everything at Lloyds of London, or when he carried a £3 million overdraft secured against everything he owned because he believed what he was doing would work out, even though he could have lost everything. Or taking on the Milk Marketing Board, knowing they would chase for millions at some time and he would have to find the money. All massive gambles. Another huge contradiction.

Massively confident in his own abilities to solve problems

yet rarely preaching that his way was the right or only way.

He is happy to organise holidays, parties, golf days, gatherings and events but rarely wants to be at the centre of the event. Happier to observe others having fun rather than actually having the fun himself.

A spiritual man who has dedicated his life to his Church in terms of service but never pushing anyone else towards his very private calling. I could not tell you if he believed in God and I would not ask him. I do know now, that like his father, he says his prayers every evening but only he knows who listens to them.

Uncomfortable accepting praise but happy to praise others.

Meticulous in recording his thoughts in his endless diaries, in setting his annual goals, in reviewing his previous year's achievements but haphazard to the point of carelessness in his investments and private businesses. How is that even possible?

All these things make David Pickering the person he is. There is one thing for certain though; those who call him a friend think very highly of him and him of them. Their friendship has been enduring and they have each benefitted from the other.

Of his relationships with family that is a harder one for an outsider to gauge. His was a generation that found it hard to say, "I love you", to show or talk about their feelings, to give someone a hug, to crave or to give physical contact. It is not a fault of the individual it was just the time in which they were raised. If time spent together were the measure of family success, then there is no doubt he and Sue have done an outstanding job but is that testament to David or Sue? In truth it takes two to make a relationship work and this one certainly does.

I have also reached one other, what might appear to be unpopular, conclusion. I believe David now recognises, that from a young age, he lived a very selfish life. He did what he wanted to do and thanks to the understanding and backing of his wife and children, he has been able to live the life he did. Were there casualties along the way? Undoubtedly. Relationships only flourish with time invested in them. Time, as we all find out with age, being the most precious commodity in the world. I am certain he now understands that.

Of his earlier life, I am sure he would argue, you do what you must do to provide for your family and those you love. In his eyes, the endless meetings, the fundraising trips, the golf, the horses, the Presidencies and Chairmanships, were all part of the making of the brand that has become — David Pickering. A sacrifice worth making, or an indulgence, you decide.

Now that he has wound down his commitments outside the house, I get the feeling he is comfortable with what he has done but that now is the time to right some wrongs. Time to show his gratitude to his family and pay back some of their incredible investment in him and his brand. Because that is what this has been for his wife and family: the biggest emotional investment they have made, backing their husband, their father, and their grandfather.

Never, ever, one to welch on a deal, I think that the payback has started, and I hope those closest to him reap the benefits of who he has become. There is an awful lot of learning through experience inside one human being. Knowledge that needs passing on to those who care to take the time to listen and perhaps now read. As I said at the start of this book, this is the story of what appears to be an ordinary person, doing extraordinary things. I hope he keeps doing more extraordinary things for a long time to come.